**363.23 R263r
Rethinking community policing /**

Criminal Justice
Recent Scholarship

Edited by
Nicholas P. Lovrich

A Series from LFB Scholarly

Rethinking Community Policing

John M. Ray

LFB Scholarly Publishing LLC
El Paso 2014

Copyright © 2014 by LFB Scholarly Publishing LLC

All rights reserved.

Library of Congress Cataloging-in-Publication Data

Library of Congress Cataloging-in-Publication Data

Ray, John M., 1963-
  Rethinking community policing / John M. Ray.
      pages cm. -- (Criminal justice: recent scholarship)
  Includes bibliographical references and index.
  ISBN 978-1-59332-762-0 (hardcover : alk. paper)
  1. Community policing. I. Title.
  HV7936.C83R39 2014
  363.2'3--dc23
                                          2014019395

ISBN 978-1-59332-762-0

Manufactured in the United States of America.

Table of Contents

List of Figures vii

Preface ix

Acknowledgements xi

Chapter 1: Introduction 1
    Research Questions 3
    Organization of the Book 5
    Contribution to the Literature 9

Chapter 2: Conflict and Conflation: Community Policing's History and Related Concepts 11
    Community Policing 12
    Pluralism 21
    Democracy, Democratization, and the Police 32

Chapter 3: The Idea of Deliberative Democracy: Theory and Practice 41
    Origins 41
    The Early Thinkers 43
    Development of Deliberative Democratic Theory 63
    Deliberative Democratic Principles and Practice 72

Chapter 4: The Idea of Community Policing: Practice Without a Theory 77

American Policing's Origins and Early history 79

Birth of Police Organizations and Emergence of Professional Policing 91

The (Alleged) Demise of Policing's Professional Model 100

Chapter 5: The Long Slide: A Return to Efficiency-Oriented Policing 105

Common Features of Community Policing Programs 107

Problems with Community Policing's Implementation 119

The Assailable Practice: Unstructured and Ambiguous 133

Post 9/11 Policing: COMPSTAT, Evidence-Based, and Intelligence 139

Chapter 6: Reflections 147

The Legitimacy Question Revisited 151

Deliberative Democratic Theory and the Practice of Community Oriented Policing 155

Community Policing as Democratic Policing: Democratization in Progress 162

Steps in the Right Direction 165

Avenues for Future Research 174

References 179

Index 203

List of Figures

Figure 4.1. COPS Grant Funding and Inflation Adjustment.............. 127

Preface

The community policing enterprise is beginning to founder. Community policing scholarship and innovation has slowed as scholars' and police practitioners' efforts focus on new data-driven initiatives that seemly deliver on the crime-reduction promises community policing had hoped to realize. In fact, when discussing the research for this book with a respected colleague – one who wrote extensively on the subject of community policing in the 1980s and 1990s – he confided his belief that "community policing was an idea that had run its course." Can this truly be? Has history taught us nothing?

The social and political turmoil of the 1960s and early 1970s greatly affected all levels of government. The era marked a change in thinking about the relationship between the government and the governed. Citizens demanded a new standard of legitimacy based on access and voice for all. The demands extended to all levels of government, particularly the police. During the 1960s, the police received unprecedented scrutiny and criticism concerning their response to high profile incidents as well as commonplace routine encounters with citizens. A series of presidential commissions and blue ribbon committees investigated and recommended changes in practices for improving the relationship between the police and the citizens they serve. Scholarship supporting and furthering these recommendations ensued, ultimately ushering in the era of community policing. The central feature of this new model of policing concerned methods and practices designed to both engage and involve citizens in police matters that, by the 1980s, evolved into community policing.

Emerging from the same tumult, but at a considerably slower pace, was a new way of thinking about democracy, deeply rooted in *critical theory*. Known as *deliberative democratic theory*, it also had citizen involvement as its principal feature. Yet forty years later, community policing is waning while deliberative democratic practices are growing in other various institutions of government. It is argued here that community policing's community engagement component was in major part founded on a pluralist understanding of society popular in the 1960s that did not serve it well. Ironically, the alternative theoretical foundation of the community engagement component offered in deliberative democratic theory did not receive full articulation until decades later when the practice of community policing was largely faltering.

The following pages contain an analysis of popular and successful programs as well as widely accepted concepts that, when zealously over-emphasized, may have a deleterious effect on community policing practice. Three deserve mention here. First, data-driven models of policing have clearly delivered positive results in many localities. It is hard to argue against decreasing crime, nor will I. However, despite the reductions in crime, why has (as recent research suggests) citizen support not increased correspondingly? How were these programs adopted, executed and engrained into the police culture so quickly? Second, the pluralist understanding of American society as a host of overlapping and conflicting groups is canonical. Nevertheless, pluralism has its limits. While it appears to have great explanatory powers, it is not good at effecting change. Finally, government efficiency is a worthy value and goal. However, it is an elusive and misunderstood ideal in the context of democratic governance. Governmental action in the democratic context is notoriously inefficient, a fact realized over two-millennia ago by philosophers in the Golden Age of Greek philosophy. Balance is needed.

These programs and concepts are not bad in and of themselves; they are worthy of support. The words of caution and criticism offered herein are aimed at helping the reader realize that a balanced approach is in order. What is suggested herein is a rethinking of community policing's community engagement component as an opportunity for the actualization of deliberative democratic practice. Once recast in this light American policing may be able to strengthen its democratic legitimacy in the eyes of citizens. Moreover, doing so allows the community engagement component of community policing to transcend its programmatic status and become institutionalized democratic policing and a foundation upon which both current and future models of policing practices may thrive.

Acknowledgements

The six years it has taken to produce this work has been marred with nearly incomprehensible personal tragedy. This work would not have been possible without the patience and persistence of a number of people at The University of Texas at Dallas, not the least of whom were Edward J. Harpham, James W. Marquart, L. Douglas Kiel, and Donald R. Arbuckle. They never gave up on me or my work when I was struggling to think and write while so much else was crowding my mind.

This research is the result of a decades-long blending of an academic and professional career. Exposure to scholarship on policing, politics, and philosophy, while at the same time engaged in a career as a police officer, inspired this work. I owe a debt of gratitude to the police executives who, through their vision and leadership, created the environment that allowed me to have the community policing experience upon which much of this work is built. Longview Police Department chiefs Johnny Upton, A.J. Key, J.B. McCaleb, and Don Dingler are particularly important in this regard, as well as Tarrant County Sheriff Dee Anderson. Moreover, Sheriff Anderson's personal support of this research effort has been invaluable.

My heartfelt thanks go also to my longtime professional and academic colleague Eric S. Metcalf, whose stirring discussions and critical eye helped produce this work. He and I have been a team for over a decade, and many of our highest professional accomplishments are the result of shared efforts and sacrifice.

In that same vein, I should like to thank my editor, Nicholas Lovrich. He has shown great enthusiasm for this rather unique look at community policing. Moreover, his suggestions have made this book even better than I had ever imagined.

I also wish to thank the faculty and staff of The Institute for Law Enforcement Administration in Plano, Texas. The institute's environment and quality leadership curriculum provides an unmatched educational experience, merging state of the art practice with academic rigor.

I am deeply indebted to many other scholars and colleagues at a variety of institutions who over the past two decades have helped shape my thinking. While there are many, three deserve particular notice. First, Edward J. Harpham particularly aided and expanded my thinking in the area of democratic theory. Moreover, his critical reviews helped think of ways to present this information in a manner that would be beneficial to scholars and practitioners alike. The second is John Randolph "Randy" LeBlanc of The University of Texas at Tyler. It was his discussions on Habermas's *Discourse Ethics* that provided the *gestalt* moment for this work. Twelve years ago, that moment provided insight into community policing's missing component and was the animating force behind this thinking. Finally, my deepest thanks to my friend and mentor, R. Stephen Krebbs of The University of Texas at Tyler. For nearly as long as I have been a police officer I have been a philosophy student under his tutelage. All academic roads lead back to him, and everything that followed our time together bears evidence of his profound influence. He truly changed my world; he is the older brother I never had.

Above all, I thank my wife Julie, who has been my rock, my hero, and my best friend. She inspired me to persist when I did not think I had another step in me. She proofread the messy musings of my muddled mind until it sounded like the voice I had so long ago when these ideas first occurred to me. Not one breath I have taken in the last six years would have been possible without her.

April 2014

CHAPTER 1

Introduction

The transformative effect of social and political turmoil in the late 1960s and early 1970s on American institutions is well chronicled and studied. The quest for justice and equality for all citizens was met by some with hostility. The police, often viewed as agents of the majority, responded to enforce laws and ordinances that seemed designed to preserve the *status quo*. Too often, these responses involved violence. As the fight for civil rights came to a *crescendo*, many citizens registered objections to government's decision to send their young to fight in Southeast Asia on the grounds there were not sufficient reasons of national interest or moral right, to commit blood or treasure to the task. A perceived lack of governmental responsiveness led to protests. Sent once more into the conflict between the parties was the police, who again in some instances exacerbated the situation and provoked violence (Terris 1967, 61; Sklansky 2008, 76). In this era of increased attention to the machinations of government, citizens asked probing questions and demanded greater accountability on a variety of public policy issues. Fearing corruption and stymied by the lack of transparency and accountability, unease and mistrust grew between the people and many of their institutions of governance. Moreover, these institutions appeared to constitute a pervasive "threat to justice" (King [1963] 1999, 361). It was clear that the nation was changing and its institutions were not keeping pace. In fact, these institutions appeared to be actively thwarting efforts at reform.

Unlike upheavals of the past, many were able to see the conflict for themselves as it played out unfiltered and unedited on national television (Kelling 2003, 12). All too often, the face of the adversary to justice in the eyes of many was that of the police (Germann 1969;

Goldstein 1979, 3-5; Rumbaut and Bittner 1979, 241; Goldstein 1990, 9-10; Trojanowicz and Bucqueroux 1990, 64-67; Pelfrey 2000, 86).

Away from the fray, the image of policing fared no better. Crime was on the rise, particularly in the larger urban centers (Trojanowicz and Bucqueroux 1990, 66). The police practices of the era seemed unable to stem the tide, and more often than not the enforcement tactics employed left a wake of substantial social damage (Pelfrey 2000, 86). The dominant strategies and accepted practices placed more distance between the citizens and their supposed protectors than one would have expected in an advanced democracy (Germann 1969). In short, it seemed at times that the cure for crime was as bad, if not worse, than the disease itself. Like many institutions of government, the police faced a crisis of legitimacy (Trojanowicz and Bucqueroux 1990).

It was in this environment that scholars and public policy experts began working on a new model of policing; one that sought to reconnect the police to the community, thereby reducing violence and restoring legitimacy (Rumbaut and Bittner 1979, 262; Trojanowicz and Bucqueroux 1990; Goldstein 1987). The model and its associated practices became known as "community policing." Central to this new model was the practice of involving the community in its policing in significant and substantial ways (Trojanowicz and Bucqueroux 1990). With the assistance of Federal grants and programs designed by leading scholars, this new model of policing was deployed across the country with varying levels of success (Moore 1994; Weisburd *et al.* 2010).

Also emerging at about the same time in the field of political science was a revised and revitalized deliberative democratic theory (Held 2006). This theory has as its central feature the actualization of democratic outcomes and legitimization through citizen input and active deliberation (Held 2006). Though there is debate among scholars on the particulars of this theory, there is significant agreement on certain key issues – meaningful discourse, legitimacy of outcomes, etc. – to suggest clear relevance to the community policing model (Fearon 1998; Dryzek 2000; Chambers 2003; Gutmann and Thompson 2004). This connection is especially timely now as the community policing model has come under attack for failing to deliver on the promises made in the 1980s and early 1990s (Carter and Albritton 1999; Weisburd *et al.* 2003; Herbert 2006b). However, this book will demonstrate that this criticism is unfounded. An honest examination of community policing's development will show that its most important requirement was underspecified and ill-suited to be the cornerstone of a new crime control model (Zhao and Thurman 1997; Harcourt 2001; 46-47; Herbert 2006b). This most important requirement was the clear need to rethink the relationship between the citizen and the police and to engage in civil society-building practices that create governmental legitimacy by involving citizens in the community's policing.

RESEARCH QUESTIONS

As previously mentioned the principal component of the community policing model – its core practice as originally conceptualized – was the requirement of community input and involvement in policing affairs. The emphasis on this practice was born out of the hard lessons of the not so distant past, and at a high cost. However, with the passage of time this practice has diminished so much so that the community policing model is now struggling to defend its position against more quantifiable results oriented programs (Weisburd *et al.* 2003; Walsh and Vito 2004; Kubrin 2008). The analysis that follows will show that much of the criticism of community policing was brought on by "false promises" of law enforcement administrators who asserted that they could use the model to control crime (Harcourt 2001). The expectations of the community policing model have thus changed over time due to promises made by practitioners. As originally conceptualized, community policing was intended to be a broad philosophy; a strategy of policing designed to restore legitimacy through decidedly democratic means (Kelling and Moore 1988; Trojanowicz and Bucqueroux). In the estimation of many, the core practice has become a perfunctory subcomponent of other efficiency driven programs and more quantitative in nature.

Interestingly, the practices recommended by the community policing model as originally – though weakly – specified are very much in keeping with those submitted by deliberative democratic theorists. However, I find no evidence where the community policing and deliberative democracy literatures have spoken to each other. The origins of the core concepts in both literatures have a normative base. An important component of this research will be to examine the normative assumptions underlying the idea of community involvement and participation in the delivery of police services and identifying similarities in the deliberative democratic scholarship. I will demonstrate that in addition to a weak theoretical foundation, what foundation community policing does have reflects the prevailing bias of the social science paradigm from which it originated. Particularly, I maintain that elements of utilitarianism and pluralism are uncritically assumed in the normative basis of community policing practice (Held 2006, 158-160). These were precisely the theories many deliberative democratic scholars were arguing against (Manin 1987, 344, 355; Rawls [1993] 2005, xv-xvii; Freeman 2000, 372-382; Held 2006).

The principal question of this study is whether the community policing model as originally specified can be re-conceived as a practical application of deliberative democratic theory. At the center of both the community policing model and the deliberative democratic theory literature is a concern for a shared relationship. It is the relationship between the police and the policed in one, and the government and the governed in the other. This examination will explain how pluralism was uncritically adopted in the community policing model, resulting in a form of hyper-pluralism with an elevated sensitivity to the effects of interest group politics. Furthermore, this work will show that resistance to the effects of hyper-pluralism, accompanied by strong tendencies toward efficiency-oriented models of policing, has worked against the ultimate success of the community policing model.

Deliberative democratic theory emerged as a reaction against pluralism. The goals of the community policing model are better served when founded on deliberative democratic theory. There is strong convergence between the two. What with community policing in decline, it may be possible to salvage its most important component – the community engagement component – and the object of the hardest lessons of the 1960s. Using deliberative democratic theory, it may be possible to recast community policing's community engagement imperative as an exercise in deliberative democracy, and therefore actualize democratic norms of American policing.

Because this research focuses on both literature's originating ideals and concepts with the intent of re-founding the community policing practice, rigor requires a conscious exploration of the common underlying norms. Consequently, this research is primarily normative in nature. It will take a historical approach to identify and examine the underlying norms of community policing and deliberative democratic thinking, pointing to important points of agreement between the two.

Introduction

To support arguments concerning community policing, this research relies on a series of original commission reports that give rise to community policing practice, the early and later scholarship that arose to further that practice and subsequent evaluative scholarship and government reports. In exploring deliberative democratic theory, this research relies on founding scholarship produced around the same time the earliest scholarship on community policing was being produced. Also considered is more recent deliberative democracy scholarship, which has as its goal creating means for the practical application of that theory. In the end, this examination will show that the potential expressed by community policing and deliberative democratic scholars are realized when joined. More importantly, through deliberative democratic processes community policing's community engagement component can become the very definition of democratic policing. Conversely, deliberative democratic theory can be understood as a practical mid-range democratic theory as evidenced in the daily practice of community policing (Chambers 2003). This work should be of value to public affairs scholars and practitioners alike.

ORGANIZATION OF THE BOOK

This book will contain six principal chapters to address the research question, which explores the possibility of refounding community policing practice on deliberative democratic theory. After this brief introduction, Chapter Two includes a review that considers two distinct bodies of literature. The first focuses on the community policing literature, identifying three broad themes that are pertinent to the arguments advanced herein. The first theme concerns community policing's lack of a theoretical foundation at its inception. Community policing is a practice that owes its origins to a series of presidential commissions and blue ribbon panel recommendations, all seeking to ease social and political tensions in the late 1960s and early 1970s. Secondly, lacking a theoretical foundation, the scholarship that emerged to support and advance the practice may be characterized as an evolutionary history of community policing practice. The final theme concerns the identification of pluralistic assumptions of social and political action that appears deeply intertwined with community policing practice.

Any argument that seeks to link policing with democracy should explain how these ideas have been treated in the past. The goal of the literature review's second part is to examine how several disciplines view the relationship between the police and democracy, and the character of policing in a democracy. I find evidence of clear differences between academic disciplines in the way this relationship is treated. Democratic policing scholarship had gained greater attention in the last twenty years in policing scholarship. I argue here that there is much to build on in any effort to move community policing practice toward a more deliberative model.

Chapter Three consists of an exploration of deliberative democratic theory. That chapter will attend to deliberative democracy's early thinkers and ideals because those particular contributions were written contemporaneous with the burgeoning scholarship on community policing. Literature foundational to deliberative democratic scholarship emerged during the turmoil of the late 1960s and early 1970s, just as policing scholars were working to solve problems rooted in the same troublesome social phenomenon. Additionally, more recent works that emphasis the practical application of deliberative democratic theory will be examined in that belief that such works may have direct practical application to the enterprise of community policing.

Chapter Four seeks to address the development of the idea of community policing practice. Because the practice of community policing was conceived as a method to solve a practical social problem, a look at the historical record will be enlightening. Furthermore, I contend that a deeper examination of the history shows two important and largely counterproductive ideas became uncritically embedded in the practice. The first of these is the longstanding bureaucratic bias toward efficiency at the expense of legitimacy and effectiveness. The second concerns the bias toward a pluralistic understanding of society that breaks people into groups with dichotomous interests and interacting in constant conflict – even if a state of equilibrium were possible. Furthermore, democratic ideals associated with the enterprise of American policing receive cursory attention in community policing literature, but they are seriously underspecified. Therefore, the chapter has two important and interconnected goals necessary to the development of this book.

Before attempting to connect community policing practice to deliberative democratic theory, the connection between the institution of American policing and democratic ideals must be established. This book treats American policing as an institution situated within a democracy that over its history has employed several models of service delivery (Kelling and Moore 1988). Therefore, the first goal of Chapter Four will be an examination of the relationship between policing and democracy. In order to achieve this, it will be necessary (and enlightening) to discuss pertinent aspects of the historical development of American policing. I argue here that the analysis of the historical record does not support as clear a connection between democratic governance and American policing as many might think. Restated, there is nothing unique about the founding or development of American policing that automatically gives it special standing among the policing systems of the world. That American policing can be made more democratic – that it continues to evolve in keeping with democratic principles – is another matter entirely. This examination builds on the first chapter's development of the idea of a democratic police and its treatment in various fields of study.

Chapter Four's second goal proceeds from the first. Having contextualized community policing in the broader historical development of American policing, I explore the development of community policing with an eye toward pinpointing the theoretical assumptions, which I argue, are imbedded in the original conception of the practice. This is an important point because these assumptions about social groups and how they form preferences inform so much of the subsequent scholarship and evaluative research on community policing. Specifically, existing scholarship on community policing will be reexamined for its treatment of citizen involvement in the belief that it will evidence a bias toward interest aggregation theories of group action. In this regard, the exercise and analysis of community input received less than rigorous treatment because a coherent idea of democratic policing did not yet exist in the case of American policing. Additionally, I believe the literature exhibits a devaluation of the citizen participation component. A cursory review of the studies revealed an example wherein one researcher admits cutting short their attendance at community meetings, opting for more face time with officers in interviews (Willis, Mastrofski, and Kochel 2010).

The final important goal of Chapter Four concerns the place of efficiency as an ideal to the institution of American policing. The historical review in this chapter demonstrates the impact of the

Progressive Era of late 19th Century and early 20th Century on policing. During that era, government agencies at all levels underwent reforms promoted by advocates such as Woodrow Wilson, which emphasized efficiency in its operations and deemphasized politics in administration (1887). The history of American policing shows tremendous growth associated with the reforms of this era. Some scholars, such as David Bayley, argue that the impact of this era was formative and helped propel American policing to the status of profession (1979, 133). The historical record reveals that two ideals continue to evidence a high degree of continuity that last to this day – namely, the elimination of political influence in enforcement agencies, and the emphasis on operational and administrative efficiency.

Chapter Five of this book explores the slow decline of community policing and the emergence – or re-emergence – of previous models of policing. These earlier models emphasized results and efficiency, stressing the crime-fighting activities of the police over nearly any other role (Kelling and Moore 1988). The effects of technological advances in accelerating this devolution back toward earlier models of policing cannot be overlooked either. This noteworthy trajectory has been particularly acute in the post-9/11 era. To make sense of this trend, I find it necessary to discuss countervailing influences. For instance, I argue that some trends in public administration theory and practice play an important role in the development of rival modes of policing that threaten to eclipse community policing. To further the point, recent criticisms of some social and political actors' strategic use of the phenomenon of crime as a tool of governance are discussed. Reports and studies published by various recognized authorities demonstrate this shift away from community policing and toward more traditional models. Scholarly assessments of community policing grants show the slow decline of community policing as originally conceived, and a clear shift toward earlier models of policing that emphasize crime fighting over community engagement.

The final chapter in this book offers a reflection on the idea of community policing in light of deliberative democratic theory. A more balanced approach is identified, one that avoids the peril of trading democratic legitimacy for efficiency. To that end, the issue of legitimacy is revisited. The similarity in the way the legitimacy is discussed in community policing and deliberative democratic scholarship is an important clue as to their relevance to each other. The

Introduction

conclusions and recommendations offered provide a synthesis and proposal, one calling for rethinking community policing as more than a model of policing. When applying deliberative democratic principles and practices, community policing becomes a theory and model of democratic policing. Fortunately, a few initiatives currently underway implicitly reflect the principles, values and processes suggested herein. These steps in the right direction are briefly discussed. Finally, avenues for further research are set forth. The most important of these avenues is the suggestion that historical institutional analysis of community policing's history may be enlightening. That research will likely be of interest to students of change management. The point of such work would include understanding the conditions under which change that appears to have clear and broad support nevertheless fails in spite of having the best chances at success. This type of research may also be useful to American Political Development scholars.

CONTRIBUTION TO THE LITERATURE

In sum, I examine how citizen involvement came to be a central feature of the community policing philosophy, and I trace its treatment since. In a similar manner, I demonstrate that around the same time deliberative democracy scholarship – also featuring citizen participation – was in active development. The analysis shows that when the practice of community policing was in need of the theory guiding its central feature – citizen involvement – that an appropriate political theory was still in development. Had deliberative democratic thought achieved its current level of articulation, the trajectory of community policing scholarship may well have been quite different. Absent a strong theoretical foundation, and a commitment thereunto, the structure of incentives helped push the promising reform model away from its central tenets.

Deliberative democratic theory presents an interesting opportunity for the domestic security enterprise of democratic regimes. It also speaks on matters of importance to leaders and stakeholders concerning issues of state-building, governance, and the administration thereof. Domestic security concerns and their relationship to democratic ideals are timely topics, as clearly evidenced by current events in Afghanistan and Mexico. Presently, journalistic evidence indicates citizens in those countries are losing confidence in the official organs of internal safety and pose problems that threaten to undermine the state. This inability to provide basic public safety threatens the legitimacy of the police, leading the people to turn to other avenues for safety. The search for alternatives can range from the engagement of private forms of security to affiliation with criminal gangs. Both forms of "exit" may have a deleterious effect on democratic regimes (Hirschman 1970).

To summarize, the goal here is to demonstrate that community policing and deliberative democracy share many of the same concerns and they identify a way forward together. In the end, we should find that community policing, as originally conceived, finds its voice through the mechanisms of deliberative democracy. In order to achieve this, efficiency arguments will have to be accorded far less importance in our evaluation of community policing – specifically the citizen and community engagement component – and replaced with deliberative practices designed around the ideals of justice and legitimacy. When fully actualized, community policing becomes the philosophy of democratic policing it was originally intended to be.

CHAPTER 2

Conflict and Conflation: Community Policing's History and Related Concepts

In order to support the claim that community policing's community engagement component obtains better grounded when viewed as a practical application of deliberative democratic theory, a discussion and synthesis of two distinct bodies of literature is required. Specifically, I am referring to the community policing literature and the deliberative democratic theory literature. In subsequent chapters, I will discuss the ideas of each in depth. However, before proceeding, an overview of the community policing literature is in order. In this chapter, I identify three themes in the community policing literature that are important to this investigation. These include community policing's lack of a theoretical framework, the historical character of the tome, and the introduction of pluralism as the principal lens through which social phenomena is assessed. The second part of this chapter extends the discussion on pluralism, specifically addressing its influence in the social sciences, of which the academic fields of political science and criminal justice are a part. The third part considers the variety of treatments the relationship between policing and democracy receives in several disciplines. The section concludes with a discussion of the more recent developments concerning the manner in which democratic norms are addressed in the policing literature. We shall find that the bulk of the literature concerning policing's relationship to democracy developed subsequent to the most prolific period of community policing scholarship. With this overview completed, I take up the idea of deliberative democracy and the idea of community policing in the subsequent chapters.

COMMUNITY POLICING

Extensive reviews of the community policing literature abound. While a more focused examination of works foundational to the idea of community policing will be undertaken in the analysis portion of this book, a broad review of the literature yields three important themes pertinent to this research. First, as will be demonstrated in later chapters, one of the deficiencies in community policing literature is the lack of an explicit theoretical underpinning (Leighton 1991; Oliver and Bartigis 1998). That community policing does not have a coherent underlying theory is often a point of criticism for the practice as evidenced in the remarks of Barry Leighton, who observed, "a comprehensive theory of community policing has yet to emerge and [...] community policing as it is currently constructed, is a theoretically undeveloped set of policing principles and practices" (1991, 515). Evidence to this fact is seen in the scholarly debate over concept definitions and persistent complaints of vagueness in this regard (Trojanowicz and Bucqueroux 1990, 4; Eck and Rosenbaum 1994, 5; Oliver and Bartigis 1998; National Research Council 2004, 232-233; Palmiotto 2011, 215). This conceptual ambiguity is particularly distressing for efforts toward postulating a theory of community policing because the process of theorizing in social science research requires precise definitions and conceptual clarity before systematic theorizing can begin (Bailey 1994, 41). In the recent struggle to find the appropriate place of community policing theory some scholars have suggested it is a "unifying" theory encompassing all other modes of policing (Scheider, Chapman, and Schapiro 2009, 694-695). Though an attempt to place the practice on firmer theoretical foundation has been a more recent goal of scholars, the fact remains that in the case of community policing the practice precedes theory. This is largely attributable to the fact the practice emanated from the recommendations in a series of presidential and national commissions in the 1960s and in the early years of the 1970s. Therefore, understanding the particular circumstances in which the practice emerged aids in an understanding of the literature.

As stated, the practice emerged as a recommendation in a series of commission reports. The first of these documents – the 1967 *Report of the President's Commission on Law Enforcement and Administration of Justice* – reflected the general sense of the times that at the center of the problem was the community's relationship with government. When conflict presented itself in a myriad of venues between the people and their government, the face of government was the police (*President's Commission on Law Enforcement and Administration of Justice* 1967b, 91-95). The commission members noted that the police always seemed to be on the "front line" and in the spotlight of these conflicts, be they robberies or riots (1967b, 92). Moreover, in an era where news cameras were beginning to deliver images of the social chaos on nightly news, the scrutiny of police actions was constant and pervasive. The sense of the times is expressed in the opening paragraph of the commission's report and recommendations on the police:

> The police [...] are the part of the criminal justice system that is in direct daily contact both with crime and the public [...] charged with enforcing the law and maintaining order. What is distinctive about the responsibility of the police is that they are charged with performing these functions where all eyes are upon them and where the going is roughest, on the street. Since this is a time of increasing crime, increasing social unrest and increasing public sensitivity to both, it is a time when police work is peculiarly important, complicated, conspicuous, and delicate. (1967b, 91)

It is against this backdrop the commission recommended that American police departments develop sophisticated "community-relations machinery" designed to appeal to the concerns of the "minority population" (*President's Commission on Law Enforcement and Administration of Justice* 1967b, 100-101). Though the report warned, "a community-relations program is not a *public*-relations program to 'sell the police image,'" many persistent assumptions about the police – and policing – remained in place (1967b, 100). Prominent community policing scholar Herman Goldstein made this observation, noting that early efforts "reflected a continuing belief that the way to improve policing was to improve the organization, staffing, education, training, and equipping of the police" (1990, 10).

The 1969 report of the president's *National Commission on the Causes and Prevention of Violence* spent much less effort on the matter of citizen involvement and tended to focus on the economic and social causes of violence. However, to its credit, the report did make important observations about the risk of government institutions losing legitimacy in the eyes of segments of the community (*National Commission on the Causes and Prevention of Violence* 1969, 41-42). Most notably, the report recommended increased social spending at the federal level to help ease the stress experienced by economically disadvantaged groups that tended to be statistically more likely to be victims and perpetrators of violence (1969, 27-43, 271-282). Though expending less energy on the matter than did the 1967 commission report, the body restated a call for "increased police-community relations activity in the slum ghetto areas in order to secure greater understanding of ghetto residents by police, and of police by ghetto residents" (*President's Commission on Law Enforcement and Administration of Justice* 1967b,46).

By the time the *National Advisory Commission on Criminal Justice Standards and Goals* issued the last of these reports in 1973, the crisis had not yet fully subsided. However, the thinking on the police-community relationship did evolve slightly. The earlier 1967 commission report had recommended that the community and the police enter into a sustained dialogue, stating that "in a minority-group neighborhood there should be a citizen's advisory committee that meets regularly with police officials to work out solutions to problems of conflict between the police and the community" (*President's Commission on Law Enforcement and Administration of Justice* 1967b,101). The 1973 commission built on this, admitting, "[t]he relationship between the police and the people they serve is the single most important concern" (4). Furthermore, this commission believed "the people-police relationship to be the foundation of any policy or procedure of a police agency" (4). Significantly evolved from the earlier report, this report called for citizen-police collaboration in the provision of public safety. It recommended the implementation of the "team policing" concept; a method of community policing that Herman Goldstein would spend the better portion of his academic career honing (*National Advisory Commission on Criminal Justice Standards and Goals* 1973, 154-161; Goldstein 2008, 16-21). In the rudimentary form proposed by the report, officers would work a fixed geographical area in partnership with the residents. Collaboratively, they were supposed to resolve community crime issues. However, rather than an actual partner, the citizen continued to be viewed as an informant of sorts who owed cooperation to the police (*National Advisory Commission on Criminal Justice Standards and Goals* 1973, 161).

Goldstein marks the issuance in 1973 of the last in a series of reports as the point at which the tide turned in thinking about the police (1990, 10-12). It ushered in a decade of new research between "1972-1982" that had as its focus "questions about the police that had never been raised in the past – about their function, their accountability, and their relationship to the community" (Goldstein 1990, 10, 12). Moreover, questions were being asked about the prevailing professional model's tenability. Its preoccupation with efficiency seemed to some, including Goldstein, to be contributing to the problem. In his estimation, "to achieve a high level of efficiency, operating procedures were adopted that, in retrospect, irritated citizens on whose cooperation the police depend[ed] and reduced the effectiveness of the police in meeting community expectations" (Goldstein 1990, 10).

The series of reports in question pushed for a new form of law enforcement practice that saw policing as something done *with* citizens, and not done *to* citizens. This new form of practice required a new citizen-police relationship and many police departments began experimenting with various programs and organizational configurations (*National Advisory Commission on Criminal Justice Standards and Goals* 1973, 156-158). The early research on community policing – the basis for much of the current literature on community policing – centered on evaluations of, and recommendations for, these pioneering efforts by innovative police departments attempting to do anything to help the situation (Goldstein 1990, 10-13).

The second theme is closely related the first. Because of this lack of grounding, much of the literature can be characterized as an evolutionary history of the *practice* of community policing. In an effort to perfect the practice, scholars argue for the application of a variety of theories thought to bolster the program, such as organizational change theory (Gaines 1994; Redlinger 1994; Maguire 1997; Oettmeier and Wycoff [1997] 2000) and social capital theory (Pino 2001; Martin 2002; Scott 2002; Ferguson and Mendel 2007; Hawdon and Ryan 2008). In many ways, the literature can be characterized as a chronicle, recording the evolution of the practice of community policing, with each proposed version seeking to improve on and correct the shortcomings identified in the last.

Fortunately, because the practice of community policing issued from practical and political concerns rather than applied theory, the practice was (and remains) open to continuous revision. Therefore, the literature on community policing may be viewed as a chronicle of the continuing evolution of the practice through ongoing trial and error. As mentioned earlier, in the more recent literature, American policing is generally discussed in terms of three distinct eras; each subsequent era is a reaction to the earlier one (Kelling and Moore 1988). Community policing evolved in response to the perceived deficiencies of the traditional "professional model" that dominated during the "reform era" of the "late 19th and early 20th centuries" (Kelling and Moore 1988, 4, 6). Scholarship designed to be corrective formed the path of transition, lighting the way toward the new "philosophy of policing" and a new era generally referred to as *community policing* (Trojanowicz and Bucqueroux 1990, 5). The developing literature is particularly enlightening in that it follows the evolving relationship between the police and the policed. More to the point, the literature traces how citizen involvement gradually increased in importance and focus along the path of reform.

In response to the earliest calls for police reform, many agencies established public relations units. The goal was to ease the tensions that had begun to arise in the mid-twentieth century (Berkley 1969; Germann 1969; Trojanowicz and Bucqueroux 1990). However, that initiative was not successful, since it was perceived as an attempt to give the appearance of improvement without actually improving (Germann 1969). What is more, it involved engaging in more talking and doing less active listening. The community relations divisions that sprung up were intended to take citizen complaints and conduct damage control and image repair rather than make any substantive change to the way the police thought about their work (Trojanowicz and Bucqueroux 1990). It treated the fundamental problem of how the police related to the community as principally a public relations issue in that the police believed that they were being misunderstood. This tactic would be ineffective and downright harmful during the chaos of the 1960s in that it was taken as evidence of stonewalling in the face of needed reforms (Germann 1969; Trojanowicz and Bucqueroux 1990).

In an effort to move toward a more thoroughgoing citizen-police interaction, some agencies established "team policing" initiatives (Goldstein 1979; Sherman 1986; Trojanowicz and Bucqueroux 1990). These were the earliest precursors of community policing efforts. Team policing programs sought to establish a collaborative relationship between the police and neighborhoods with chronic problems, though not as well developed as in later iterations (Shanahan 1975). The fundamental characteristic of this initiative – and one that endured through all subsequent developments on the way to community policing – was that it required a dialogue with the community (Goldstein 1987). Goldstein notes the significance of the changes that took place over the years, stating:

> [T]here are some important distinctions between the older community-policing projects and those that have been launched within the past several years. The newer projects have been started at the initiative of the police in an attempt to improve the quality of police service, rather than primarily as a means of giving the community more direct control over police operations. (1987, 7-8)

Neighborhoods involved in these initiatives were viewed as laboratories, and were seen as important test grounds for the development of community policing. There were three problems with team policing initiatives, however. First, they lacked funding, in comparison to levels later available in the 1990s (Worrall and Zhao 2003; 69-70). Second, they were viewed as a short-term program to address the specific crisis at hand – that is, a tactic rather than a broad strategy (Trojanowicz and Bucqueroux 1990). Third, these initiatives still relied heavily on the expectation that citizens should cooperate with the police rather than collaborate with the police (*National Advisory Commission on Criminal Justice Standards and Goals* 1973, 161). This initiative appears to have served as a stopgap measure rather than serving as a fundamental shift in the way policing was conducted.

"Problem-oriented policing" (POP) proposed to enhance the effectiveness of the "team policing" concept (Goldstein 1979). Goldstein's work is important in that for the first time police work meant looking beyond the obvious criminal activities and working to resolve fundamental problems to improve the quality of life in neighborhoods (Goldstein 1977, 1979, 1987, 1990). The thinking was that crime was actually a manifestation of deeper problems and that officers should use analytical skills to diagnosis root causes and develop creative strategies to address core problems (Goldstein 1990). However, this was still a tactic and not a fundamental shift of the police mindset. The *Law Enforcement Assistance Administration* (LEAA) made some funding available for developing programs to increase an agency's capacity that included training officers in the application of the Problem-Oriented Policing (POP) method (Worrall and Zhao 2003, 69-70). The new and growing body of scholarship developed techniques for solving problems, but it required no changes to the institution of policing or its administration. The problem-oriented policing initiative retained an emphasis on community collaboration the earlier team policing program had, but the thoroughgoingness of this police-community relationship would not be fully articulated until the advent of community policing literature of the late 1980s and 1990s (Goldstein 1987; Trojanowicz and Bucqueroux 1990).

Community policing receives its best expression in the 1990 work of Robert Trojanowicz and Bonnie Bucqueroux. Their work was significant in that it identified the citizen and the community as the central feature in American policing, a fact missed in each generation of police reform in the previous 100 years. They describe the clearly revolutionary and transformative difference between this and previous models, stating:

> The Community Policing philosophy provides an organizational strategy that challenges police officers to solve community problems in new ways. It says that the police must form a partnership with people in the community, allowing average citizens the opportunity to have input into the police process [...]. Community Policing rests on the belief that contemporary community problems require a new decentralized and personalized police approach, one that involves people in the process of policing themselves. (Trojanowicz and Bucqueroux 1990, ix)

This statement hints at a new vision for policing in a democracy. The next step in the evolution of this philosophy of policing might well have been to consult with deliberative democratic theorists had they existed in their current state.

However, community policing scholars and practitioners turned to organizational adjustments, and particularly to "decentralization" (Goldstein 1990, 159-161; Trojanowicz and Bucqueroux 1990, 5-6). The focus on decentralization may have aided the return to efficiency models of policing, inadvertently contributing to the truncation of community policing's democratic development. Some scholars and practitioners, such as Larry Gaines (1994), William Bratton (1998) and David Weisburd et al. (2003; 2010), argue that the first step of this long slide was the poor execution of organizational decentralization. They contended that it allowed administrators to abdicate their responsibility under the guise of decentralization (Gaines 1994; Weisburd et al. 2003; 2010).

To advance community policing, the federal government began offering incentives for agencies to adopt the practice when the Violent Crime Control and Law Enforcement Act of 1994 established the Office of Community-Oriented Policing Services (Worral and Zhao 2003). In exchange for more resources to combat crime and improve the quality of life for citizens, the police had to adopt policies and practices that included the citizens in important law enforcement decisions. These deliberations were to be authentic and genuine and help set priorities; they were also intended to affect the distribution of resources. These programs funded technology and additional staffing (Worrall and Zhao 2003). Community policing initiatives so funded met with varying levels of success (Zhao, Scheider, and Thurman 2002). A review of the literature suggests their ultimate failure may be attributable to unwillingness by personnel at several of levels of the organization to embrace one of the central tenants of the model. That central tenant mandates the substantive involvement of citizens in important program or policy discussions (Dicker 1998; Novak, Alarid, and Lucas 2003; Cordner and Biebel 2005; Vito, Walsh, and Kunselman 2005; Glaser and Denhardt 2010).

Within the community policing era several refinements have been advanced, each ostensibly to advance the goals of community-policing. During the 1990s, scholarship began to emerge that stressed the need to address quality of life issues in neighborhoods. The "broken-windows" argument offered by Kelling and Moore in 1982 reinvigorated scholarship in the older order-maintenance theory, proposing that the reduction of citizens' perception of crime requires a focus on minor offenses related to small incivilities (Wilson and Kelling 1982). The thinking was that when a neighborhood accepted a certain level of minor disorder, it made the area ripe for crimes that are more serious. More simply, the community's appearance of indifference seemed to invite serious if not violent crime. Kelling and Coles proposed that taking a zero-tolerance stance toward these petty offenses might reduce the probability of onset of serious criminal behavior (1996). However, knowing where to direct these zero-tolerance initiatives was dependent on criminal intelligence, and therefore the approach is quite technology-intensive (Weisburd *et al.* 2003; 2010). To make this work required an administrative structure that was more "command and control" oriented (Weisburd *et al.* 2003; 447, 448). These requirements seemed to be at odds with the prevalent character of community policing thinking (Harcourt 2001). As a result, the intelligence-led policing and COMPSTAT initiatives began taking flight. These initiatives will be discussed at length in the chapters that follow. For now, it is important to understand that this change would begin to have an effect on the citizen-police interaction.

There is general agreement that citizen involvement in policing and matters of public safety is essential in the early community policing literature and in subsequent derivatives. These models differ on the treatment of the citizen-police interaction. The research herein will show that community policing as originally conceived seeks to treat the individual as a citizen, and not a source; or as deliberative democratic thinkers would say (echoing Immanuel Kant), treat them as *ends* and not *means*. In subsequent models created to address the perceived deficiencies of community policing, the citizen-police interactions changed. Increasingly, citizens are treated as an intelligence source. This is especially pronounced in the models that rise to prominence after the 9/11 terrorist attacks. The dynamics of this type of citizen interaction is different in that it does not involve the kind of dialogue normally associated with the authentic civil discourse required for democratic deliberation. In fact, in order to be effective and efficient, it may be necessary to mislead the citizen-source of information.

Third, and finally, much of the evaluative research on community policing practice reflects assumptions of pluralist theories of group social and political activity. These studies generally focus on either the citizen's satisfaction with the police or police satisfaction with the practice of community policing. In both cases, researchers use survey instruments that evidence a pluralistic bias. Assumed in the goal is that a stasis can be realized. At work is a classic utilitarian assumption that if properly specified and executed, community policing is a practice that can win the "hearts and minds" of the public and the police, thereby providing a reasonable amount of happiness to a greater portion of the people (Dicker 1998, 79).

This theme in the community policing literature is probably the most important and complex. It concerns the literature's demonstrated tendency toward pluralism in its understanding of social and political behavior. Much of the evaluative research on community policing suggests a bias towards pluralism, as evidenced by the frequency with which scholars in this area rely on citizen satisfaction surveys. This predisposition toward pluralism is seen at nearly every stage of the development of the community policing practice; from its inception in the various commission reports, to later evaluative efforts directed toward diagnosing problems with its acceptance. Before discussing the grounds for this assertion, a brief review of what is meant here by *pluralism* is in order. It is also important in that the story of its ascendency as the dominant explanatory social and political theory in the 1960s is very much in keeping with the themes of the times.

PLURALISM

"Pluralism" emerged in response to a version of democratic theory called "competitive elitism" advanced by Joseph Schumpeter in the 1940s (Held 2006, 158). Seeing democratic theory prior to 1940 as engaging in "excess speculation and arbitrary normative preferences," Schumpeter "sought to develop an empirically based 'realistic' model of democracy" that reflected how democracy actually worked (Held 2006, 141). He saw democracy more as a "political *method*" – a *practice* if you will – "for arriving at political – legislative and administrative – decisions by vesting in certain individuals the power to decide on all matters as a consequence of their successful pursuit of the people's vote" (Held 2006, 142). Those in power – the elites – were those who had ascended by virtue of resources and legacy power from family and associates, and therefore presumed to have the requisite skills and abilities to lead (Held 2006). They were necessary because the average citizen lacked the special knowledge and abilities the elites had access to, and the ability to exercise. Therefore, in Schumpeter's view, democracy is the institutionalized process of deciding which elites will rule (Held 2006, 143).

Schumpeter argued that market forces play an important part in the political process. These forces influence the citizen's role, which is primarily to show up at the polls and vote for whichever elites have the greater appeal. Furthermore, to his way of thinking, complex and highly evolved government administrative institutions were inevitable and necessary in order to achieve a high degree of stability for a sustained period (Held 2006, 152-157). This thinking places public issues and matters of governance out of the reach of the individual; little room remains for the ordinary citizen (Held 2006, 152-157). To summarize, "in Schumpeter's theory [...] the citizen" is relatively powerless and "portrayed as isolated and vulnerable in a world marked by the competitive clash of elites" (Held 2006, 158).

Pluralism arose in the "1950s and 1960s" as a reaction to the belief that "Schumpeter's theory is partial and incomplete" in that it failed to account for groups (Held 2006, 158). In the pluralist's view, his elite theory is faulty because "scarcely any attention is paid to 'intermediary' groups [...] which cut across people's lives and connect them in complex ways to a variety of types of institutions" (Held 2006, 158). Thus, "a school of political analysts, widely referred to as empirical democratic theorists or 'pluralists', attempted to remedy this deficiency by examining directly the dynamics of 'group politics'" (Held 2006, 158). What is important to note about these groups is that they can be either formal or informal, meaning that they can be organized groups such as "business organizations, trade unions, [or] political parties" or un-organized – but readily identifiable – blocks of individuals sharing a common social characteristic, such as "ethnic groups, students, prison officers, women's collectives, and religious groups" (Held 2006, 160). When defined this way, we see why some pluralist scholars make the case that "government departments are sometimes best conceived as just another kind of interest group" (Held 2006, 161). This line of thinking gives rise to the observation that, in many instances, individuals belong to more than one group at a time; a confounding factor that scholars endeavor to resolve anyway (Held 2006, 161).

Of particular interest to pluralists are groups that are "structured around particular economic or cultural 'cleavages', such as social class, religion, or ethnicity" (Held 2006, 160-161). As is the case with elite theorists, pluralists seek "to describe the *real workings* of democracy and [assert] nearly every group has some advantage that can be utilized in the democratic process to make an impact" (Held 2006, 159, 160). What that looks like – that is to say, how groups leverage this power – will vary from group to group and "issue to issue" (Held 2006; 160). Power is of particular concern in pluralism. "In the pluralist account, power is non-hierarchically and competitively arranged," meaning that while elites enjoy substantial power, other groups too have the ability to (and do) coalesce to exert influence in a competitive manner, with no one group's power being credited with institutionalized superiority to the other's (Held 2006, 160).

Pluralists owe an intellectual debt to James Madison's work on the value of factions, and John Stuart Mill's utilitarianism (Held 2006). First, Madison argued in the *Federalist Papers* that factions were a naturally occurring political phenomenon, but one that was capable of destabilizing a government (Held 2006). Therefore, structures had to be created that mediated and mitigated their deleterious effects (Held 2006, 159). The pluralists agree in part, but contend, "factions are a structural source of stability and the central expression of democracy" (Held 2006, 159). Utilitarian assumptions observed in pluralist thought show evidence of Mill's thought. It is through the competition among these factions that "individuals maximize their personal interests," which are shared with others of their ilk, and realized through joint effort (Held 2006, 159). As Held puts it, "Accordingly, a very particular utilitarian conception of individuals as satisfaction maximizers, acting in competitive exchanges with others in the market and in politics, is also presupposed" (Held 2006, 159).

Evidence of pluralism is seen in community policing scholarship in several ways. First, in the formative works from which the practice of community policing emerged – the analysis and recommendations of the presidential commissions – groups are identified by their location, interests and demographic characteristics. In the earliest presidential commission report (*President's Commission on Law Enforcement and Administration of Justice* 1967b), the task force investigated a wide array of social disturbances under the broad umbrella of crime. The phenomena studied included campus demonstrations, riots, and violent crime in general. Early in the report, these activities were linked to the "social conditions" observed at the specific geographical point in which they occurred (1967b, 5).

For example, they note that the "slums, with all their squalor and turbulence, have more and more become ghettos, neighborhoods in which racial minorities are sequestered with little chance of escape" (1967b, 6). The now identified group inhabiting characteristically similar geography (slums) are observed to be bonded by common experience and interests, such as "poverty and racial discrimination, bad housing and commercial exploitation" (1967b, 6). The U.S. Riot Commission Report (*National Advisory Commission on Civil Disorders* 1968) echoes this identification. In discussing the riots taking place in several urban areas between 1964 and 1968, they note that "abrasive relationships between police and Negroes and other minority groups have been a major source of grievance, tension and, ultimately, disorder" (1968, 299).

Further evidence of pluralistic assumptions is the assertion that the police themselves are a social group with distinct and divergent interests that apparently conflict with minority groups. The report goes on to note that "it is wrong to define the problem solely as hostility toward police," but that the "policeman in the ghetto is a symbol […] of the entire system of law enforcement and criminal justice" (*National Advisory Commission on Civil Disorders* 1968, 299). Both reports were probably more accurate in the sections in which they take a more global view by noting that the police were the first point of contact – at the point of conflict – between these disadvantaged groups and the larger political system (*President's Commission on Law Enforcement and Administration of Justice* 1967b, 92; *National Advisory Commission on Civil Disorders* 1968, 135).

Other evidence of pluralism in these early reports is found in the identification of students as another distinct interest group. Student demonstrations of the 1960s supported the civil rights movement as well as protested U.S. involvement in the ongoing hostilities in Vietnam (*President's Commission on Campus Unrest* 1970, 3-5). For example, in the 1969 report by the *Commission on the Causes and Prevention of Violence*, the task force took testimony from a campus administrator who noted that "civil disobediences are mainly responsible for the present lawbreaking on university campuses" (*National Commission on the Causes and Prevention of Violence* 1969, 88). The frequency and intensity of these campus protests increased until May of 1970 in which violent demonstrations caused the loss of life at Kent State University and Jackson State University. President Johnson formed another commission in reaction, and by September of 1970 it had produced its findings and recommendations (*The Report of the President's Commission on Campus Unrest - 1970*). The findings were similar in character in that they identified the issues of the group at hand – students – and their grievances, generally believed legitimate. With legitimate concerns and an acknowledged right to engage in peaceful protest, the commission recommended that the university and law enforcement officials engage in greater coordination.

Additionally, it is worthy to note a thematic consistency between *The Report of the President's Commission on Campus Unrest* and all the earlier reports (1970). As evidenced by the testimony of the campus administrator cited in the 1969 report, the events that were unfolding were seen as criminal acts and therefore involving a moral issue. Even though the earliest commission was beginning to take a different tack in its view of criminal phenomena, they acknowledged that at the time "the people are more inclined to think of crime in moral than in social terms" (*President's Commission on Law Enforcement and Administration of Justice* 1967b, 50). In the subsequent 1969 report by the *National Commission on the Causes and Prevention of Violence*, the commission noted the then-current national discussion on the justification of presumably criminal activity on social and not moral grounds. In describing the character of that national discussion, they noted that:

> The […] idea – that disobedience to the law is justified in a good cause which can be furthered in no other way – is […] widely held by students, black citizens and other groups pressing for social change in America today. It is the illegal and sometimes violent activities of these groups that have been most perplexing and disturbing to the great majority of Americans. Their actions have prompted the most intense interest in the ancient philosophical question of man's duty of obedience to the state. Business lunches and suburban cocktail parties have come to sound like freshman seminars in philosophy, as an older generation has argued back and forth over the rightness and wrongness of 'what the kids and the

Negroes are doing.' (*National Commission on the Causes and Prevention of Violence* 1969, 92)

Increasingly, we see the prevalence of the argument that crime is a social issue rather than a moral one. Evidence of pluralism can be seen here as the discussion of norms begins to change from moral absolutes to normative ideals relative to identifiable interests (Gutmann and Thompson 2004, 91). At the center of the discussion are the pluralists' concerns for the group.

Evidence of pluralism can be observed as well in still other recommendations of these early reports. For example, the 1967 and 1973 reports recommended that police departments increase their minority recruiting activities and that minorities be represented at all levels of the police organization (*President's Commission on Law Enforcement and Administration of Justice* 1967b, 101-102; *National Advisory Commission on Criminal Justice Standards and Goals* 1973, 107). This represents a clear example of attempts to create "overlapping membership" as discussed earlier (Held 2006, 161). Even clearer evidence of pluralism can be found in the 1973 report by the *National Advisory Commission on Criminal Justice Standards and Goals*, a report in which the commission recommended the creation of police-community relations activities. Therein they defined the term "community," and connect it to the prevailing pluralistic thinking, stating: "Community as used in the report means the people for whom the police agency provides service. Within that broad framework are diverse groups which have special needs or interests" (1973, 5).

The second way pluralism can be seen in the community policing literature is in the way community policing is evaluated. The literature makes extensive use of survey instruments directed toward the groups aimed to gauge satisfaction, which again evidences an assumed utilitarian goal. Indeed, failure to appropriately construct survey samples that include groups can cause validity problems for a study's findings (Weisberg, Krosnick, and Bowen 1996, 15-17). In other words, survey research of this sort is predicated on pluralistic assumptions about social and political phenomena and their findings are valid only if accommodations for it are made.

As the practice of community policing began to spread to agencies across the country throughout the 1980s and 1990s, attention began to turn to assessing its effectiveness. Thurman and Reisig were among the many who recognized "[...] social science research methods have become useful tools upon which police agencies can rely to assess citizen satisfaction, generate ideas for improvements, and plan future service delivery" (1996, 571). In particular, survey instruments became popular tools "to systematically assess public attitudes toward the police and the services they provide" (1996, 577). The surveys were distributed to the "members who reside in an affected area," usually at the neighborhood level (1996, 571, 575). These surveys measured a number of "individual-level variables [that] "include race/ethnicity, age, gender, and socioeconomic status" (Thurman and Reisig 1996, 574). In their survey of quantitative assessments of community policing, Thurman and Reisig find that "the current literature holds that the most important individual-level variables are race/ethnicity and age" (1996, 577). Demonstrating a further tilt toward a pluralistic understanding of the community, they argue that "contextual variables" such as "neighborhood culture, type of police-citizen contact, and a citizen's evaluation of a police contact," may hold explanatory powers in assessing the level of citizen satisfaction (Thurman and Reisig 1996, 577).

Much of the survey research carried out reports finding that the practice of community policing has failed to yield the results anticipated in the form of sustained satisfaction and cooperation with the police by the wide array of groups and community members served (National Research Council 2004, 234-235). Scholars have spent considerable effort to account for community policing's shortcoming through the deployment of surveys designed to measure a particular researcher's pet theory about particular explanatory contextual variables. Different aspects of "neighborhood context" are frequently argued for and analyzed (Thurman and Reisig 1996, 574-577). A study conducted by Hawdon and Ryan (2003) sought to determine if the level of community solidarity was a confounding factor unaccounted for in a handful of analysis that concluded with positive results for community policing practice. Again, we see evidence of pluralism as the variable under consideration – "solidarity" – seeks to measure some assumed attribute of the group (Hawdon and Ryan 2003, 55). The negative conclusion reported in that study led the researchers to conclude that their "study adds to a growing list of evaluations that find the assertion of community policing advocates to be somewhat overstated" (Hawdon and Ryan 2003, 67).

Examples of other analyses of group characteristics under the guise of neighborhood context includes Pattavina, Byrne, and Garcia's assessment of "the risk level of a particular neighborhood" to have relatively higher or lower crime (2006, 203). In what might be construed as another version of the neighborhood solidarity argument, Lord, Kuhns, and Friday seek to measure the effectiveness of community policing practices in a variety of neighborhoods located in a "small city" (2009, 574). Finally, some researchers question the usefulness of neighborhood context altogether, asserting that other descriptors such as age and race are of greater value (Dai and Johnson 2009). In effect, pluralism can be seen in this identification of a latent group.

In a similar way, we see police officers treated as an interest group. This is the third observation on the literature's evidence of a bias toward pluralism. As mentioned previously, pluralism maintains that because the state has interests too, it can be conceived of as an interest group as well. Furthermore, because the organs of the state have power disproportionate to other groups, "the state cannot be regarded as a neutral arbiter among all interests" (Held 2006, 171). The police are such a group exercising unequal power. Therefore, in the pluralist's view, the police can be treated as an interest group, and one that can also be studied through sociological methods.

Scholarly sociological research that sought to treat police officers as an interest group began in the early 1960s, before the commission reports were produced. Jerome H. Skolnick was among the first to look at the social aspects of police officers as a group in his seminal *Justice without Trial: Law Enforcement in Democratic Society* (1966). That the 4th edition of this work was produced in 2011 gives testament to its enduring importance. The work is based on field observations of police officers (beginning in 1962) in two un-named cities; one on the East Coast to which he refers as "Eastville" and another on the West Coast, which he calls "Westville" (1966). Through his observations he comes to some unflattering conclusions, and proposes a "sketch of the policeman's 'working personality'" (1966, 42). In building the "sketch," Skolnick ties the policing type to other groups (and therefore their interests) when he identifies them as overwhelmingly "white" and "conservative, emotionally and politically" (1966, 59). As for other interests and preferences, they are obtained through the socialization process in the training phase and reinforced through experience in the profession (Skolnick 1966). Disturbingly, Skolnick found officers were intensely interested in preserving their authority, which appears to be taken on as a personal attribute of the individual (1966, 231).

Another of the earliest researchers to conduct this type of inquiry was Albert J. Reiss, Jr. who, in 1963 and 1964, started conducting field research in a variety of large metropolitan departments (Reiss 1971, x). Working in concert with these agencies in 1965 and 1966, he and a team of researchers undertook observations of police officer's interactions with the public on the streets during their tour of duty. Reiss's work "came to the attention of the National Crime Commission in 1965" and he and his team were retained to do further work (1971, x-xi). However, little of that research appears in those commission reports. As one reviewer explained: "His report to the Commission, emphasizing a high incidence of observed police misconduct, proved controversial and little of his findings are included in either *The Challenge of Crime in a Free Society* or the *Task Force Report: The Police*" (MacNamara 1972, 410). The data and his findings would not be lost, however; instead, they would be published in a rather uncomplimentary study of the police entitled *The Police and the Public* (Reiss 1971). It would be among the earliest attempts to describe the social characteristics of the police, both as individual officers and an interest group.

Reiss's work entailed a description of what he actually saw police officers do during the course of their duties. Though one reviewer criticizes him for not going far enough in analyzing "the socio-psychological factors which perhaps underpin much of the defective structure," his important contribution is in beginning the dialogue about the social aspects of the police as a group in American society (MacNamara 1972, 410). What Reiss does accomplish in furthering the pluralists' argument is point to the citizen-police social group dichotomy when he observed that while "police are locally organized and controlled in a society [it] does not necessarily imply that they are highly integrated with the local populace" (1971, 214).

James Q. Wilson reports similar research in his *Varieties of Police Behaviors* ([1968] 1978). In that work, he too reports findings from field observations conducted in a variety of police departments. Wilson not only reported general sociological characteristics in "how the police patrolman behaves," he found noteworthy variations between groups of police and between police departments (Wilson [1968] 1978, 4, 138-

139). He recognized that different police departments had a "distinctive character or 'feel,'" and that for individual officers the "process of socialization is especially important in organizations like the police" (Wilson [1968] 1978, 139). Wilson reports finding "three distinctive police styles" among the agencies studied ([1968] 1978, 139). The styles are not as important to this research as the fact that variation within groups is present, much like the variation discussed as the explanatory social variable *neighborhood context* (Thurman and Reisig 1996, 574-577).

Subsequent works by Manning in 1977 (*Police Work: The Social Organization of Policing*) and Klockars in 1985 (*The Idea of Police*) continued to build upon the earlier works which sought to establish the social aspects of the police as a group. Their individual findings are also not as important to this research as the fact of their existence. These studies demonstrate the persistence of pluralist thinking on the part of researchers who continue attempts to socially define police officers by their interests and specify the boundaries within which group behavior takes place. They further support the claims that the community policing research evidences a bias towards pluralism in that it portrays the police as a social group often times diametrically opposed to the citizenry. In sum, each of these four works point to a tendency toward antipathy in the police attitude toward citizens. In the end, we see that while many argue the practice of community policing is the solution to mediate the positions of these groups, much of the research expresses a deep-seated skepticism of police – both as individual officers and as a collective group.

While the evaluations of community policing's effectiveness in the eyes of the citizens centers on their satisfaction with the police, surveys of police satisfaction with community policing generally revolve around their satisfaction with the practice itself. Generally, the same social science research methods are deployed, most often taking the form of surveys and interviews (Rosenbaum, Yeh, and Wilkinson 1994; Dicker 1998; Novak, Alarid, and Lucas 2003; Cordner and Beibel 2005; Glaser and Denhardt 2009). For example, in a series of surveys taken of police officers in Joliet, Illinois over a period of years, no real significant change in officer attitudes toward community policing practice was detected, despite several years of training and exposure (Rosenbaum, Yeh, and Wilkinson 1994). Dicker directly addressed the tendency toward recalcitrance in officer's attitudes about community policing (1998). Also using survey data, he concluded that the overt organizational culture was less predictive of community policing's acceptance than the individual officer's predispositions toward the job of policing (Dicker 1998, 79).

Also focusing on the "officers' acceptance of community policing," Novak, Alarid, and Lucas administered surveys to 445 officers of all ranks in the Kansas City Police Department (2003, 57). They found that despite years of engagement in community policing practices, extensive exposure, and specialized training in the methods of community policing, acceptance was lower than anticipated (Novak, Alarid, and Lucas 2003). Surveys administered by Cordner and Beibel (2005) to officers at San Diego Police Department, and by Glaser and Denhardt (2009) in another "Midwestern city," likewise found low support for community policing practices. The later study noted that in many instances "the bonds of the 'brotherhood' of police are stronger than officers' connections to community" (Glaser and Denhardt 2009, 312).

This disjunction between citizen and officer view on community policing was uniquely demonstrated in survey research conducted by Liederbach, Fritsch Carter, and Bannister (2008). In that study, citizens and officers were given the same survey. This "direct comparison between the views of citizens and officers within a jurisdiction [...] largely influenced by the community-oriented policing movement" demonstrated that "officers and citizens significantly differed in their assessment of the importance of specific crime problems [and] the value of community policing programs" (Liederbach, Fritsch, Carter, and Bannister 2008, 271).

Because pluralism was the predominant social and political theory of the 1960s, its principal assumptions became uncritically incorporated in the formulation of community policing practice. Moreover, because tension and conflict between competing interest groups is a persistent characteristic of pluralism, the community engagement component of community policing was the target of claims of inefficiency. Of pluralist thinkers writing in the political context, Held observes, "While their influence is by no means as extensive now as it was then, their work has had a lasting effect on contemporary political thought" (2006, 158). This is particularly true with regard to much of the scholarship on community policing, as the legacy of pluralism has served to stall any further development. As demonstrated previously, the practice is set up to involve perpetual conflict between the police and citizens, as the interests and preferences of each group are presumed to be rather fixed and naturally dichotomous. As we will see in the subsequent chapter, this is precisely what deliberative democratic theorists argue against – namely, the assumption that an individual's preferences are fixed and anchored solely to some aspect of their identity, and that they are always utilitarian in their drive to maximize their interest, even at the expense of others.

DEMOCRACY, DEMOCRATIZATION, AND THE POLICE

Because the key ideals and norms of democracy were in place before the development of modern policing organizations, American policing is treated in much of the literature as presumptively democratic. Unfortunately, the idea of democracy is discussed within much of the policing literature with little precision (Berkley 1969; Remington 1965; Marx 2001; Sklansky 2008). Though this deficiency is being addressed with increasing frequency (Bayley 2001, 2006; Pino and Wiatrowski 2006b; Sklansky 2008; Manning 2010), a more precise discussion of democracy as it relates to policing would have been very helpful in community policing's formative era. This is especially true when considering community policing's most fundamental precept is the involvement of citizens in the public's safety. Democratic theorists still to this day wrestle with conceptions and measures of democracy (Held 2006, 231). Similarly, scholars are still grappling with definitions of "community" in community policing (Herbert 2006b). While recent work shows a more concentrated effort to connect democratic theory to policing, evidence of the stilted and disjointed treatment of the notion of democracy in policing (or police-related) literature remains. Moreover, very little of it is presented in a manner that could help a practitioner inform practice.

Scholarship on the nexus of the key concepts at play – democracy, democratization, and policing – is often oblique. A review of the scholarship reveals considerable diversity in its treatment of these key concepts and their role in policing. These configurations account for the divergence in the extant scholarship in two ways. First, each of these concepts receives varying levels of treatment depending on the scholar's base discipline (sociology, criminology, history, public administration, political science, etc.). Each discipline's treatment has different goals, depending on their target audience (be they practitioners or other scholars). Secondly, concentration on one of these concepts is often accompanied by a heavy reliance on assumptions concerning the others. This is not altogether unforgivable. Research cannot be all things to all people. Assumptions allow for a starting point from which to begin the dialogue without rebuilding the whole of democratic theory and its predicating philosophy. In the space of a single word – *democracy* – a large amount of context and meaning are transmitted. The term is a valuable and powerful culturally informed heuristic (Rawls 1989, 234-35; Wedeen 2002). When considered in this manner, the available scholarship can be classified into three broad spheres: literature directed toward practitioners and administrators; country studies that evaluate regime performance against democratic standards; and, scholarship on democracy and the process of democratization. With few exceptions, each of these areas of scholarship proffers a theory of democracy (explicit or implicit) and evidence a belief that that those ideals can be spread through the process of democratization.

The first sphere contains scholarly works – largely produced by criminologists and some sociologists – seeking to inform practitioners and their policies. Because these works have practical aims in that they seek to influence practice, they may not go into significant detail about democratic theory, and pay only a little more on the process of democratization (Berkley 1969; Kohn 1997; Marx 2001; Amir and Einstein 2001; Pino and Wiatrowski 2006a). Discussions of democratic policing did not appear in the literature frequently accessed by practitioners until the late 20th century (Loader 2006). Much of the earlier scholarship concerned effectiveness and professionalism under presumptively democratic institutions operating under constitutional restraints (Loader 2006; Berkley 1969). The literature often contains assumptions about the purpose of law enforcement in a democratic context. That is to say, the police were simply to enforce the law and maintain order as effectively and efficiently as possible (Loader 2006; Wilson 2000).

Democratic assumptions, however, force us to take a closer look at the police culture, as it is argued the current arrangement could exist without regard to whether the regime is democratic or not (Loader 2006, 210-15). Neither the police nor the military are inherently democratic institutions. Moreover, once employed by previously undemocratic regimes they may prove difficult to retool due to the heavy influence of the cultural normalcy of violence (Loader 2006; Kohn 1997; Pino and Wiatrowski 2006a). When an individual joins such institutions, they do not come already imbued with the cultural norms of the institution – they become infused with the culture and integrate these ideals (Selznick [1957] 1984; Stone and Ward 2000, 11-13). This is consistent with the pluralists' understanding of group politics, yet supportive of the deliberative democratic theory proposition that preferences and interests can change through genuine discourse and persistent dialogue. This kind of institution and its culture becomes particularly troublesome during the process of democratization if the police and military predate the democratic regime (Bayley 2001and 2006; Pino and Wiatrowski 2006a).

Scholars writing within the first sphere – the sphere directed toward administrators and practitioners – also tend to distill democratic theory and institutions into one or more principles that their prescriptions are intended to support. Some of these summaries are helpful in forming policy, but their characterizations of practice tend toward on an overly simplified notion of democracy. For example, one early effort of this type of scholarship condensed from the combined works of Locke, Dahl, and Morganthau projects a notion of democracy built upon the principle of "consensus," and postulate this idea as the foundation of democratic policing (Berkley 1969, 1-5). Later scholars seem to infer these principles (and a few others) from observed arrangements of Western democratic institutions and surmise the core principles of democratic policing to include the ideals of accountability, responsiveness and transparency (Bayley 2006, 19-21; Marx 2001; Pino and Wiatrowski, 2006a). Other ideals incorporated into notions of democratic policing include the rule of law, independent judicial procedures, and the consent of the governed (Sherman 2001; Pino and Wiatrowski, 2006a; Sklansky 2008). The writers in this area often advance policy positions intended to promote and protect one or more of these principles through professional training (Marenin 2004), policy initiatives aimed at institutional reform (Stone and Ward 2000; Bayley and Shearing 1996) and reforming the government as a whole (Bayley 2001; 2006).

Area studies scholarship is found within the second sphere. These works describe and evaluate the institutions and processes of regimes transitioning to democracy. They focus their analysis on critiquing the activities of a regime's coercive elements (military or police), spending little time suggesting policy reforms, a little more time developing their theoretical assumptions of democracy, and a great deal of effort explaining democratization processes (Diamond 1997; Giliomee 1995; Hiskey and Bowler 2005).

Giliomee's (1995) scholarship in the area of the democratization of South Africa is an example of an area study that is grounded in the real-time context of political activity. Written in the era immediately after the fall of apartheid, he suggests that certain cultural requisites are missing – principally a civic culture, economic stability, and national identity – all argued to be needed to make the transition work (Giliomee 1995). His analysis makes almost journalistic use of the key actors and the interplay between them in forming his analysis and observations of obstacles (Giliomee 1995). Similarly, Diamond (1997) explores the problems of Central and South American countries that for years have been in transition to democracy, but are finding it difficult to complete the task. Before identifying a host of broad features that are missing (such as "elite" and "mass" acceptance of liberal reforms), he grounds his views of democratic theory in the works of Schumpeter and Dahl (Diamond 1997, 12-13). Diamond's work serves as an example of consolidation literature, directed at those areas that are nominally democratic, but feature nations within which the commitment seems weak (1997). This literature offers an analysis of the progress made, identifies missing features, and suggests necessary steps to be taken in order to strengthen Central and South American democracies at the national level (Diamond 1997). Hiskey and Bowler (2005) take this analysis one step further, conducting a more detailed analysis of a single country (Mexico) within the scope identified by Diamond (1997). They focus on the impact of "local effects" of democratization instead of "national-level processes" in their analysis (57).

Other work in this sphere centers on specific institutions within the countries or regions in democratic transition. A great deal of work is available on reforming the military in a democratic context, considerably more so than on policing (Barany 1997; Ruhl 2004; Winkates 2000; Kohn 1997). For example, Barany undertakes an examination of the post-Soviet era difficulties encountered in the democratization of Eastern European military forces (1997). He concludes that variation in the manner in which the military related to the former regimes explained the degree of difficulty faced by the new regime in getting the military to adapt to its new role in a democratic government (Barany 1997). In countries where the military was more "professionalized" (Hungary and Poland) the transition was easier than in countries where the military was "politicized" (East Germany, Romania, Czechoslovakia) (Barany 1997, 21-22).

Some works speak to the risks posed by confusion between the military and the police as to their role in the new regime. Winkates, for example, studies the democratization of the South African military and expresses concern about its increasing involvement in domestic law enforcement (2000). Ruhl expresses similar concern about the declining role of the military in external matters, and its increasing role in domestic affairs (2004, 138-39). He concludes that the lack of responsiveness on the part of military leadership to civilian oversight is a serious risk to democratic advances (Ruhl 2004, 141-142). In another example, Davis points out the threats posed to democratic consolidation in Mexico by police corruption (2006). Failure to control this threat is leading to the deterioration of "the rule of law" and represents a significant risk to democracy in that country (Davis 2006, 57-60). Wilson, on the other hand, points to successful reforms of Kosovo's police as an example of how to achieve "internal security" and consolidate democracy (2006, 155-56).

Other scholarship falling within this sphere, though not entirely neatly, is research on peacebuilding and peacekeeping (Celador 2005; Doyle and Sambanis 2000). Whereas Wilson (2006) reports positive progress in Kosovo's policing reform efforts, Celador (2005) reports that similar reform of Bosnia's police force – even under the close supervision of U.N. peacekeepers – has not advanced the goal of democratic consolidation. In fact, what ended up developing there was a *de facto* form of apartheid within the community. Nevertheless, U.N. policies and programs are enjoying a moderate level of success assisting countries through the difficult transition (Doyle and Sambanis 2000).

The third sphere includes the literature concerning the study of democracy and democratization. The literature on democracy and democratization tends to confine itself to generalities, saying little about specific countries and contexts except in occasional convenient examples and anecdotes. This sphere consists mostly of work by political scientists, and at times sociologists working from the perspective of the political sociology (see Diamond, Lipset, and Linz 1987). It would be an error to conceive of these concepts as connected in a linear fashion – that is, that we first concern ourselves in a programmatic fashion with democracy, followed by democratization, and then finally the police. However, it may well be that policing has a closer connection with democratic theory than previously thought. Furthermore, this understanding may adapt itself to the current expectations in what is best described as the process of democratization (Almond *et al.* 2001; Dahl 1998; Locke [1690] 1980; Mill [1861] 2001; Rousseau [1762] 1987; Whitehead 2002). The gaps in the political science research regimen present an opportunity for exploration. What I refer to here is the hitherto limited engagement of the political scientist with the criminologist on the matter of what could be described as the forcible acquisition and maintenance of internal security to democratic ends – that is, the police. Whitehead states it the best when he observes:

> [...] citizen security lurks in the background of most democratic theory. It tends to get included – if only tacitly – in the definition of 'democracy'; it is often assumed, taken for granted, or even enters as an unstated presupposition. (2002, 171)

Several similar examples supporting Whitehead's premise present themselves in a body of literature that stretches back for centuries. Locke suggested that the use of force for the protection and security of a citizen's life, liberty and property is a legitimate exercise of government power, and that failure of the government to protect these (life, liberty, property) is grounds for revolt ([1690] 1980). Arguing generally from a different theoretical position than Locke, Rousseau also comes to a similar conclusion, noting that the "executive power" as a "public force must have an agent of its own that unifies it and gets it working in accordance with the directions of the general will" ([1762] 1987, 49). In advocating for a representative form of democratic government, Mill contends that the "security of person and property, and equal justice between individuals, are the first needs of society, and the primary ends of government" ([1861] 2001, 176).

Theorists writing in the last several decades continue to note the importance of the police to individual security, even if only vaguely so (Dahl 1998). It appears that the provision of individual security is a basic assumption as the analysis has now processed to second order problems such as control and oversight about such issues as discursion, coercion, and the use of too much force (Dahl 1998). The advice of more contemporary scholars consists mostly of warning citizens to be vigilant with regard to instances of excessive uses of force by police, and recommending the formation of independent citizen review committees to judge the actions of police in contentious cases of alleged police misconduct (Dahl 1998).

Comparative theory does not restrict itself to the concerns of the democratic theorists. Concerned primarily with the characteristics and structures of political systems, they list the authority to use force as one of the legitimating characteristics of a government (Almond 2001). Here legitimacy is linked to the ability to carry out the will of the regime (regardless of type), without consideration as to the moral appropriateness of the ends to which that action is directed (Almond 2001). Differentiations between the force used by police or the military are distinctions without any real difference where this theory is concerned. The comparativists see security as a necessary aim of any government that can be realized by force, and is independent of any one regime's type or ideology. Meanwhile, the political scientists appear reluctant to address the issue beyond admitting its existence.

A theoretically grounded analysis differentiating between the conceptions of force as "*a* problem *for* the government" versus "*the* problem *of* government" may aid political analysis (Whitehead 2002, 173). Criminologists and sociologists ordinarily take the former approach, formulating policy recommendations consistent with their understanding of democratic principles (Bayley 2001, 2006; Diamond 2002; Loader 2006; Stone and Ward 2000; Diamond, Lipset and Linz 1987). Area studies scholars tend to take the later approach, taking up the issue of force when it appears as evidence of a regime's failure to conform to democratic principles (Celador 2005; Barany 1997; Davis 2006; Diamond 1997, 1999, 2005; Hiskey and Bowler; 2005; Ruhl 2004; Wilson 2006; Winkates 2000).

The variety of theories and positions demonstrate that citizen security is important to democratic stability, and a topic warranting exploration in the democratization literature. Whitehead acknowledges this, observing that "theories of democratization need to include some explicit account of how citizen security can be constituted or constructed out of conditions in which it is normally absent" (2002, 171). Diamond also admits citizen security is important, emphatically noting the role of the police, observing:

> A crucial and commonly overlooked arena of state strengthening involves the system of justice and especially the police. Not only do order and personal safety constitute one of the most basic expectations people have of government, but the police are the agents of state authority whom ordinary citizens are most likely to experience in their daily lives. If the police are corrupt, abusive, unaccountable or even lazy and incompetent, this cannot but affect popular perceptions of the authority and legitimacy of the state. If new democracies are to deliver the balance of freedom and order their peoples want and to keep the military out of the business of internal security (and thus politics), they must develop professionalized, disciplined, resourceful, and accountable police forces. (Diamond 1999, 94)

Some scholars have paid cursory attention to the role of police in democratization (Huntington 1991; Whitehead 2002; Bayley 2006; Diamond 1999), but those in this research space are few in number. Research in this area is important as it is often foundational to the policy initiatives of agencies such as the United Nations, the U.S. Agency for International Development, and the U.S. Department of Justice. These entities are often involved in aiding foreign governments in transitioning their force elements to democracy (Bayley 2001; Diamond 2002; Hume and Miklaucic 2005; see U.S. Agency for International Development 2002).

The manner in which policing develops in the United States – from the colonial period to the present – evidences a concern for practical matters more than theoretical ones. Plainly stated, policing was created to achieve the practical aims of public order and security rather than further fundamental democratic principles. That the police can be made to serve democratic practices and principles is another matter entirely. The manner in which the Founders structured the institutions and processes of democratic governance places American policing in a context where it is amenable to reforms consistent with an ever-evolving understanding of democratic principles. The fact that policing – particularly American policing – has been in a near-constant state of reform since its very inception serves as evidence that it can indeed be molded in a manner more conducive to democratic norms.

CHAPTER 3

The Idea of Deliberative Democracy: Theory and Practice

Deliberative democratic theory offers a new view of the relationship between the government and the governed as well as the citizen and the democratic administrative state. Emerging from the criticism of pluralist theory, deliberative democratic theory offers new explanations and understandings of the importance of community engagement in the modern administrative state. In particular, it focuses on the idea of deliberation and transformation for both the citizens and agents of the state. Deliberative democratic theory proposes a new way of thinking about community engagement. Rather than simply engaging citizens for the purposes of aggregating preferences, expressed as the interests of identifiable groups, it proposes community engagement for the purposes of forming and discerning preferences across groups through discourse and deliberation. In the process, both the citizen and the state are transformed. The legitimacy for state action resulting therefrom is based on a deeper understanding of the issues in dispute shared by all parties rather than the superficial and transient satisfaction of interest groups at one point in time.

ORIGINS

Deliberative democratic scholarship is a relatively new field of research, the term finding its first mention in a 1980 work by Joseph Bessette (Held 2006, 232; Dryzek 2000, 2). Though Bessette was the first to use the term, the arguments advanced in that early work are not considered foundational and have largely been subsumed into the critique of pluralism offered by deliberative democratic theorists (Held

2006). In that work, Bessette submits that interest aggregation through elected representatives is accomplished through deliberative means in Congress, thus making the U.S. a deliberative democracy (1980). However, critics of this perspective maintain that this type of interest aggregation does not go far enough or deep enough (see Chambers 2003; Gutmann and Thompson 2004, 13-21). These scholars speak of the "quality of democracy," (Held 2006, 232) which begins with the process of the individual's preference formation and change (Chambers 2003). If placed on a continuum, the arguments advanced by Bessette, and others like him (Dryzek and Niemeyer 2010), would be on the opposite end of the scale from those who advocate a more radical form of deliberative democracy that approaches direct democracy (Fishkin 1991). In its most radical form, deliberative democracy borders on a near direct democratic model with "deliberative opinion polls" and "citizen juries" compelled to hear evidence and make decisions on significant policy matters (Fishkin 1991, 81, 97; Beetham 2005).

However, in its most commonly argued formulation deliberative democracy is primarily a "political approach" – an idealized "model of democracy" – in much the same way community policing is a practical model of policing (Held 2006, 232). Further still, whereas community policing is marked by community engagement and participation, deliberative democracy is also characterized by citizen involvement in a discursive manner. Deliberative democracy takes its starting point from the importance of the people, and their consent to be governed. In order to arrive at this starting point for democracy, there is need of an initial engagement. In most models of democracy, this engagement is sustained and ongoing through a variety of practices, of which voting is just one. Deliberative democratic thinkers submit that the best policy decisions are arrived at through reasoned and ongoing argument in an open dialectical process (Held 2006). Public policy decisions arrived at through reasoned open discussion are believed more legitimate than those arrived at by elites and policy experts in back rooms or through parliamentary sophistry (Dryzek 2000). Parkinson summarizes it well, stating, "Above all, [...] deliberative democracy in its classical formulations is an account of political legitimacy" (2006, 4).

The first point of concern for deliberative democratic scholars concerns preference formation. Because political power and, ultimately, the authority of the state is involved, justification is an important step on the path to legitimacy. When speaking of

The Idea of Deliberative Democracy

justification, the idea of justice cannot be avoided. This conflict of preferences tends to shape the political discourse along the path to public policy. If public policy is intended to further the common good, differences in preferences need to be resolved. This engagement is a principal concern for deliberative democratic practitioners and scholars. For its philosophical foundation, deliberative democratic theory primarily relies on the works of two thinkers: John Rawls and Jürgen Habermas.

THE EARLY THINKERS

Rawls and Habermas are paradoxically early entrants and late arrivals to the development of deliberative democratic theory. They were early entrants in that other scholars in the 1980s and 1990s regularly appealed to their earlier works in developing the foundation of deliberative democratic theory (Bohman and Rehg 1997; xii). Moreover, as is normally the case with the rigorous scholarship, still other scholars sought to discredit the invocation of one or the other or both (Held 2006, 242). In the case of Rawls, the most often invoked work was *A Theory of Justice*, a classic study that first appeared in 1971. In the case of Habermas, most often cited was his "Discourse Ethics: Notes on a Program of Philosophical Justification," (often referred to simply as "Discourse Ethics"). This is a chapter in his book entitled *Moral Consciousness and Communicative Action*, published in 1983. However, some scholars reference an earlier work, *Legitimation Crisis* (1973), because they argue it provides important insight for the famous "Discourse Ethics" and its imperatives concerning the most appropriate rules for deliberation (Chambers 2003, 98-101 & 163-168). I submit that Habermas's *Legitimation Crisis* (1973) and Rawls's *A Theory of Justice* (1971) give important context as they reflect important themes of the times in which they were written. "Discourse Ethics" merits special attention and will be explored in far more detail as I argue it should figure prominently in any program advancing a "deliberative turn" (Dryzek 2010, 3) in community policing.

Throughout the 1980s, both scholars were drawn into the fray to make clarifications of their oft-cited thoughts, and eventually compelled to produce works that addressed deliberative democratic theory head-on. In this sense, they are late entrants. Dryzek notes their later contributions, stating "John Rawls and Jürgen Habermas, respectively the most important liberal theorist and critical theorist of the late twentieth century, lent their prestige to the deliberative turn by publishing major works in which they identified themselves as deliberative democrats [...]" (2000, 2). He identifies Rawls's contribution to deliberative democratic theory as *Political Liberalism* (1993) and Habermas's as *Between Facts and Norms: Contributions to a Discourse Theory of Law and Democracy* ([1992] 1996) and not their earlier classic works. Though there are differences between the two (see McCarthy 1994; Chambers 2003, 101-102), there is much more convergence than divergence on the central issues of concern (Elster 1998, 5; Gutmann and Thompson 2004, 9, 26). As Elster puts it (with his emphasis), "[...] the arguments advanced by Habermas and Rawls do seem to have a common core: political choice, to be legitimate, must be the outcome of *deliberation about ends among free, equal, and rational agents*" (1998, 5).

John Rawls

Notions of freedom, equality and reason naturally lead us to a discussion of justice. Social and political concerns are the animating force behind his most famous work, *A Theory of Justice* (Hampton 1997, 133; Pogge 2007, 19-21). While some elaboration is in order later on, for now we can summarize Rawls's principal contribution by saying it concerns the ethical implications of preference formation and decision making by individuals who are constituent members of a larger society (Chambers 2003). In *A Theory of Justice*, Rawls advances a Kantian argument for a universal moral imperative without resorting to metaphysics, ultimately proposing a process for determining how that imperative might be determined (Sturba 1998, 401). Rawls is famous for advancing the idea of the "veil of ignorance," from behind which one would have to form preferences (Rawls [1971] 1999). Without knowing one's interests or position in a given situation, one would then have to rely on the rationale of the argument presented in order to make decisions (Rawls [1971] 1999). A decision arrived at in this manner is presumed to be impartial, which is an important goal of one strain of deliberative democratic thinkers (Held 2006).

Because Rawls's greatest contribution came during the turmoil of the late 1960s and early 1970s, certain biographical facts of Rawls's life are instructional in understanding the content and timing of *A Theory of Justice* (Pogge 2007). First, Rawls was a veteran of Second World War, having seen combat in the Pacific (Pogge 2007). Having observed the loss of life on a vast scale in the conflict influenced his thinking on the idea of justice (Pogge 2007). After military service, he resumed his academic pursuits, receiving his doctorate in 1950 from Princeton. He held posts at Cornell University and the Massachusetts Institute of Technology before arriving at Harvard in 1962 (Pogge 2007). His early work evidenced a scholarly concern for justice, having sketched out an ethical decision model in "Outline of a Decision Procedure for Ethics" (1951). Though he was not among the activist scholars of the 1960s who demonstrated against the war in Vietnam or for civil rights, he did have related concerns and expressed them through his writings (Alterman 2002). In a reflective piece published upon Rawls's death, Alterman noted that many believed he was in a position to do more to advance correctives for injustices he witnessed during his times. Instead, he chose to express himself through his political philosophy (Alterman 2002). Relying on a quote from Thomas Nagel, Alterman argues that the Rawls's method of addressing injustice through his political philosophy would take generations to effect; he felt Rawls was needed in a more active role during his own time (Alterman 2002).

Nevertheless, Rawls did take up the matter of social justice through his seminal 1971 work. Keeping in mind his rather oblique way of addressing the issues of the times, I suggest that *A Theory of Justice* (1971) is about as emphatic a statement as we could expect from the mild-mannered Rawls (Alterman 2002; Pogge 2007). One need only look to the preface of that work to find out that many of the important chapters were essays puolished in the preceding "dozen years or so" and germane to the times in which they were written (Rawls [1971] 1999, xvii).

Among the included essays are "Justice as Fairness" (1958), "The Sense of Justice" (1963), "Distributive Justice" (1967), and "Civil Disobedience" (1966). Evidence that Rawls was engaged at some level with important issues of his day is particularly found in "Civil Disobedience" (1966), which was reproduced as a chapter in *A Theory of Justice* concerning the definition of civil disobedience. Therein, he references Dr. Martin Luther King's famous "Letter from Birmingham Jail" (Rawls [1971] 1999, 321). That he saw the need for radical and thoroughgoing change can be seen in the opening paragraphs of *A Theory of Justice*, when he observes: "Justice is the first virtue of social institutions, as truth is of systems of thought. [...] [L]aws and institutions no matter how efficient and well-arranged must be reformed or abolished if they are unjust" (Rawls [1971] 1999, 3). In this one passage, Rawls takes aim at efficiency-oriented arguments made at the expense of justice. The work found broad audience and influenced a generation of scholars and practitioners in a variety of fields (Alterman 2002; Pogge 2007). As Hampton put it, "Influenced by the political turmoil of the 1960s, Rawls's vision of the just state is deeply egalitarian in spirit in a way many have found compelling" (1997, 133).

As previously mentioned, *A Theory of Justice* was the starting point for a great deal of the development of deliberative democratic theory in the 1980s and 1990s (Bohman and Rehg 1997; xi). Many scholars appear to have been compelled to incorporate, or refute, but in any case, address Rawls's thoughts. Though Rawls's thoughts are original and generative, he relied heavily on the contractarian philosophies of Rousseau, Kant, and Locke, hoping to perfect them (Rawls [1971] 1999, 10). In Rawls's view, the social contract was not constitutive of the relationship between the individual and the state or some other abstract aggregation, but rather between individuals (Hampton 1997, 133). In his estimation, the legitimacy of the initial agreement requires unanimous consensus on certain foundational principles that will govern all future interactions between individuals (Rawls [1971] 1999, 10; Hampton 1997; 133). If these can be determined, under these circumstances they would form the principles of justice, but not in any metaphysical sense.

In the context of cooperation – or political society – Rawls qualifies principles of justice by referring to them as "justice as fairness" (Rawls [1971] 1999; 1985). He argues that the nature of individuals capable of entering into such an agreement (ultimately forming a society) would include a capacity for reason as well as envy, balancing envy with reason to deduce an enlightened sense of self-interest. Individuals so disposed would ultimately come up with and agree to two principles of justice (Palmer 1996). However, these two principles materialize only if – prior to the agreement – the individual had no knowledge of their "place in society, [their] particular religious or metaphysical views, [their] moral beliefs, [or] social theories"

(Hampton 1997, 137-138). Rawls called this blinded vantage point the "original position" and the blinding device, the "veil of ignorance" (Rawls [1971] 1999, 15-19). Therefore, without knowledge of one's advantages, disadvantages, or other accidental qualities, prejudice loses its grip on reason in the decision making process (Hampton 1997, 137). Rawls supposes that individuals (with the character described above) would admit to principles of justice. In their initial formulation, they are:

> First: each person is to have an equal right to the most extensive scheme of equal basic liberties compatible with a similar scheme of liberties for others. [...]Second: social and economic inequalities are to be arranged so that they are both (a) reasonably expected to be to everyone's advantage, and (b) attached to positions and offices open to all. (Rawls [1971] 1999, 53)

Though Rawls maintains some resource redistribution to the most underprivileged members of society is justified, he does not argue for an unqualified Marxist-style distribution. If the unequal distribution is of greater benefit to the whole than equal distribution, then the demands of justice as fairness are met (Palmer 1996; Hampton 1997). Specifically, Rawls calls for "wealth and power to be distributed equally except where inequalities would work to the advantage of all and where there would be equal opportunity to achieve advantageous positions of equality" (Palmer 1996, 362). On a continuum, Rawls would fall somewhere between the communism of Marx, and the libertarianism of Nozick (Palmer 1996; Hampton 1997). While an in-depth examination of Rawls's thoughts on economic theory and policy are not relevant to the thesis advanced here, having a general fix on this position is important for two reasons. The first pertains to his rules of priority concerning judgments about the principles of justice. We will see below that justice cannot be shortchanged in the interest of efficiency (Rawls [1971] 1999, 266). Secondly, understanding his idea of cooperation is important. It is this enterprise to which the principles of justice are directed and particularly to the construction of just social institutions.

In Rawls's scheme, the principles of justice are listed in their order of importance and priority (Rawls [1971] 1999, 53). Moreover, the subparts of the second principle are also listed in order of priority (Rawls [1971] 1999, 77, 266). Rawls goes to considerable lengths to make distinctions between equality and efficiency and specify their respective roles in the principles of justice. He relies on the understanding of Pareto efficiency to assert that efficient distribution is not synonymous with an equal distribution ([1971] 1999, 57-65). Inefficiency occurs when there are unallocated goods that could be distributed, but are not. This is waste. The distribution of those goods to any party does not result in a reduction in the goods to another. Once this is reached – all goods are distributed without consideration to the size of that distribution – efficiency is realized. Rawls admits an inequality in the distribution of goods is justified under the condition that it somehow works to the benefit of the least well off, does not disadvantage another, and most importantly, does not come at the expense of rights specified in the first principle. Included in that first principle, "are political liberty (the right to vote and to hold public office) and freedom of speech and assembly; liberty conscience and freedom of thought; freedom of the person, which includes freedom from [...] assault and dismemberment [...] the right to hold personal property and freedom from arbitrary arrest and seizure" (Rawls [1971] 1999, 53). The distributions of these goods are equal and therefore efficient. That is to say, there is no way to shift the distribution of these goods between the parties that do not work to disadvantage other individuals. Disadvantaging some may be efficient, but not justified when it violates the first principle. In Rawls's view, efficiency arguments must come in second to basic human rights that constitute the first principle of justice.

One of the main reasons deliberative democratic scholars cannot avoid speaking about Rawls's work is due to the context in which he demonstrates the validity of his process. He devotes some effort to explaining the concept of *cooperation*, which sets the social foundations for engaging in the deliberative model proposed in *A Theory of Justice*. This idea has many facets. First, Rawls conceives of cooperation as the basic activity of organized society. He states that individuals come together and form cooperative groups because they can obtain more together than they can alone ([1971] 1999, 4). Secondly, this activity is guided by "rules of conduct," that we can infer to represent group norms, which emanate from human association and guide decision making ([1971] 1999, 4). Rawls argues that these rules (or norms) come to form the "system of cooperation designed to advance the good of those taking part in it" ([1971] 1999, 4). However, these rule sets can lead to conflict if there is disagreement about the distribution of benefits. For these reasons, it is in need of regulation. Therefore, it is necessary to choose widely acceptable rules that are demonstrably valid for all individuals. Finally, the principles of justice specified above serve as the basis for the "scheme of social cooperation," and thus stabilize the social system ([1971] 1999, 6).

The principles of justice are directed toward guiding decision making on fairness. These are the rules of the game that outline what is acceptable and what is not with regard to social cooperation. To summarize, cooperation is a necessary and fundamental activity of organized society that is structured on the principles of fairness in a manner that gives the activity – and the participants – stability. Interestingly, it is the idea of stability that gives insight into a host of problems with Rawls's thought that will be discussed later in this chapter as we explore deliberative democracy.

This discussion brings us back to the idea of justice as fairness. When deliberative democratic scholars of the 1980s began issuing criticisms of the relevancy of Rawls's model to the real world of politics, Rawls issued a series of corrections and restatements in a series of lectures and articles. Generally speaking, most of these criticisms centered on the impossibility of achieving the ideal conditions and outcomes advanced by his method (Gutmann and Thompson 1996; Chambers 2003). In one of these defenses, he indicated that his conception of fairness was a political – not metaphysical – notion, and that the model and position (original position) was merely a device by which more just decisions could be made (Rawls 1985). Further still, he goes into some detail about the idea of cooperation in that article, noting that cooperation is political and very real, as opposed to being abstract. However, a threat to cooperation emerges in the real world when there are multiple "moral doctrines," none of which may claim primacy over the other. When this is the case, questions arise as to the attainability of a "stable" and "well ordered society" (Rawls [1993] 2005; xvi). As Rawls puts it, "[a] modern democratic society is characterized not simply by a pluralism of comprehensive religious, philosophical, and moral doctrines but by a pluralism of incompatible yet reasonable comprehensive doctrines" ([1993] 2005, xvi). Reasonable people will disagree, yet when strictly applied, Rawls's method in *A Theory of Justice* is supposed to yield an obviously correct and singular result. Rawls's counter was to admit the plurality of divergent views that constitute society and one accommodated upon understanding his notion of justice as fairness in a political and not metaphysical sense. However, critics like Manin (1985) contend – and Rawls admits – this does not go far enough. In order to understand this political conception of justice as fairness, the recognition of several other concepts and assumptions must be specified in the arguments that constitute *A Theory of Justice* (Rawls [1993] 2005, xvii). In short, to fully understand justice as fairness as a political conception, the predicate ideas of "overlapping consensus" and "public reason" would be needed (Rawls [1993] 2005, xlv). These ideas and several other elaborations would constitute the principal contributions of Rawls's 1993 work, *Political Liberalism*.

In January 1985, Manin issued a critique of Rawls's ideas in *A Theory of Justice* as they apply to the practice of deliberation in politics. That article, "On Legitimacy and Political Deliberation," was originally published in Manin's native language (French) in the journal *Le Débat*. Deliberative democratic scholars Elly Stein and Jane Mansbridge translated it into English in 1987 for publication in the journal *Political Theory*. Manin's work deserves some discussion for two reasons. First, in Manin's criticism he addresses the problem of unanimity as the basis of legitimacy. Rawls will later amend his thoughts on this matter in *Political Liberalism* ([1993] 2005, 144). Secondly, Manin's work is seen by many as an important step in the development in deliberative democracy theory because he suggests practical and reasonable modifications to the idealistic solutions proposed by Rawls by criticizing his understanding of Rousseau. The best way to summarize Manin's contribution is that he brings to the forefront the idea and importance of deliberation to the process of will formation in the less-than-ideal circumstance that is society.

Manin's critique begins by highlighting the difficulty, if not impossibility, of Rawls's "original position" ([1985] 1987, 339-340). He notes that in the liberal tradition of which Rawls is a part, "by nature, every individual is free and equal to every other individual" and that this sovereignty is self-evident and cannot be abridged ([1985] 1987, 340). However, the primacy of the individual runs into practical difficulty in organized society where rules governing action must "arise from the will of all and represent the will of all" ([1985] 1987, 340).

The Idea of Deliberative Democracy

Rawls, he observed, is theoretically consistent when he observes that "unanimity alone is the basis of legitimacy" ([1985] 1987, 341). The task at hand for Rawls in *A Theory of Justice* is finding this single point or position of unanimity upon which legitimate political decision can be made. Quoting *A Theory of Justice*, he recalls that Rawls conceives, "the original position is so characterized that unanimity is possible" ([1985] 1987, 340). However, as Manin points out, "individuals behind the veil of ignorance are supposed to deliberate […] but what does deliberation mean in this situation" ([1985] 1987, 348)? Because they are alone, ignorant of their interest or prospects, and stripped of all differentiating characteristics, "only one point of view exists, which is the same for all" ([1985] 1987, 348). Therefore, if "they all have the same point of view […] deliberation is nothing but the calculation of the classic economic agent" ([1985] 1987, 348). Manin asserts that the real world is not like this.

A practical problem remains – namely, how "to reconcile the principle of decision making (by majority) with the principle of legitimacy (by unanimity)" ([1985] 1987, 341)? Relying on the work of Sieyes, Manin suggests that if the "sum of all individual wills is what is meant by unanimity […] practical necessities of political life […] make it essential to settle for a majority" ([1985] 1987, 342). Using Sieyes's words, "plurality becomes legitimately a substitute for unanimity" ([1985] 1987, 342). Likewise, he recalls that Rousseau observes a link between "principle and practice" in his famous "distinction between the general will and the will of all" ([1985] 1987, 343). Using Rousseau's word, Manin points out "the general will is […] deduced by counting the votes" ([1985] 1987, 343).

However, Manin remains unconvinced that we can completely abandon the "individual will" ([1985] 1987, 344). The problem for him lies in the fact that for Sieyes and Rousseau (and Rawls), the individual will upon which legitimacy is dependent is already formed ([1985] 1987, 344). Deliberation, as we saw above, is mere calculation. Manin wants to recall a more Aristotilean conception of deliberation. He explains in this regard:

> Following a usage that goes back to Aristotle, philosophic tradition generally takes deliberation to mean the process of the formation of the will, the particular moment that precedes choice, and in which the individual ponders different solutions

before settling for one of them. Rousseau uses the term *deliberation* in a different sense, one that is accepted in common language, and uses it to mean "decision." We can see the difference that separates these two definitions: in the vocabulary of philosophy, deliberation describes the process that precedes decision; in Rousseau's writings, it signifies decision itself. (Manin [1985] 1987, 345)

What Manin admits to the process of decision making is all that Rawls and Rousseau painstakingly removed – the exchange of information that is dialogue; the give-and-take that is deliberation ([1985] 1987). Therefore, "the source of legitimacy is not the predetermined will of individuals, but rather the process of its formation, that is, deliberation itself" ([1985] 1987, 351-352). As such, "a legitimate decision does not represent the *will* of all, but is one that results from the *deliberation of all*" ([1985] 1987, 352).

In reality, "political decision making is by its nature a choice under uncertainty" ([1985] 1987, 349). Therefore, it is necessary to consider as many viewpoints as possible prior to making a decision. The minority opinion must be considered and no one should be excluded from participation ([1985] 1987). The ultimate end of the decision making process is not to determine the majority opinion and eradicate the minority opinion. In fact, Manin maintains, it is the responsibility of the majority to continually engage the minority in deliberation ([1985] 1987, 361-363). In this specific way, we can see politics – deliberative democratic politics – as the constant engagement and perpetual questioning through the process of deliberation, in which the majority is "compelled to justify itself before the public" ([1985] 1987, 361). Manin keenly observes, "the procedure preceding the decision is a condition for legitimacy, which is just as necessary as the majority principle" ([1985] 1987, 360). It is precisely to this concern that Habermas speaks in developing his method for deliberation that is set forth in "discourse ethics" ([1983] 1990). This contribution to our understanding will be explored further in the next section.

Other pertinent criticisms of Rawls's exist and will be presented. However, they pertain mostly to his later works, particularly *Political Liberalism* (1993), which is his most direct contribution to the theory of deliberative democracy. Subsequent scholars took Rawls's thought in *A Theory of Justice*, as well as the associated criticism, utilizing relevant aspects to formulate a practical theory of deliberative democracy. Much of the criticism centered on the limited utility of a highly idealistic internal dialogue that was supposed to constitute deliberation. These subsequent scholars believed Rawls's thinking was formative to deliberative democratic thinking, but not consisting of deliberative democracy itself. Rawls admitted this in part in *Political Liberalism* (1993), and offered an interpretation of what he believed his earlier seminal work (and subsequent clarifying articles) contributed to the development of deliberative democratic theory ([1993] 2005, xliv-lx). In the next section, I discuss Habermas's contribution to deliberative democratic theory, the criticisms (which are very similar to those made in Rawls's case), and a solution proposed by Chambers (1996) that I maintain works for Rawls's as well, though in a somewhat limited sense.

Jürgen Habermas

Habermas's contribution concerns the manner in which deliberations take place. From his conception of "discourse ethics" in his work *Moral Consciousness and Communicative Action* ([1983] 1990), deliberative democratic scholars advance the idea that the process of deliberation and engagement has an ethical component as well. In order for action arising from public deliberation to be considered legitimate, nothing but the "force [...] of the better argument" must prevail (Habermas [1973] 1975, 108; Habermas [1983] 1990, 159; Held 2006, 238). Deliberative democratic scholars observe that in order for the deliberative enterprise to work, there has to be a belief that the participant's preferences are not fixed and that they are amenable to change when presented with new information and alterative frames of thought. This transformation takes place through communication processes. Because the process is so dependent on communications, the mode of conveyance and veracity of its content is important (Held 2006). These rules are important and will be discussed later. Though many reference his observations in *Legitimation Crisis* (1973) as a precursor his notion of "discourse ethics" set forth in *Moral Consciousness and Communicative Action* (1983), others see evidence of this line of thought developing as far back as 1962 in his *The Structural Transformation of the Public Sphere: An Inquiry into a Category of Bourgeois Society* (Bohman and Rehg 1997; McCarthy

1994; Bohman and Rehg 2011). In *Legitimation Crisis*, Habermas describes the conditions and requirements that necessitate a process for reasonable discourse. As was the case with Rawls, a discussion of that work gives evidence of the historical period in which he was writing as well as demonstrates the thought that was to lead to his very important 1983 work concerning discourse ethics.

At about the same time and within the same social context in which Rawls published *A Theory of Justice*, Habermas was working on *Legitimation Crisis*. This work was originally published in German and translated into English by Thomas McCarthy two years later. However, whereas Rawls was writing here in the U.S., Habermas was writing in Germany. Consequently, the turmoil that constituted the context in which he was writing had more to do with European political upheaval than with a foreign war (Bohman and Rehg 2011). Nevertheless, both were writing in the context of their times, a period which was characterized by crisis.

In *Legitimation Crisis*, we find an early call for the use of discourse to resolve societal disagreement. In fact, for him it was the method by which legitimacy is conferred on collective action. Habermas sketches out how crisis erodes legitimacy and how discourse can be used to restore it. He begins by explaining what he means by the term *crisis* within the context of systems theory, stating that in the "systems approach, crises arise when the structure of a social system allows fewer possibilities for problem solving than are necessary to the continued existence of the system" (Habermas [1973] 1975, 2). However, systems in and of themselves do not experience crisis. It is the individual who feels crises. Therefore, "only when members of a society experience structural alterations as critical for continued existence and feel their social identity threatened can we speak of crises" (Habermas [1973] 1975, 3).

But what causes the crisis? Habermas explains crises "issue from unresolved steering problems" (Habermas [1973] 1975, 4). Steering mechanisms are, in systems theory, those facets of the system that help it correct itself and that the individual may or may not be conscious of, but that in any case "endanger social integration" when they fail (Habermas [1973] 1975, 4). These include naturally occurring or purposefully created institutions of social control. To the degree the social system relies on these mechanisms determines the degree to which a state's legitimacy is threatened when they fail. The market is one such mechanism in advanced capitalist societies (Habermas [1973] 1975, 33). Under these conditions, "the state actually *replaces* the market mechanism whenever it creates and improves conditions for the realization of capital" (Habermas [1973] 1975, 33). This is accomplished in a variety of ways, to include "transportation, education, health, recreation, urban and regional planning, housing [...] unemployment compensation, welfare" and the like (Habermas [1973] 1975, 35). It is this "re-coupling [of] the economic system to the political [that] creates an increased need for legitimation" (Habermas [1973] 1975, 36). However, Habermas observes a problem. Because the state is now in competition with the private sector, the state will need insulation for its activities. He submits that a system of "formal democracy" is substituted for "substantive democracy," meaning that voting is the only voice the individual has in the decision making process (Habermas [1973] 1975, 36). This will only last so long. The state's supply of legitimate pretext will run out; "questioning will break out" and failure may result (Habermas [1973] 1975, 69). Habermas observes, "[t]he penalty for this failure is withdrawal of legitimation" (Habermas [1973] 1975, 69).

His answer to the problem of legitimacy is the idea of a "discursively formed will" (Habermas [1973] 1975, 108). In his oft-cited passage from *Legitimation Crisis*, he asserts that in this process "no force except that of the better argument is exercised" (Habermas [1973] 1975, 108). This is a consistent theme in Habermas's work. It can be seen in his earlier work, *The Structural Transformation of the Public Sphere: An Inquiry into a Category of Bourgeois Society* (1962), and again in a later work, *Moral Consciousness and Communicative Action* (1983), wherein he outlines his "Discourse Ethics" ([1983] 1990, 43-115). In the earlier work he highlighted the value of the "*salons* and coffeehouses" in 19th century Europe and their contribution to the development of a democratic "public sphere" ([1962] 1991. 36). Habermas explains that it was in these venues that the bourgeoisie created culture rather than consumed it as is the case in the modern day ([1962] 1991, 175). The salons served a valuable function in that they served to influence activities external to themselves rather than find themselves the object of them.

Here we see evidence of Habermas's early interest in the deliberative capacities of private individuals on matters of public interests, which would continue in subsequent works. He explains that though they were in varying European nations and enjoyed different levels of success, these deliberative venues shared some common elements (Habermas [1962] 1991). "First, they preserved a kind of social intercourse" that treated all participants as equals ([1962] 1991. 36). In the salons title generally held no sway, though the lower social strata generally did not participate ([1962] 1991, 33). Second, the subject matter for discussion was wide ranging; from politics to literature and art. Contemporary issues and latest news as well as all matters of "common concern" were the subject of discussion ([1962] 1991. 36). Third, though the salon was "exclusive [...] it could never close itself off entirely and become consolidated as a clique," rather it needed to be "inclusive [...] of all private people, persons who – insofar as they were properties and educated – as readers, listeners, and spectators could avail themselves via the market of the objects that were subject to discussion" ([1962] 1991. 37). A mature and rigorous expression of these ideas are found a little over twenty years later in his "discourse ethics;" concepts some deliberative democratic scholars hold as important to the program (Chambers 1996). A discussion of his *discourse ethics* is central to this thesis. However, an overview of his philosophy is in order first because it sheds light on his relationship to Rawls.

In the introduction he prepared for his translation of *Legitimation Crisis*, Thomas McCarthy admits, "Habermas can be quite difficult to read" (1975, vii). We can be grateful that in his 1994 article "Kantian Constructivism and Reconstructivism: Rawls and Habermas in Dialogue," McCarthy provides a clear and concise summation of Habermas's "moral and political theory" (45-49). The goal of the article is to assess both Rawls's and Habermas's efforts at reviving the Kantian moral enterprise. Like Rawls, he attempts to avoid transcendentalism in establishing a universal moral imperative. Because of its uniqueness to the human species, he chooses the act of communication as his focus, citing it as the most fundamental evidence of rationality in humans. In addition to the ability to intersubjectively determine what is *valid*, humans have the ability to defend these positions through reasonable discourse. In this way, McCarthy explains, "Habermas's idea of a 'discourse ethics' can be viewed as a reconstruction of Kant's idea of practical reason in terms of communicative reason" (1994, 45). McCarthy goes on to expand, stating:

The Idea of Deliberative Democracy

> [I]t involves a procedural reformulation of the Categorical Imperative: rather than ascribing to others as valid those maxims I can will to be universal laws, I must submit them to others for purposes of discursively testing their claim to universal validity. The emphasis shifts from what *each* can will without contradiction to what *all* can agree to in rational discourse. (1994, 45)

Rather than a Kantian exercise, wherein the individual considers within themselves what they would will *others* to do (the golden rule so to speak), the whole question is placed before those *others* in a "procedure of practical argumentation" (1994, 46). When rigorously followed, the process "reconstructs the moral point of view from which questions of right can be fairly and impartially adjudicated" (1994, 46). In a footnote, McCarthy asserts that instead of "discourse ethics" a more appropriate term might have been "'discourse morality' or 'discourse justice'" (1994, 46).

Because issues of fairness and justice are the focus of the deliberation, the procedures for argumentation as well as the predicate conditions are extremely important. By predicate conditions, Habermas means that there are stipulations as to who may participate and how they conduct themselves on those deliberations (1994, 47). For instance, anyone that is subject to the outcome of the deliberation should have a voice if they so choose (1994, 47-48). Furthermore, the participants must exhibit a "concern for the common good in [...] that each participant take[s] into account the needs, interests, and feelings of all others and give them equal weight to her own" (1994, 47-48). This stands clearly in contrast to Rawls's "original position" in that moral reasoning is conducted in communicative interaction rather than in isolation.

In this regard, we can see that Habermas has a "proceduralist conception of deliberative democracy" in that decision making occurs through "justification by appeal to generally acceptable reasons [...] of free and equal citizens in a constitutional democracy" (McCarthy 1994, 48). These procedures govern what he refers to as "practical discourse," the aims of which are to resolve three kinds of problems: practical problems pertaining to means of reaching goals, ethical issues, and moral issues (McCarthy 1994, 48). The venues of these deliberations are not merely applicable to formal institutions, but also to the informal social institutions of civil society (McCarthy 1994, 49). Habermas maintains that it is to these secondary associations that formal institutions of the government and bureaucracy should pay attention as they give clues as to the sovereign will of the people (McCarthy 1994, 49). The dialogue that takes place in these casual venues forms the basis of public opinion and provides legitimating cover for official action if heeded. Quoting Habermas in a 1993 conference paper, McCarthy recounts, "the power available to the administration emerges from a public use of reason.... Public opinion worked up via democratic procedures cannot itself 'rule,' but it can point the use of administrative power in specific directions" (McCarthy 1994, 49).

The structure for arriving at legitimate social decisions is at the heart of Habermas's classic 1983 work, *Moral Consciousness and Communicative Action*. In particular, the chapter entitled "Discourse Ethics: Notes on a Program of Philosophical Justification" spells out the conditions that must be met in order to have a valid and legitimate decision at the close of what he terms "practical discourse" (Chambers 1996, 98). The first standard that must be met concerns the use, or misuse, of language itself. Habermas refers to them as the "logical-semantic [...] rules," which are: (Habermas 1983, 87).

(1.1) No speaker may contradict himself.
(1.2) Every speaker who applies predicate F to object A must be prepared to apply F to all other objects resembling A in all relevant aspects.
(1.3) Different speakers may not use the same expression with different meanings. (Habermas 1983, 87)

The second tier of rules he refers to as "procedural" rules, which pertain to "accountability and truthfulness" (Habermas 1983, 87-88). This set of rules bars strategic communications, deception, or other forms of misrepresentation of the individuals true position, designed to steer the decision making process away from the fundamental goal of achieving an agreement that all will, or could assent to. They include:

(2.1) Every speaker may assert only what he really believes.
(2.2) A person who disputes a proposition or norm not under discussion must provide a reason for wanting to do so. (Habermas 1983, 88)

The Idea of Deliberative Democracy

The final rule set Habermas terms "process" rules, which largely constitute what he characterized in earlier works as the "ideal speech situation" (Habermas 1983, 88). They include:

(3.1) Every subject with the competence to speak and act is allowed to take part in a discourse.
(3.2) a. Everyone is allowed to question any assertion whatever.
b. Everyone is allowed to introduce any assertion whatever into the discourse.
c. Everyone is allowed to express his attitudes, desires, and needs.
(3.3) No speaker may be prevented, by internal or external coercion, from exercising his rights as laid down in (3.10 and (3.2). (Habermas 1983, 89)

Habermas's goal was not to create a decision making structure to derive universal norms. What he instead proposed was that this decision structure was the universal norms – namely, the "ideal speech situation" (Chambers 1996, 69, 155-166). As Chambers explains, "the ideal speech situation represents the *formal* conditions [...] that would have to hold if we wanted to say that an agreement was reasonable and authentic [...] like Rawls's original position, it is a device" (1996, 166). However, it differs significantly from Rawls's project as he was trying to determine what the universal norms were using the method laid out in *A Theory of Justice*. Habermas, on the other hand, is not as concerned with the outcome as much as he is with respecting the process. As Chambers puts it, "the ideal speech situation, by itself, has no content" (1996, 166). In short, the *ideal* is not the norm that is produced; it is the rigorously created *situation* in which the decision was arrived.

There are a number of criticisms to Habermas's contribution to deliberative democratic theory. Most criticism distills down to the impossibility of the *ideal speech situation* proposed by the rules detailed above (Chambers 1996). Held summarizes the critics' arguments, stating that "an account of deliberation in unattainable conditions following very abstract argumentative rules" does not advance the very practical enterprise that is political and social problem solving (Held 2006, 241). More useful would be "a better grasp of the nature and meaning of deliberation under non-ideal conditions" (Held 2006, 241-242). Held identifies Gutmann and Thompson as leading critics, though there are others who are noteworthy. Some of the specific criticisms are worth discussion, but summarized that they all turn on the questions of the impossibility of the ideal condition.

Though Gutmann and Thompson give Habermas the bulk of the credit for "reviving the idea of deliberation," they have concerns about his method and what it entails (2004, 9). One of the important issues they take up is the problem created when a process or procedure is more important than the outcome it produces (Gutmann and Thompson 1996, 17). This is a somewhat Kantian position, which argues that form matters more than content. In the "ideal speech condition," norms are provisional outside the structure of the argument (Gutmann and Thompson 1996). In fact, "principles such as basic liberty and opportunity […] are valued only for their contribution to deliberation, not as constraints on what counts as a morally legitimate resolution of disagreement" (Gutmann and Thompson 1996, 17).

The issue of impartiality – rather the impossibility of the ideal of impartiality – is also a point on which Habermas receives criticism. In his "Discourse Ethics" he argues, "the idea of impartiality is rooted in the structures of argumentation" (Habermas [1983] 1990, 75-76). Again, we recall that the force of the better argument should determine decisions. However, this idea of an impersonal argumentative force has a coercive tone. In summarizing the position of Gutmann and Thompson on the concept of impartiality, Held states that "impartiality entails a type of moral absolutism […] instead [of] accommodation consistent with mutual respect" (2006, 242). Gutmann and Thompson submit that dilemmas resolved impartially do not really require deliberation, but instead demonstration (1996, 52-55). This is an important distinction because without the introduction of true "moral disagreement" there is no real deliberation (1996, 52). The removal of partiality makes the matter impersonal, which is a problem for Gutmann and Thompson in that "impartiality […] does not take moral disagreement seriously enough" (2004, 152). Therefore – as was the case with Rawls – all that is needed is the time to run the calculation.

A third important criticism of Habermas suggests that he ignores the important and practical role played by institutions in organized society (Dryzek 2000, 24). The Habermasian apologist John S. Dryzek acknowledges that if implemented strictly as proposed, "we end up with a political theory that has little to say about political structure – except to condemn it as an agent of distortion" (2000, 24). In its most radical "transformative mode," citizens in a deliberative democracy might well have to be experts in all matters of public life (Held 2006, 252). Moreover, while more radical deliberative democratic theorists have suggested a set of practices they believe resolve this difficulty – such as "citizen juries" (Fishkin 1991, 87; Beetham 2005) and "deliberation days," (Ackerman & Fishkin [2002] 2003) – in the end they are new institutions substituting for old ones. The fact is we rely on institutions to play an important and efficient role in a democracy. On the less radical end of the spectrum are theorists who commend "deliberation [...] as a supplement to liberal institutions" and "a way of improving the quality of existing political institutions" (Held 2006, 252). Because this book strives for a very similar goal – to demonstrate the applicability of deliberative democratic theory to the already established institution of policing – it relies largely on this particular strain of deliberative democratic theory.

The rehabilitation of Habermas's "discourse ethics" offered by Simone Chambers in *Reasonable Democracy: Jürgen Habermas and the Politics of Discourse* (1996) is entirely suited to this enterprise. This rehabilitation is a significant element in this book and requires serious exploration here. First, it should be noted that in her opinion Rawls does have something to contribute that is complementary to Habermas, though it is of somewhat limited utility (1996). In accordance with a few other scholars mentioned above, she believes the two legendary theorists are not all that far apart (Chambers 1996; Elster 1998; Gutmann and Thompson 2004). Specifically, she maintains that Habermas's thought, though not in complete agreement, does not negate Rawls's contribution, but instead "goes much farther" with it (1996, 13).

Secondly, she argues for a more global applicability of "discourse ethics" to deliberations. In her estimation, Habermas's thought does not necessarily entail the radical revision of organizations and institutions of the state, though it could if the parties so choose. To her way of thinking, Habermas's arguments are "not simply a matter of setting up the right institutions," possessing the proscribed deliberative processes (Chambers 1996, 194-195). Instead, she notes that, "many existing institutions are well suited to discourse" (Chambers 1996, 194-195). Moreover, she makes the argument that the procedure mapped out in

"Discourse Ethics" was intended to apply to a wide array of formal institutions and informal groups, which are crucial to the creation of legitimacy (1996).

Finally, Chambers offers an alternative view of the "ideal speech condition" that is similar to Rawls's later clarification of the "original position" wherein he characterized it as a "device" and not an actual position (Rawls 1985). Chamber's creative solution is to characterize Habermas's "ideal speech condition" as an "approximation" necessary for the conduct of "practical discourse" (1996, 193-211). She affirms, "[t]he ideal speech situation is a presupposition of argumentation, never fully realized in the real world but approximated in a sincere search for consensus within a practical discourse" (1996, 156). Further still, "practical discourse is a long-term consensus-forming process and not a decision procedure" (Chambers 1996, 171). Chambers admits that the process and the outcomes likely will be flawed, but the dialogue should go on; the ideal is never attained on any account. Therefore, "in the real world, the question becomes the degree of approximation" (Chambers 1996, 171).

Before moving forward, it is important to note Habermas's direct entry into the tome on deliberative democracy in his *Between Facts and Norms* ([1992] 1996). It was published about the same time as Rawls's *Political Liberalism* (1993). (Later editions of both works contain responses to each other.) In his preface to the English translation of *Between Facts and Norms*, translator and Habermas scholar William Rehg characterizes the work as "the culminating effort in a project that was first announced with the 1962 publication of his *Strukturwandel der Offentlichkeit;*" in English his *The Structural Transformation of the Public Sphere: An Inquiry into a Category of Bourgeois Society* (Rehg 1996, ix). Though this long work seems to blend a string of works, it does not specifically recreate them as much as it seems to recast them in a new context. This work almost requires familiarity with his prior thought, particularly his two-volume *The Theory of Communicative Action* (1981). For instance, when discussing "discourse ethics," he does not recreate those arguments, but instead offers commentary on them (Habermas [1992] 1996, xl). It is here that he solidifies his position on the matter of impartiality for which he is criticized by both Gutmann and Thompson. Therein Habermas asserts, "the discourse principle is only intended to explain the point of view from which norms of action can be *impartially justified*" (his emphasis) ([1992] 1996, 108-109).

THE DEVELOPMENT OF DELIBERATIVE DEMOCRATIC THEORY

Considerable attention has been given thus far to the works of Rawls and Habermas. Their original contributions to liberal theory and critical theory, respectively, spurred democratic scholar's thinking toward a new and better way of making social and political decisions. This new way of making such decisions countered the negative and overly simplistic notions offered by pluralist thinkers on how people formed preferences. Rather than viewing preferences and interests as fixed, this new class of thinkers saw the preferences and interests of individuals as dynamic and subject to change when exposed to new information alternative framing. The problem for these theorists was to determine how this occurred naturally in society and to establish formal mechanisms for intentionally bringing about this type of change. They believed the importance Rawls and Habermas placed on dialogue – on discourse – and deliberation, provided a critical starting point. However, Rawls's method for decision making through highly reasoned internal deliberation, and Habermas's decision making method requiring perfect conditions under which to conduct deliberations with others, did not translate well to practical application. Nevertheless, their contributions remain foundational.

Arguments exist for the inclusion of others in the class of original thinkers contributing to founding deliberative democratic theory. For instance Chambers (1996) includes Thomas Scanlon's 1982 essay "Contractualism and Utilitarianism" as among the foundational works. However, I believe that confining the early emphasis to Rawls and Habermas is warranted. Evidence of their continued relevance is found in the tendency by subsequent deliberative democratic thinkers to incorporate, extend or refute the ideas of Rawls and Habermas. Other scholarship offers apologies, amendments and expansions by their acolytes. The famous quote attributed to Alfred North Whitehead comes to mind. It was he who famously and succinctly summarized western philosophy when he said, "[t]he safest general characterization of the European philosophical tradition is that it consists of a series of footnotes to Plato" (Whitehead [1929] 1979, 39). Though it might be an overstatement in the case of Rawls and Habermas, the general ethos certainly applies, that it is fair to say that deliberative democratic scholarship consists of a series of footnotes to Rawls and Habermas.

The examination thus far has sought to emphasize these earliest works by Rawls and Habermas for another reason. It concerns the need to connect the era in which they wrote to the community policing scholarship that was produced around the same time. This will be important in the next chapter's examination of the evolution of the idea of community policing. The concerns Rawls and Habermas express are echoed in the early community policing literature. For example, Rawls and Habermas were concerned with ideas of legitimacy and justice; matters of particular importance to political philosophy and philosophy proper. Discussions of legitimacy and justice had yet to gain (or regain) traction in the social sciences, which was on a trajectory largely shaped by the behavioralist tradition (Almond 1990; Susser 1992, 1-2; Theodoulou and O'Brien 1999, 1-12). Swept up in the empiricism of the times was the social science subfield of criminology, which played no small part in formulating criminal justice policy in response to the crisis of the 1960s (Barlow 1984, 24). Deliberative democratic theory had not yet matured. The result, I argue, was a missed opportunity to ground the community policing scholarship of the 1970s in the theory of deliberative democracy, a literature that would not reach its peak for another twenty years. Nevertheless, a look at the development of deliberative democratic theory throughout the 1980s and 1990s is needed.

The idea of *legitimacy* is a consistent theme addressed in the deliberative democracy literature throughout the 1980s and early 1990s. As mentioned previously, most scholars credit Bessette for the first use of the term "deliberative democracy" in his 1980 essay, "Deliberative Democracy: The Majority Principle in Republican Government." However, that work took a more institutional perspective. In it, he argued that the institutions of American government were fundamentally deliberative in nature. Specifically, Bessette argues that because Congress is a body that meets and deliberates before making decisions, American government is *ipso facto* a deliberative democracy (1980; 1994). I argue that the link between deliberation and democracy he suggests is as tenuous as the link many make between American policing and democracy. Both contentions are based on simple geographical fact. Merely situating policing in a democracy does not necessarily mean that by nature it is democratic. He uses a framers argument, relying heavily on the U.S. Constitution and the *Federalist Papers* to support his claim (Bessette 1980). However, many like Dryzek remain unconvinced (Dryzek 2000, 12). Bessette's 1994 restatement in *The Mild Voice of Reason: Deliberative Democracy & American National Government* emphatically reasserted the thesis that Congress is the highest form of, and forum for, democratic deliberation. Evidencing a belief in the perfectibility of pluralism, Bessette submits "analyzing U.S. national government as a deliberative democracy both enhances our understanding of the real workings of American democracy and provides us with a set of norms or standards for assessing how our governing institutions *ought* to work" (1994, 5).

Most scholars of deliberative democracy do not take the view that formal government institutions are the sole venues of deliberative democratic activity. Dryzek (1987) was among the first to point to Habermas in advocating for a broader conception of deliberation that extends beyond the boundaries of institutions. Without relying on Habermas, Elster (1986) also makes an argument similar to Dryzek's, noting the difference between the way "markets" make decisions through aggregation versus the "forum" which uses discourse (24). Elster argues for a more civic-minded citizenry engaged in the "political process" (1986, 26). However, for most deliberative democracy scholars, the political process that had been allowed to grow without critical reflection was not enough to guarantee legitimacy. Manin (1987) and Cohen (1989) were among those who suggested that legitimacy was predicated on reasoned exchange – discourse – wherein the participants publicly justified their positions to each other before coming to a collective decision. In short, legitimacy is tied to deliberation. This line of argument was to have important implications for the character of democracy. The question that remained was how to develop a practical process for engaging in substantive deliberations.

A generation of democracy scholars following Rawls and Habermas turned their attention to developing methods and forums for deliberative democratic practice. Finding the early thinking of Rawls and Habermas useful but too ideal and too abstract to be of practical use, they sought to develop a theory that would inform deliberative democratic practice. Throughout the 1990s and 2000s, greater attention was paid to processes, procedures, and venues of deliberative democracy in practice, though attention was still given to the predicate conditions as well. These developments retained their grounding in the ideas of legitimacy developed in the earlier literature. Amy Gutmann and Dennis Thompson were among the leading scholars in the 1990s advocating a more practical and less idealized approach to discourse and deliberation (Held 2006). In their classic 1996 work, *Democracy and Disagreement*, Gutmann and Thompson argue "the persistence of moral disagreement" constitutes a practical real-world problem that idealized schemes of discourse will never dispose of in a world of fallible beings (7, 11-26). This being the case, deliberation must be a constant activity in a healthy democracy. Believing that disagreement should be accepted as a permanent feature of democracy, they propose three "principles that express the conditions of deliberation" (1996, 7). These three principles include "reciprocity, publicity, and accountability" (Gutmann and Thompson 1996, 8). They are worth noting here because they dovetail with – if not mirror – subsequent work by David Bayley (2001) on democratic policing's core principles. Briefly, Bayley's work advances the idea of a democratic police that embodies the principles of *accountability, transparency*, and *responsiveness* (2001, 13-15). Bayley's contributions to democratic policing are detailed in subsequent chapters.

First, Gutmann and Thompson develop the idea of "reciprocity [as] the leading principle" in deliberative democracy "because it shapes the meaning of publicity and accountability" (1996, 52). Reciprocity is a key predicate to a valid process in that it requires "citizens and officials to justify public policy by giving reason that can be accepted by those who are bound by it" (Gutmann and Thompson 1996, 52). In order for reciprocity to work, a tolerance for diverse views must be present (1996, 62-63). This tolerance, which Gutmann and Thompson call "mutual respect" (1996, 63) does not in Bohman's opinion go far enough (2003). Bohman submits that his notion of "toleration" goes deeper than Gutmann's idea of respect because it calls on individuals to be open to points of view that are so far in opposition to their own they may not have much respect for them (2003, 758). The idea of reciprocity put forward by Rawls appears to be even narrower. It pertains solely to the political realm, and is "expressed in public reason," which are those grounds publicly expressed, "reasons we would offer for our political actions [...] are sufficient [...] and we also reasonably think that other citizens might also reasonably accept those reasons" (Rawls [1993] 1997, 766-771).

Secondly, Gutmann and Thompson advance the idea of *publicity*, meaning "the reasons that officials and citizens give to justify political actions [...] should be public" (1996, 95). To their way of thinking, transparency is a two-way street. Private and public figures should justify their positions before each other. Initiatives that foster open government interest Gutmann and Thompson. They do acknowledge that the effectiveness of government can be compromised in some situations if secrets are not maintained. However, these exceptions are relatively rare and should be restricted. Furthermore, they recommend various mechanisms of oversight to make sure that no abuses are taking place. In addition, the question concerning what issues belong in the public domain is itself a topic for deliberation.

The third principle Gutmann and Thompson offer as indispensable to the deliberative enterprise is the principle of *accountability*. Their sense of accountability is not bound up in a notion of punishment. Instead, it is concerned with a mutual reason-giving process (Gutmann and Thompson 1996, 128-129). Gutmann and Thompson argue that the "scope of accountability" cannot consist only of elected officials giving reasons to the electorate for their decisions (1996, 128). However, opening up to a generalized accountability poses two problems for Gutmann and Thompson. They observe the "problem of specialization" in that some individuals have more information and their decisions will be of a different quality than the uninformed (1996, 132). The second issue concerns "the problem of constituency" (1996, 144). Here it is required that the deliberation participants must be those who are "bound by" the decisions or are "affected by them" (1996, 128). A final difficulty raised by Gutmann and Thompson concerns the standards by which this accounting is given. What are the parameters of good decisions? They contend that an accounting is a public justification wherein the decision must "survive such scrutiny as a necessary condition and a substantial reason for making their conclusions the law of the land" (1996, 164).

What are these considerations? Gutmann and Thompson maintain that Rawls has some relevance here, and believe his later work relevant (1996, 160). In their own words, they maintain, "the deliberative principle of accountability holds representatives accountable not only for satisfying the interests of their constituents but also for action in a way that can be justified to future generations (161). Offe and Preuss said it better and more comprehensively when they assert "a 'rational' or 'enlightened' political will [...] would ideally have to be at the same time *'fact-regarding'* (as opposed to ignorant or doctrinaire), *'future-regarding'* (as opposed to myopic) and *'other-regarding'* (as opposed to selfish)" (1991, 156-157).

Scholars continued to produce works centering on the importance of legitimacy throughout the 1990s and 2000s. As mentioned previously, one of the principal criticisms of the early scholars concerns the premium placed on the idea of impartiality. The connection of impartiality to legitimacy is similar to the connection unanimity shares with legitimacy, though the connection is frequent fodder for scholars. The belief that decisions arrived at impartially are in fact legitimate is largely grounded in the Western philosophical tradition's faith in human reason, which can be observed in everything in the post-enlightenment world from science to jurisprudence.

However, like unanimity, impartiality suggests an ideal that is virtually impossible to achieve. Critics contended the over-emphasis on the philosophical ideal left the enterprise with little practical value. Yet, all around it appeared to many scholars that some form of deliberative democracy was indeed taking place, and was working. Amy Gutmann and Dennis Thompson argued that just because the ideals identified by Rawls and Habermas seemed un-attainable, the enterprise should not be abandoned. As Held (2006) observes, the process of deliberation never takes place in the ideal situation. Gutmann and Thompson realize this and seek "a better grasp of the nature and meaning of deliberation under 'non-ideal' conditions" (Held 2006, 241-242).

While Gutmann and Thompson build upon Rawls and Habermas, they actually extend their notions of legitimacy further than either Rawls or Habermas did. Legitimacy understood as unanimity and impartiality impose high thresholds for everyday social and political decision making. Gutmann and Thompson introduce a type of legitimacy that enjoys a provisional character; it is conditional and does not last forever. If one accepts the proposition that deliberations that take place under non-ideal conditions – real world conditions – then one must also admit they are subject to error. Upon presentation of new and disconfirming information, decisions must be revisited. Therefore, all questions must remain open, subject to new debate, and eventually substantive revision. Legitimacy is provisional in that it is subject to revocation upon receipt of new information. Unlike the version of legitimacy offered by Rawls and Habermas, this notion of legitimacy offered by Gutmann and Thompson is within reach. In the end, they argue that Rawls and Habermas are important to the development of deliberative democratic thinking, but are of rather little practical significance now that the deliberative democratic discourse literature has come into being (Held 2006; Gutmann and Thompson 2004, 9).

Other scholars concur that the idea of complete impartiality is not realistic; the absence of any universal mechanism governing discourse is of concern and constitutes a further threat to legitimacy. Because deliberation relies on the communicative act, social and cultural features may contribute to advantaging some and disadvantaging others (Tully 2002, 224). Moreover, those with particular skill can take advantage of those less well versed in the art of argumentation, engaging in what are effectively deceptive "language games" (Fearon 1998, 223). Deliberative democracy scholar James D. Fearon discusses at length the problem of "private information" in group decision making (1998, 45). Private information is essentially one's primary preferences, which can be masked or lied about in order to advance one's true preference (Fearon 1998). This tactic reduces the deliberative process to a sort of linguistic gamesmanship. Fearon observes that failure to disclose one's true preferences can lead to suboptimal decisions and less than full disclosure can threaten to undermine the deliberative process, causing participants to "exit" in a manner described with insight and sophistication by Hirschman (1970).

A final point worthy of mention in the evolution of deliberative democracy scholarship pertains to the development of new practices in furtherance of the concept. Among the earliest entry to this body of literature was James S. Fishkin's *Democracy and Deliberation* (1991). One of the first recommended practices proposed involved "deliberative opinion polls" (Fishkin 1991, 81). These polls would differ from normal opinion polls in that they would be taken after participants were immersed in an environment where they would be exposed to good information and varying opinions on important issues. The participants would engage in discourse and debate and conclude the multi-day deliberation event with a poll (Akerman and Fishkin 2002). It is supposed that rather than indicate the unreflective preferences of the participants, the poll would now evidence the considered opinions of individuals who had carefully studied the issues. In a similar recommendation, Fishkin and others suggest the formation of "citizens' juries," which consists of a panel of citizens routinely assembled to hear expert testimony, consider the evidence on a single issue, and render recommendations (Fishkin 1991, 87; Beetham 2005). Fishkin in particular argues that these practices are not intended to supplant the current institutions of government, but simply augment them with informed citizen opinions. In fact, Fishkin maintains that these practices might serve to stem what he believed to be the slow "march toward direct democracy" in America (Fishkin 1991, 54).

It is difficult to discuss the practice of deliberative democracy without mentioning the various venues for formal deliberation. Throughout the 1990s and 2000s, scholars discussed directly, and indirectly, the sites where democratic deliberation characteristically takes place. These venues also have a connection to concerns of legitimacy. When taken seriously, the norms of deliberative democracy place different strains on the concept of legitimacy. If conducted in the wrong arena with affected people absent, claims to legitimacy of outcomes are dubious. And, as we have seen, elected representation alone does not meet the standards for legitimacy set by deliberative democracy since elections focus more on interest aggregation and less on informing policy preferences (Gutmann and Thompson 1996). Most deliberative democracy scholars appear to have in mind large-scale issues to which they would direct deliberative practices. Rawls, for instance, is taken to task for his method, which critics maintain is better suited to exiting the Hobbesian state of nature (Gutmann and Thompson 1996). As detailed above, Fishkin and his colleague Akerman sees deliberative polls and citizen juries as mechanisms to address large and small-scale problems. However, limited attention is paid to who decides. For the sake of effectiveness, even small-scale deliberative exercises, such as planning boards and commissions, have to address the question of who gets to participate (Forester 1999). As we see, bound up in the idea of venue for deliberation is the problem of scale, which in turn is also a problem for legitimacy (Parkinson 2003). Leading thinkers in this regard are Dryzek and Parkinson.

Dryzek described three possible solutions to the problem of "deliberative legitimacy under conditions of large scale" (2001, 2010, 24). First, Dryzek suggests we might "limit the times when deliberation is needed" to only those occasions that involve matters of "basic justice," such as constitutional matters or major laws that affect every person in the polity (2001, 653). Secondly, we could consider, "limiting deliberation to a small number of representatives" who are elected, selected at random, or simply summoned as is the case with jury duty (2001, 653). Here he refers to these select bodies as "mini-publics," which seem to operate much like focus groups (2010, 27). Finally, the problem of scale might be resolved by "limiting deliberation to those best able to discern the public's interest" (2001, 654). In this scenario, he uses the operations of the U.S. Supreme Court as an example. However, none of these seems satisfactory to Dryzek in the end. He suggests, "the best way forward here involves detaching the idea of legitimacy from a head count of (real or imaginary) reflectively consenting individuals" (Dryzek 2001, 657). Substituted is a notion of legitimacy that is rooted in a Habermasian ideal, which is that of a "discursive democracy that emphasizes the contestation of discourses in the public sphere" (2001, 657). In short, he does not view a narrow set of venues or practices as having a monopolistic claim to deliberative democracy, but rather sees them as part of a broad spectrum in the public sphere.

Parkinson (2006), on the other hand, "is not convinced that legitimacy can be so easily disconnected from head-counts" (28). Individuals are composite beings which no doubt affect judgment and deliberation; "identity" can inform deliberation (2006, 28). Practical problems remain. Dichotomous forces such as "majority rule and minority rights, inclusion and exclusion, power and interests," all have a shearing effect on legitimacy (2006, 28). Parkinson retains a belief that institutional makeup and processes have a bearing on legitimacy. He notes that "deliberative institutions, macro and micro, are affected by the legitimacy problem in different ways" (Parkinson 2006, 7). Interestingly, he maintains that the problem of scale affects the smaller deliberative bodies more that the larger. For the macro issues, the matter is resolved by either allowing all to participate, or agreeing on a method of representation. Here, the onus is on the procedure. However, in the smaller venues, "the insider/outsider distinction is most sharp," making deciding who gets to participate possible and important (2006, 8). In these cases, who gets a voice often times boils down to the politics of inclusion. In short, deliberative discourse in smaller venues, while logistically possible, can be politically problematic.

DELIBERATIVE DEMOCRATIC PRINCIPLES AND PRACTICE

Some scholars contend summarizing deliberative democracy in a concise definition is a difficult task as there is no general agreement on what the essential features are (Freeman 2000, 373; Chambers 2003, 308; Elster 1998, 8). In many ways, it appears that we are "arguing over arguing" (Elster 1998, 9). However, Elster attempts to do so, observing that scholars "give explicit and implicit definitions of deliberative democracy that differ widely from one another. Yet [...] they are talking about the same object" (1998, 8). Using a term that reminds us of Rawls's *overlapping consensus*, he notes that among these definitions "there is extensive overlap" at the center of which "is a robust core of phenomena that count as deliberation" (1998, 8). He characterizes this core as "collective decision making with the participation of all who will be affected by the decision" and who engage in "decision making by means of argument [through] rationality and impartiality" (Elster1998, 8). As seen above, some hold the view impartiality is an unattainable ideal that should not find its way into any definition of deliberative democracy.

One of the least troubling attempts at a definition is offered by Bohman, who asserts, "[d]eliberative democracy, broadly defined, is any one of a family of views according to which the public deliberation of free and equal citizens is the core of legitimate political decision-making and self-governance" (1998, 401). A number of important democratic norms are embedded in this definition. The examination of the literature has thus far enabled us to extrapolate much from this concise statement. For example, democratic notions such as fairness, reason, reciprocity, inclusion, active participation, transparency, accountability and responsiveness, emanate from this conceptualization. The thoughts presented suggest an idea of a rational discourse conducted by affected people, wherein they publicly justify their positions to each other, constituting the object of deliberative democratic practices. We have learned that citizens are expected to carry with them into their deliberations their unique perspective and life experiences that inform their interests. However, they should be open to considering differing viewpoints from others who may have different values shaped by different experiences (Gutmann and Thompson 2004). The dialogue envisioned must be continuous and participants should not lose confidence if impartiality, unanimity, or even consensus cannot be reached. The participants should be prepared to walk away from such deliberations without making decisions, yet always leave with new information, a fresh perspective, and an appreciation of the other's point of view. When options are presented, they should be legitimately available for action. An idea of legitimacy that is based on engagement and not efficiency is what will, in the end, serve to strengthen communal bonds and thereby help establish a well-ordered society.

Despite scholarly disagreement on the essential features of deliberative democracy that would inform a concise definition, themes do emerge that expose underlying democratic principles. As several briefly mentioned above, the norms espoused in the deliberative democracy literature are consistent with recent literature on democratic policing's principles. David H. Bayley's work in support of democratizing police forces around the world is just as relevant in the U.S. as anywhere else in the world. In *Democratizing the Police Abroad: What to Do and How to Do It* (2001) he offers three principles of democratic policing which I maintain find their complement in Gutmann and Thompson's thinking. First, Bayley notes, "the most dramatic contribution police can make to democracy is to become responsive to the needs of individual citizens" (2001, 13). This responsiveness is different from that seen in many parts of the world, where some police are required to be responsive solely to an official party organ of the state. Secondly, Bayley asserts, the "police must be accountable to the law rather than to the government" (2001, 14). This notion of accountability also finds its equivalent in Gutmann and Thompson's idea of accountability. Finally, Bayley maintains, the "police should be transparent in their activities" (2001, 14). This idea also finds its match in Gutmann and Thompson's idea of *publicity* discussed above.

These democratic norms of policing would appear to suggest a relationship between the police and their citizenry that is amenable to a deliberative character. All that is left is to determine the process and venue of the citizen – police interaction, but this remains an open question. As Held (2006) observed, "[w]here deliberation should be sited, and the extent of popular participation, are not questions about which there is a consensus among deliberative thinkers" (252).

Deliberative democracy in practice appears to be available on a wide array of public issues in a variety of forums and at various scales.

Many deliberative democratic theorists have attempted to create deliberative mechanisms and forums for decision making on a large scale (Fishkin 1991). However, the practice of deliberative democracy appears to be most at home in the smaller venues, hence the early criticisms that it borders on direct democracy (Held 2006). The use of neighborhood crime watch meetings by the police is an example of a small-scale deliberative venue. It is in venues of this limited size that deliberative democratic practice originated. Recall the earlier discussion by Habermas, recounting the origins of small-scale public discourse in the *salons* of France. Mansbridge's suggestion that "everyday talk" in a variety of small-scale venues adds up to a larger deliberative arena recalls the idea of the *salons* (1999, 212).

A survey of the major contributors to the literature shows evidence of optimism that deliberative democratic practices can be implemented on a national and global scale (Gutmann and Thompson 2004, 36-39; Dryzek 2000, 115-139). The difficulties of achieving this have been detailed above. However, it appears that deliberative democratic thinkers are trying to resolve the problem of scale by reconstructing smaller bodies called "mini-publics" that function like informed focus groups that simulate large-scale deliberative processes (Dryzek 2010, 167-170). As early as 1991, Fishkin proposed national deliberation polls and deliberation days to address wide-ranging issues of regional and national importance. Nearly ignored are the small-scale settings that make frequent use of town hall meetings. This might be attributable to the belief that in these intimate small-scale settings, we get close to realizing direct democracy (Fishkin 1991, 91-92). The processes advocated for deliberations by mini-publics may work well at the neighborhood level.

Gutmann and Thompson submit, "The principle of accountability specifies that officials who make decisions on behalf of other people, whether or not they are electoral constituents, should be accountable to those people" (2004, 135). Being as most individuals have the greatest contact with their local officials, it can be argued that these agents and entities have the greatest impact on a person's day-to-day existence. It would make sense that Gutmann and Thompson's observation would apply to these officials as they are in the best position to give an account for their actions. In some ways, this is at least partially achieved through "public meetings" (Adams 2004, 43). However, because of their structure, such meetings tend toward procedures that are tightly scripted for legal and procedural reason (Adams 2004). Consequently, "they are not deliberative, and they are not an effective vehicle for rational persuasion" (Adams 2004, 52). Instead, "other devices, such as roundtables, forums, and citizens' panels, are more effective at this task" (Adams 2004, 52). "Neighborhood councils" are another instrument of deliberative democracy (Kathi and Cooper 2005, 562). Before these bodies, governments may introduce initiatives and policies to get feedback and direction before implementation. In these forums, officials have the opportunity to present information and offer justification for proposals, which may or may not change a citizen's mind.

Other uses of deliberative practices can be seen in the use of commissions for planning economic development and land use (Forester 1999). Proposals for variances and changes to building codes are brought before these bodies for consideration and the information used by policy makers in the formulation of future endeavors. Another venue where deliberative democratic practices are gaining traction is in the area of environmental policy. For example, Irvin and Stansbury evaluate the effectiveness of citizen deliberation in the EPA's program entitled *Community-Based Environmental Protection*, finding such citizen participation to be crucial to building support for initiatives; however, the public forums conducted under this program are open to manipulation if not properly managed (2004).

If we take seriously former Speaker of the House Tip O'Neill's observation that "all politics is local," then nowhere is deliberative democracy more at home than at the local level (1994). The local institution most likely to be called upon by its citizens is the police. No local institution enjoys greater scrutiny. Its legitimacy is indeed provisional, subject to review through existing institutions and formal mechanisms of accountability. However, deliberative democratic practices may well hold the key to transforming and improving the quality of the relationship between the police and the policed.

CHAPTER 4

The Idea of Community Policing: Practice Without a Theory

The term *community policing* can be confusing in that it is used in two ways. On the one hand, it refers broadly to the American policing's historical focus on the community, attributable to the tradition of local control. In the narrow sense, the term refers to a model or program of policing, one that emerged from the turmoil of the late 1960s and early 1970s. The review of the community policing literature previously presented focused on the narrow view of community policing as a model of policing. The intent was to trace the outlines of the community policing model as reflected in the literature, and place it in the foreground of the patchwork that is American policing, ignoring for the moment more recent developments in policing's practices.

However, understanding what is offered here – a new interpretation of the narrow understanding of the term – depends on a deeper appreciation of the broader picture. In this way, inconsistencies and exaggerated claims concerning the community policing model can be identified and reconciled where possible. For example, while some scholars claim that community policing is a return to an earlier time in American policing and an attempt to recapture something lost (Mastrofski 1988, 47; Crank 1994, 340; Sklansky 2008, 83), others assert it is a new path to be blazed if we would but give the effort it is due (Eck and Rosenbaum 1994; Goldstein 1990, 179). In truth, it is probably both something old and something new. The explanation behind such a contradictory assertion is dependent on knowledge of the broader context. In other words, to make sense of the idea of community policing as a practice, it will be helpful to place it in its larger historical context.

In order to support the argument that deliberative democratic theory is a proper grounding for community policing practice, it will be important to establish a connection between democratic ideals and American policing. This is an important goal of this chapter. I begin this chapter with an examination of the history of American policing. The thread that runs through this history gives interesting insight into the unique relationship in the United States between the police and democracy. The connection between democracy and American policing is rather circuitous, and in need of specification. Furthermore, I submit that the history of American policing also tells the story of American democratization.

The second important goal of this historical review is to detect evidence of two counterproductive preoccupations picked up along the way that work against community policing practice as they have enjoyed a degree of "stickiness" (Pierson 2004, 8). The first ideal concerns the issue of efficiency. This ideal made its way into public administration – and subsequently into policing – during the Progressive Era of the late 19th and early 20th Centuries (Wilson 1887; Bayley 1979). It has enjoyed a great deal of durability, but may be the single largest inhibitor of success for the practice of community policing. The second preoccupation embedded in community policing practice concerns the adoption of a pluralistic understanding of social and political phenomenon. This way of viewing social actors places them into different groups, defined by attributes or interests often presumed fixed and dichotomous. While it may be a helpful way of interpreting current events, the history of American policing shows mobility between what in the short-term may have been taken to be fixed groups.

In sum, this chapter hopes to use the historical record to demonstrate that not only is community policing a "plastic concept," (Eck and Rosenbaum 1994, 3) but American policing as a whole exhibits this characteristic as demonstrated by near continuous change and reform (Rumbaut and Bittner 1979, 240; Lane 1980, 6). American policing, at its origin, was a practical solution to common problems of living in the dynamic social environment that was – and is – the community. It is a practice born of efforts at reform that have political and social implications. This casts community policing reform as simply another chapter in a larger story of reform. It also places American policing in the middle of the on-going process of American democratization (Whitehead 2002). Because American policing is a responsive and reactive paradigm – a reform that is itself constantly undergoing reform – deliberation-oriented change is possible (Rumbaut and Bittner 1979, 240; Lane 1980, 6).

AMERICAN POLICING'S ORIGINS AND EARLY HISTORY

The advent and evolution of community policing cannot be fully understood without considering the history of American policing. There is consensus that American policing has its origins in Western European thought, specifically the development of policing in England in the early 19th Century (Manning 1977; Bayley 1979; Lane 1980; Monkkomen 1992; Crank 1994; Dodsworth 2004). It is through this lineage that American policing gets one of its most pronounced features: the enduring legacy of local control (Levett 1975; Goldstein 1977, 131; Kelling 2003, 4). In fact, many scholars assert this single feature, in addition to being the most distinguishable, it is the largest determinant factor in the delivery of police services in the United States (Goldstein 1977, 131; Bayley 1979, 130-135; Kelling 2003, 4; Manning 2010, 111). It reflects the Founder's distrust of centralized control and a preference for federalism (Lane 1980, 12).

A preference for local control in the enforcement of the law also hearkens back to an earlier time in European history, an arrangement with parallels to community policing practice. In fact, the American preference for a model of policing that exhibits decentralization and local control finds its precedent in the practices of Western European society as far back as the Middle Ages. Those arrangements and practices so long ago in many ways resemble community policing of the present. A brief look at the policing practices of the Middle Ages is important because they were substantially the same as those adopted by the American colonies and retained in large part after Independence. Furthermore, this history gives insight into the retention of certain features in American policing, even after the establishment of the modern police department in the early 19th century in U.S. cities.

In contextualizing the era in which I begin this discussion, it is important to keep in mind that while empires existed, the nation-state we are familiar with was hundreds of years in the future. As the Roman influence over Europe was waning, a new set of geopolitical actors emerged. Notwithstanding the machinations of European geopolitical history at the macro-level, the historical record suggests the responsibility for basic order in the community was the responsibility of local inhabitants (Downing 1992). Regardless of the exact geographic location, the arrangements were generally similar (Downing 1992). The "crown" granted or chartered lands to "nobility" with the expectation that they be productive with the property and be ready to respond with an adequate military force should it be needed (Downing 1992, 26-27). These grants of land included towns and villages and the economic enterprises they hosted. While the crown generally concerned itself with the larger issues of the empire, the local nobility was charged with administrative tasks in the lands bequeathed to them (Downing 1992). Though the nobility generally concerned themselves with the operation of the feudal manor, the towns and villages in their domain were also their responsibility (Downing 1992). Generally, the village dwellers were free persons not necessarily of noble title (Downing 1992). These villages established local governments that provided for the communication and enforcement of local norms and customs, as well as held individuals accountable for heinous acts. The historical record reflects that often when conflicts arose between empires and these lands became the province of a new monarch, the local community simply became a part of the new empire with local governments and customs remaining largely intact (Downing 1992).

As mentioned, American policing is particularly rooted in the development of the practice in England, but also in the broader Western European tradition (Manning 1977; Bayley 1979; Lane 1980; Monkkomen 1992; Crank 1994; Dodsworth 2004). This is noteworthy because immigrants to the American colonies did not just come from England, but hailed from other European lands as well. Yet there existed a degree of consensus on the matter of local government administration and the enforcement of community norms. Evidence of this is found in Paul Vinogradoff's review of feudalism and the important role of the manor (Vinogradoff 1913; 1922). In explaining the pervasiveness of the arrangement, Vinogradoff writes:

> The manor is peculiarly an English institution, although it may serve to illustrate Western European society in general. Feudalism, natural husbandry, the sway of the military class,

the crystallization of powers and rights in local centres, are phenomena which took place all over Western Europe and which led in France, in Germany, in Italy and Spain to similar though not identical results. (1922, 483)

The "manor" – or its equivalent – constitutes the "lowest" and "most characteristic type of such a feudal unit," as it is the most "efficient unit of medieval organization, and local justice, administration and police are all more or less dependent on its arrangements" (Vinogradoff 1922, 472). Vinogradoff notes it would be an error to imagine the nobility as having a singular purpose of exploiting the lower classes for the purposes of profit, although they did have an interest in maintaining a certain degree of local order as everyone was expected to advance the interests of the enterprise that was the manor. Both Downing (1992) and Vinogradoff (1922) observe that the nobility had an interest in keeping the local community somewhat happy as many were free persons who could permanently move from manor to manor and village to village (Vinogradoff 1922, 481). In fact, "the village community lay at the basis of the whole [and] gave rise to a very peculiar system of holding and using land [...] best indicated by the expression 'shareholding arrangement' or the term 'community of shareholders'" (Vinogradoff 1922, 473).

The arrangement of the manor and the village – or "*vill*" – is not just of critical importance for economic reasons, but for the order of the society in general (Vinogradoff 1922, 482). Vinogradoff paints a clear picture of the arrangements of local governance that includes policing, stating:

The complex machinery of the manor as the centre of economic affairs and of social relations demanded by itself a suitable organization. But besides this the manor was the local centre for purposes of police and justice; it had to enforce the king's commands and the law of the realm in its locality. It would be more correct to say that the manor and the village community or township underlying it were regarded as local centres of justice and police, because in these political matters the double aspect of the manor, the fact of its being composed of an upper and lower half, came quite as plainly to the fore as in its economic working. Indeed, for purposes of justice, taxations, supervision of vagabonds, catching and watching thieves, keeping in order roads, and the like, the government did not recognize as the direct local unity the manor, but the *vill*, the village community or *town*, as the old English term went. The vill had to look over the frankpledge, to keep ward, to watch over prisoners and to conduct them to gaol, to make presentments to justices and to appear at the sheriff's *turn*. This fact is a momentous piece of historical evidence as of the growth of manorial jurisdiction, but, apart for that, it has to be noticed as a feature of the actual administration of justice and police during the feudal period. (1922, 482).

The histories of the Middle Ages show that the matter of policing was "delegated to the care of the manor, in which the central power intervened only indirectly" (Vinogradoff 1922, 482). In fact, the variation in standards and procedures on matters of law could cause the kingdom trouble. One of the more notable achievements of Henry II's reign was "the centralization of justice" (Stenton 1926, 585). Stenton observes that by 1166, "for the first time in English history, criminal justice was to be administered all over the land in accordance with the same rules" (1926, 585).

However, lacking speedy communication and a safe transportation, coordination problems persisted with early experiments in centralized justice and policing, and as a result the king had to rely mainly on local institutions and community-based efforts (Stenton 1926, 584-586). Of particular importance was the individual. In 1166, Henry II required that "twelve lawful men of every hundred and four lawful men of every village should declare on oath if any in their hundred or village had been accused or suspected of being a robber, murderer" (Stenton 1926, 584). The king's court, now operating at the local level, retained jurisdiction in these more severe offenses, and the local "sheriff" retained responsibility and jurisdiction of the remaining host of petty offenses and violations of order (Stenton 1926, 584).

The expectation that the individual had the responsibility to police society and to turn in offenders persisted until the last century or so. The notion of a specialized and socially differentiated responsibility for policing is a somewhat recent development, as reflected in the 1967 report by the Task Force on the Police, which stated in this regard:

The Idea of Community Policing

Seen from the perspective of history, the anomalies of regarding the police as solely responsible for crime control become evident. In the preindustrial age, village societies were closely integrated. Everyone knew everyone else's affairs and character; the laws and rules of society were generally familiar and were identical with the moral and ethical precepts taught by parents, schoolmasters, and the church. If not by the clergy and the village elders, the peace was kept, more or less informally, by law magistrates (usually local squires) and constables. These in the beginning were merely the magistrates' agents, literally "citizens of duty" – the ablebodied men of the community serving in turn. (*President's Commission on Law Enforcement and Administration of Justice* 1967a, 1-2)

This, as the report indicates, was a "system [that] encouraged mutual responsibility" (*President's Commission on Law Enforcement and Administration of Justice* 1967a, 3). The system appears to have undergone several revisions between the 11th and 19th centuries to accommodate the changing times. However, some elements appear to have carried forward, even to the present day in the United States. These include the establishment of sheriffs, constables, and counties.

Klockars characterizes this form of policing as "obligatory avocational policing" in that service was mandatory, although not anyone's fulltime job (1985, 22). After the Battle of Hastings in 1066, Norman conquerors instituted the "frankpledge" wherein "every male above the age of twelve" took an oath to obey and actively enforce the law on others in their community (Klockars 1985, 23). This system was instituted in an attempt to gain a greater degree of central control for the crown, particularly in the areas of tax policy and justice (Klockars 1985). As noted above, prior to 1066 "policing and the administration of justice was almost totally under the control of local lords and nobles" (Klockars 1985, 24). The frankpledge system – sometimes referred to as "the mutual pledge system" – organized families into groups of ten, called a *tything*, and ten tythings into the *hundred* (*President's Commission on Law Enforcement and Administration of Justice* 1967a, 3; Klockars 1985, 23). The hundreds were organized into the "shire," which would subsequently be called a "county" (*President's Commission on Law Enforcement and Administration of*

Justice 1967a, 3; Klockars 1985, 23-24). A "reeve" was an official appointed by the king to administer the district known as the "shire," giving rise to the office of "shire-reeve," or as it is known today: the sheriff (*President's Commission on Law Enforcement and Administration of Justice* 1967a, 3; Klockars 1985, 24).

The shire-reeve served several roles from the same office; duties we see today as conflicting with each other. In addition to bringing offenders to justice, in many instances they served as magistrates and tax collectors (Stenton 1926, 580-584). This system eventually ran into difficulty as the populations began migrating, thus placing the membership in the tythings and hundreds in a constant state of flux. The frankpledge system was adopted rather unevenly throughout England, with some sheriffs continuing to show more loyalty to the local nobility than to the king (*President's Commission on Law Enforcement and Administration of Justice* 1967a, 3; Klockars 1985, 24). Moreover, when considering the fact that the village was becoming a more prominent fixture in society, a new method of policing was clearly needed (Klockars 1985, 25).

The "parish constable system" was adopted in accordance with the Statute of Winchester in 1285 as a reform to the shortcomings of the frankpledge system (Klockars 1985, 25). The underlying principles were still the same in that everyone remained responsible for the policing of the community (Klockars 1985, 25). However, instead of organizing families, a geographic area was established and an inhabitant was appointed "constable," charged with the responsibility for organizing the "watch and ward" (*President's Commission on Law Enforcement and Administration of Justice* 1967a, 3-4; Klockars 1985, 25-26). Night watches were a requirement for the men, and they were expected to "raise the hue and cry" whenever they detected an offense (*President's Commission on Law Enforcement and Administration of Justice* 1967a, 3-4; Klockars 1985, 26). Once the alarm was raised, it was the responsibility for everyone to respond as a posse to pursue and apprehend the offender, and if they failed in that endeavor, to pay a fine (*President's Commission on Law Enforcement and Administration of Justice* 1967a, 3; Klockars 1985, 26).

Both systems not only relied on the individual to perform policing activities, they were required by law to participate in the "watch and ward" and report crimes they were aware of even if not performing as a "citizen on duty" (*President's Commission on Law Enforcement and*

Administration of Justice 1967a, 1-3). Sanctions might be imposed for failure in this regard (Klockars 1985, 23, 26). This duty extended to all male members of the community, regardless of class. So serious was the obligation that those with the means to do so paid substitutes to perform watch duties in their place (Klockars 1985, 28-29). This led to a low general opinion of the members of the "watch" as they tended to be unskilled members of the lower class, paid to substitute, and often derelict in their responsibilities (*President's Commission on Law Enforcement and Administration of Justice* 1967a, 4; Klockars 1985; 28-29).

As the increasing sophisticated economy led to differentiation and specialization of duties, it became increasingly difficult for skilled labor to work their watch post at night and perform their normal jobs during the day (Bacon 1939, 7-8; Klockars 1985, 28). As the economic centers of activity were shifting increasingly to the village, trade depended upon mobility and moving goods to market (Bacon 1939; Klockars 1985). In addition to being unable to keep accurate track of residents and transients, the watch system introduced a degree of uncertainty into the provision of services by other important professions. For example, if the baker had watch duty, it might affect the availability of bread (Bacon 1939, 8). It was also difficult for employers to do without these employees while they performed these obligations (Bacon 1939, 8). The uncertainty in the provision of needed services of the watch – which also was on guard against the devastating possibility of fire – and its effects on the local economy made the system ripe for reform yet again (Bacon 1939; Klockars 1985).

The manor is the forerunner and prototype of the American colony, whose charter largely spelled out the structures of local governance and the enforcement of societal norms in a manner not unlike that seen under feudalism (*President's Commission on Law Enforcement and Administration of Justice* 1967a, 5). In the charters establishing the colonies, it appeared as a near standard boilerplate language that in the enforcement of criminal laws, the colonists were to set up systems of enforcement nearly identical to those found in England and enact laws that were consistent with English law. These included elements of local control and public offices like those in the homeland.

The history of New York City, and the New York Police Department, serves as a case in point. It is particularly fitting as the New York City Police Department was the first of its kind established in the U.S. in 1845, and the second of its kind in the world, following the London Metropolitan Police in 1829 (Bacon 1939; Levett 1975). The colony known as New Netherland was originally established in 1615 by a charter of the Dutch government to the New Netherland Company (Bacon 1939; 11). The charter ended after three years and the lands were not re-chartered again until 1623, at which time the Dutch government granted the lands for a forty-year period to the Dutch West India Company (Bacon 1939, 11). The charter granted the lands covering the areas that are the present-day state of New York, as well as parts of New Jersey, Delaware and Pennsylvania (Bacon 1939, 14). At the heart of this area was the city of New Amsterdam, the present-day New York City (Bacon 1939). In the early days the colony was ruled by the Director General solely, a company official with the powers of the government. However, by 1648, a representative form of government was allowed with the Director General still at its head. The changes permitted the local election of representatives from wards within the jurisdiction, but the "schout or sheriff, [was] appointed by the Director-General" (Bacon 1939, 12).

The responsibility for conducting watch responsibilities appears to have been assigned to a diffuse group that included members of the military, ordinary individuals, and company officials that usually had some form of low-level supervisory responsibility (Bacon 1939). Interestingly, the responsibility for organizing the watch seems to have rested with the elected representatives, or "schepens," and not the sheriff (Bacon 1939, 45). While it did fall to the watch to act when heinous offenses were committed, these violations were not necessarily codified and were beyond the normal scope of their duties (Bacon 1939, 12-16). Instead, they were expected to watch for fires, warn of invaders (including Indians) and enforce the rules and regulations that promoted good order toward achieving the aims of the company (Bacon 1939). This job even required them to police the timing of people's travels to and from work (Bacon 1939, 16). In fact, the earliest enforced codes of conduct did not mention "taboos against murder, rape, and the like" but instead took aim at basic social order infractions (Bacon 1939, 13-14). For example, one of the earliest dates to April of 1638, and admonishes:

> [E]ach and every one must refrain from Fighting, Adulterous intercourse with Heathens, Blacks, or other persons, Mutiny,

Theft, False Swearing, Calumny, and other Immoralities, as in all this Contraveners shall, according to the circumstances of the case, be corrected and punished, as an example to others. (Bacon 1939, 16-17)

The network of enforcement officials was expanded when the company began employing inspectors to watch the wharves and docks as well and examine the quality of goods being traded, and collect taxes as authorized by the charter (Bacon 1939, 17). These were intended to relieve the pressure on company supervisors to detect infractions and violators, freeing them to engage in their primary duties (Bacon 1939).

As the migration of the English peoples increased to New Netherland, the Director-General granted permission for immigrants to establish a township in the province and further allowed them the latitude of adopting local governance consistent with that found in England. The town became Flushing, New York, and a foothold that allowed for the eventual takeover of the province by the English (Bacon 1939). Nineteen years before the transfer of New Netherlands to English control in 1664, the Director-General granted the immigrants the authority to establish familiar local government structures, stating in that charter they may:

Elect and choose, a certain officer over them, who may bear the name or title of Scout, or Constable of Flushing, to which said officer, or Scout or Constable, we do hereby give grant and confirm, as large and ample power and authority, as is usually given to the Scout of any village in Holland, or Constable in England, for the apprehension of any malefactor, or any that shall go about to disturb the public peace and tranquility of the said town of Flushing. (Bacon 1939, 20-21)

With the transfer of New Netherlands in 1664, all colonies on the eastern seaboard that existed – or would come into existence – would do so under the terms of an English charter. The charters that established the colonies that would come to host the cities of New York, Boston, Philadelphia and Charleston, would all contain the provision that they not adopt laws that contravene the laws of England. Thus, we see a degree of uniformity develop in the establishment of law enforcement arrangements in the colonies from that point forward.

Consistent with the charters establishing local governance, "American colonists [...] brought to America the law enforcement structure with which they were familiar in England" (*President's Commission on Law Enforcement and Administration of Justice* 1967a, 5). Though largely appointed in the early years as they were in England, the constable was responsible for enforcement of the law in the towns, while the sheriff had a broader responsibility to both town and country (*President's Commission on Law Enforcement and Administration of Justice* 1967a, 5). There was no need for a large standing force of peace officers as the colonists also followed the "mutual pledge system," adopting the practice found commonly in England – namely, the rotating duty shared by every adult male to stand watch during the nighttime hours referred to as the "nightwatch" (*President's Commission on Law Enforcement and Administration of Justice* 1967a, 5).

Some of the same problems presented themselves in the colonies as in England, such as the difficulty in getting people to honor their responsibility to perform the duty of the watchman (Bacon 1939). As a result, many local governments began paying a small sum for the performance of the duty (Bacon 1939, 39). Over time, this became the sole source of income for some individuals, paving the way for corruption and abuse in the years before the reforms of the mid-nineteenth century (Bacon 1939; Levett 1975).

The duties that fell to the nightwatchmen were not necessarily crime control *per se*, rather their first mission was to ensure adherence to a host of local ordinances and codes intended to promote the good order of the community and disrupt the immoral activities of the lower classes (Bacon 1939; Levett 1975). For example, in colonial Boston we see the watch not only charged with regulating orderly behavior of citizens, but also setting standards for the conduct of watchmen. Bacon quotes an ordinance issued in1662 to illustrate this. That order decreed, "for as much as the watch is to see to the regulatings of other men [sic] actions and manners, that therefore they be exemplary themselves neither using any unclean or corrupt language" (Bacon 1939, 329). Furthermore, consistent with the public role religion played in local governance, the watch was responsible "to apprehend all Saboath breakers and [...] carry them before a magistrate or other authority, or comit to prison" (Bacon 1939, 338).

The Idea of Community Policing

In Philadelphia, the watch appears in 1700, one year before that city was chartered under English rule (Bacon 1939, 498). Those watchmen were responsible "to go round ye town with a small bell in ye night time, to give notice of ye time of the night and the weather, and if anie disorders or danger happen by fire or otherwise in the night time to acquaint the constables thereof" (Bacon 1939, 499). Furthermore, watchmen were responsible for monitoring the movements of visitors, sailors, and immigrants after hours and to insure they were not outside of the areas they inhabited (Bacon 1939). This method of social control went a long way toward helping establish somewhat homogenous neighborhoods and wards as local ordinances requiring the watch monitor a variety of activities of immigrants. Violations could, in some instances, result in banishment from the city (Bacon 1939, 375).

The duty to detect, apprehend, and bring to justice offenders of the criminal law was the responsibility of the constable, who was working for a magistrate (Bacon 1939, 43). If an offender was not caught in the act by a nightwatchman, the individual harmed by a criminal act was responsible for seeking out the offender by soliciting information and paying a constable to have them brought to justice (Bacon 1939; Lane 1980, 5). As a result, few individuals could afford the cost of seeking justice (Lane 1980, 6). Therefore, it was highly desirable that the nightwatchman catch offenders in the act. Added to this was an influx of immigrants from a variety of countries, whose varied cultural norms placed a strain on the peace (Levett 1975). Local governments responded with an increased emphasis on regulating behavior, increasing the number of nightwatchmen, and increasing their pay (Bacon 1939; Levett 1975).

After Independence was declared, little changed with regard to the operation of the watch at the municipal level, but "sheriffs and constables tended to be selected by popular elections, [Crown] patronage then being on the wane" (*President's Commission on Law Enforcement and Administration of Justice* 1967a, 5). With the constitutional founding of a federal form of government that left the enforcement of criminal laws to the local governments, the precedent of local control in these matters was affirmed.

Decentralization was more thoroughgoing than most recognize, as the responsibility for staffing the various watches (which in many cities now included a day watch) fell to the local elected representative within the precinct or ward, rather than the central city government (Bacon 1939; Levett 1975, 1-3). As a result, the award of these positions was a highly treasured prize of elected officials as they were able to grant these paid positions to supporters (Levett 1975). The arrangement – rife with cronyism – was increasingly ineffective, inefficient, and ripe for exploitation by corrupt politicians (*President's Commission on Law Enforcement and Administration of Justice* 1967a, 5-6; Levett 1975; Lane 1980; Monkkonen 1992).

Throughout the early and mid-19th century, cities along the eastern seaboard experienced tremendous growth, much of it due to immigration from Europe (Lane 1980; Monkkonen 1992). This placed an even greater strain on local government, which struggled to maintain the peace among the diverse cultures that were coming to populate the cities (Levett 1975; Lane 1980; Monkkonen 1992). Added to this was a series of riots in the major cities; riots for which the watch was ineffective at suppressing and sometimes involved (Levett 1975; Lane 1980, 6-7; Monkkonen 1992). Pluralism and factions appear to have presented problems early on for the forerunners of local policing.

Another problem for the early policing arrangements on both sides of the Atlantic concerned the matter of efficiency. The *ad hoc* network of actors that was depended upon to provide public safety and maintain order was not necessarily reliable. Records of colonial cities indicate a persistent problem getting citizens to honor their obligations to perform watch duties (Bacon 1939). Local leaders frequently concerned themselves with issues such as numbers and deployment patterns of citizens on the watch (Bacon 1939). In an effort to compel compliance, citizens could be jailed or fined for not participating in the watch, or for failing to respond when called upon to join a posse (Bacon 1939; Klockars 1985).

The efficiency of the watch was frequently a political matter, with candidates vowing to make the arrangements more effective and efficient (Bacon 1939, 296). Positive inducements were created, such as small stipends to citizens for the performance of these duties (Bacon 1939). The creation of standing watches (both day and night) with dedicated paid employees was a step in the right direction (Bacon 1939). However, ward-level groups of untrained and quite poorly compensated individuals – often citizen volunteers – were no match for the many mass riots of the 19th century. The inefficiency of the watch and the ineffectiveness of the constables and sheriffs in addressing disorder of that magnitude further highlighted the need for a more efficient and effective arrangement (Bacon 1939, 2, 7, 311).

BIRTH OF POLICE ORGANIZATIONS AND EMERGENCE OF PROFESSIONAL POLICING

Meanwhile, in England the Industrial Revolution was changing the economic and social landscape. The development of formalized policing in England was in response to political and social strife that manifested itself as criminal behavior, many times directed against the upper class and their holdings (Manning 1977; Kelling 2003, 3). In 1829, the London Metropolitan Police began operations after many years of work by Sir Robert Peel to promote reforms (Manning 1977; Klockars 1985). The aim was to stave off pressure for political reform the likes of which the colonists fought for during the Revolutionary War. Democratic institutions and ideals were considerably more advanced in the United States than in the country where these police reforms were originating. This further supports the contention that there is nothing inherently democratic about the method of policing issuing from the London model.

In light of this historical fact, it is easy to understand how any discussion of modern policing in the United States – however belatedly adopted – would require reconciliation with the societal prevailing understanding of democracy. This is because in American policing the notion of democracy is an *a priori* ideal and imperative norm. This places American policing in a rare position among the world's policing arrangements in that it solidified its status as an institution after the formation of the democratic government. Because the context in which policing developed in England was different from that found in the U.S., it stands to reason that the adoption of policing reforms pioneered by a regime lagging behind the U.S. in its democratic development would be entered into with some degree of trepidation (Lane 1980, 12). Hence, we see the first police departments, on the scale seen in London, do not come into existence until 1845 with the founding of the New York City Police Department (Bacon 1939; Levett 1975). This was achieved by combining the day watch, night watch, and detectives into a single agency (Bacon 1939; Levett 1975). This pattern was repeated in Boston and Philadelphia in order to create those city's police departments in those cities as well (Bacon 1939; Levett 1975). By the end of the 19th century, nearly every city in the U.S. had converted its night watch into a police department, a symbol of both size and growing prosperity (Bacon 1939; Lane 1980, 13).

The differences between the two forms of government influenced how these reforms were implemented. A lengthy history with a strongly centralized government meant for the English reforms the police would be accountable to the Parliament and supervised by the Home Secretary, who was coincidently the father of these reforms: Sir Robert Peel (*President's Commission on Law Enforcement and Administration of Justice* 1967a, 4). The first of these reforms called for the consolidation of the patchwork of police services provided by "a number of civic associations," watches, constables and the like, into the Metropolitan Police force (1967a, 4). The London reforms were initially received with skepticism, but success and increased efficiency led to the spread of these reforms to other parts of England (1967a, 5). In the years that followed, centralized control of police forces throughout England was given to the Home Secretary (1967a, 5).

The American experience was quite different. As mentioned, the responsibility for enacting and enforcing most criminal laws rests with the state and local governments. This is a key feature of federalism and is reflected by the sheer numbers of independent law enforcement agencies that have since come to exist at the local level. Though modified to an extent after Independence, the same patchwork system of policing that existed in England also existed in the U.S. with the same disappointing results. However, Levett (1975) contends that the implementation of the London style reforms in the U.S. did result in a degree of centralization, just not on the scale or to the level seen in England. When the patchwork policing system in England's ward, districts and precincts were organized and consolidated, control was retained in the central government (Levett 1975). In the U.S., when the patchwork police system at the ward, district and precinct level was organized and consolidated, control was vested in the local mayor and council (Levett 1975).

While gains in efficiency were an aim of these reforms, that goal remained largely unrealized until the very late 19th and early 20th centuries (Kelling 2003, 4). Instead, the consolidation of city policing services into a single department under the mayor and elected representatives ushered in a new era of inefficiency caused by political interference and cronyism; political machines and ward bosses

The Idea of Community Policing

continued to use the perks of government employment to secure and maintain political power (Kelling 2003). One of the most significant differences between the British and American experience with the London-style police reforms concerns the role of politics. Whereas in London, the desire was to achieve a degree of "impartiality" by removing politics from policing, the opposite was the case in the U.S. experience (Lane 1980, 12). As Lane put it: "Nothing could be more alien to American political culture. Local police in the United States were supposed, like other municipal employees, to be politically active residents and voters" (Lane 1980, 12).

In fact, it appears that in the mid-to late-19th century, the London model only served to increase the efficiency of the political machines operating in the major U.S. cities. Though the departments were more centrally organized, ward-level politicians still held considerable sway in the hiring of police officers at all ranks within the local precincts (Lane 1980). Added to this was the common requirement that the police officer be a resident of the ward (Bacon 1939, 316). The fact that there was now a standing, paid cadre of uniformed quasi-military men on the streets twenty-four hours a day – with direct ties to the ward – presented new opportunities for local politicians. Given the circumstances of the urban landscape in 19th century America, it is not surprising that politicians would exploit opportunities.

As Lane observes, "nineteenth-century politicians were never a wholly homogenous group [as] continued growth and foreign immigration [...] forced members of [the] elite to share or surrender power to organized professionals drawn from the lower-middle and even lower classes" (Lane 1980, 15). The new political actors had interests not very different from the people that elected them. The durability of the political machines of the 19th century depended upon, among other things, voting behavior. Added to the duties of the police at the ward level was responsibility for "pollwatching" (Lane 1980, 15). In fact, what the "ward bosses" required was that the police – in exchange for their jobs – round up the appropriate votes in a sufficient number so as to guarantee the election (Kelling 2003, 4). This was not too terribly difficult as any significant level of homogeneity that existed was most likely found at the ward level (Levett 1975, 130).

Though under the control of the political machines, there were some positive aspects of the arrangement, and of a better organized police. In fact, as one police historian notes, after the implementation of the London model "city police almost immediately began doing things unexpected by their original creators, whose expectations were more along the lines of crime prevention" (Monkkonen 1992, 554). In addition to enforcing criminal laws and local ordinances, "the police took in tramps, returned lost children by the thousands, shot stray dogs, enforced sanitations laws, inspected boilers, took annual censuses, and performed myriad other small tasks" (Monkkonen 1992, 554). The maintenance of local order not only pertains to preserving peace and tranquility, but in many cases meeting the needs of the mass of impoverished newly arrived immigrants. This was the case in large part because "in the mid-nineteenth century, all welfare was a local responsibility," the police routinely took in everyone "from orphans to the homeless" into the "station houses [which] contained separate dorm-type rooms to house overnight 'lodgers'" (Monkkonen 1992, 555).

Most historical accounts of the development of American policing argue that while the English model was largely adopted in the U.S., this occurs for different reasons. It is generally held that the London model is employed by U.S. cities in large part to address the problem of riots and social disorder among factions that were, for the most part, within the same class (Manning 1977; Lane 1980; Monkkomen 1992). Such assessments have a sound historical basis. But these assertions were made by scholars conducting their research in the wake of the riots and turmoil of the 1960s, which may well have focused their attention on this particular pattern of violence while overlooking other equally possible justifications. In fact, there is an alternate argument that suggests that it is more plausible to believe the London model was adopted in the U.S. for political reasons as the nation's military was at the time better suited and more experienced at putting down large scale rebellion and social unrest (Bacon 1939, 466; Levett 1975, 11; Lane 1980, 7-8). Levett (1975) examines the two leading theories for the adoption of a London-style standing police force.

The first theory is a sociologically-based explanation that proposes that the influx of immigrants during the 19th century placed strain on the urban environment. Because a large number of individuals were immigrating to the U.S. with either limited or no means of supporting themselves, they resorted to crime. In an effort to gain control of the crime problem, the employment of the London model was intended to consolidate the variety of policing officials into a single department to improve the community's ability to reduce crime. However, Levett observes that in the period following reforms, crime actually goes up (1975, 18). He proposes the more likely explanation for consolidation is rooted in the politics associated with the influx of immigrants to urban centers (Levett 1975).

In examining 19th century arrest data for several of the larger U.S. cities, he concludes that the increase in crime is largely attributable to an "increase in arrests for what are called public order offenses" (1975, 19). The elites viewed the ways of newly-arrived people as aberrant and disorderly. Cultural, ethnic, and religious differences were seen as deviant on moral grounds and in need of control, if not correction. Often, immigrants were without means and were reduced to making a living in enterprises that – if not outright illegal – were on the edges of propriety. Levett suggests that the crime control argument is somewhat hollow because of a somewhat widely held agreement among all classes that property and violent crimes are injurious and undesirable (1975, 20). However, "public order offenses touch upon the life style of groups in the populations about which there is less agreement as to what constitutes correct behavior and how infractions should be handled," which means these behaviors "are more problematic politically" (Levett 1975, 20). Therefore, while it is true that elite society saw the need to reform and consolidate the police as a means of controlling the behavior of the lower social classes, the larger goal was maintaining dominance in the political arena.

A more recent example that comes to mind is the arrest of Rosa Parks in 1955 for violating a Montgomery, Alabama municipal ordinance. In the end, it may well be these two explanations consist of distinctions without a substantive difference. While both the political and sociologically-based explanations for centralization reforms in American policing appear to have some merits, many of which depend on the precise circumstances of the locality, the decision to enter into an organized effort at social control is a political decision. Any efforts at reforms – at their inception and subsequent execution – are inherently political.

The implementation of police reforms in the manner and scale of that seen in London clearly had political implications. These new organizations, under overt political control, became better and more efficient at providing traditional services that centered on community order, and even expanded the range of services. As discussed, police in

New York City took on responsibility for a host of social service responsibilities at various points in time, ranging from taking the homeless into the precinct stations at night and turning them out at daylight, to street cleaning and public sanitation duties (Bacon 1939; Lane 1980, 9; Monkkonen 1992). The idea of confining the police department to a much narrower mission – crime fighting – had not yet dawned. The Civil War and Reconstruction served to slow progress toward further reforms (Kelling 2003). This delay also allowed the entrenchment of corrupting influences that thwarted the realization of a professional law enforcement agency that had crime fighting as their overriding goal.

The efficiency in government operations has a political side as well (Bacon 1939, 477; Levett 1975, 93, 113-115). After the establishment of centralized police departments, there was a concern that a better organized and more efficient police force would represent a political threat to the party not in power (Levett 1975, 113-115). Therefore, control of the police became a political prize. Police matters, such as the deployment of resources, activities of officers, and appointments to leadership positions, were frequently the pressing subjects upon which municipal elections turned in the mid-to late-19th century (Bacon 1939, 296, 477; Levett 1975, 93). A major obstacle to efficiency and effectiveness was the spoils system (Kelling 2003). Those not pleased with the existing arrangement identified with the "Progressive Movement" of the late-19th century, which was concerned about political interference in government administration and sought reforms to end cronyism and corruption (Kelling 2003).

The roots of the movement go back to the early 19th century, but the mandate for the signature reforms that marked the "Progressive Era" gained no real traction until 1881 with the assassination of President James A. Garfield (Shafritz and Hyde 2007). The assassination was linked to the spoils system when it was learned the killer's motivation was anger arising from the fact that he did not receive appointment to a government post he thought he was due. The Progressives believed the assassination proved their concerns were valid and strengthened their resolve in advocating for greater efficiency in public administration by ending the inefficient and often corrupt spoils system. A leading voice in these efforts was a future U.S. President, Woodrow Wilson. In 1887, the future president – then a professor at Princeton – authored a now famous paper calling for a new kind of public administration and outlined measures needed for reform (Wilson 1887). Included among these reforms was a call to strengthen the civil service system, which made merit and competition the grounds for government employment and not affiliation with parties or politicians. He also advocated for a disciplined administration of government operations that emphasized efficiency, the greatest threat to which is political interference (Stillman 2005, 5). In the estimation of most scholars, Wilson's exposition of the proper role of politics in the administration of government is his most enduring contribution to this particular body of work (Stillman 2005, Shafritz and Hyde 2007).

The police proved to be a hard case for the Progressives (Kelling 2003). In an era that began in the late 19th century, meaningful reform did not reach local police departments until well into the 20th century (Kelling 2003). "Ward bosses" and the "political machines" were too deep-seated in the largest urban agencies, and "if anything, police corruption worsened with the ratification of the Prohibition amendment to the constitution in 1920" (Kelling 2003, 4). The violent crime associated with the illicit alcohol trade, and the pervasive corruption in police departments that were supposed to protect the innocent, provoked outcries for reform (Kelling 2003). President Hoover established a commission to study the situation and make recommendations (Trojanowicz and Bucqueroux 1990). The findings were an indictment of the modern urban police arrangement (Kelling 2003). The now famous "Wickersham Commission" reports suggested many of the reforms the Progressives had called for all along (*President's Commission on Law Enforcement and Administration of Justice* 1967a, 7).

The 1930s marked a transition toward a more professional policing model. Kelling characterizes the transformation, stating in this regard:

> Efforts by social reformers, both in the nineteenth and early twentieth centuries, to detach the police from ward politics largely failed. Not until the 1930s were internal reformers, aligned with Progressives, able to achieve significant success in wresting control of police organizations from ward politicians. During that decade, U.S. policing as we know it began to take shape. (2003, 4)

It was only a matter of time before the changes in public administration practices would work themselves into the management of police departments. Internal reformers and Progressives eventually succeeded in "dismantle[ing] station house lodging" and by 1920 returned the department to a "focus [...] on crime control" (Monkkonen 1992, 555-556). However, "the narrowing focus of police on crime in turn came with a new set of external pressures, including demands for efficiency, honesty, and crime control" (Monkkonen 1992, 556).

A prominent internal reformer was Oakland California Police Chief August Vollmer (Trojanowicz and Bucqueroux 1990, 55). Widely regarded as the "father of modern policing," Vollmer, a longtime advocate of modern police reforms, was largely responsible for the content of the Wickersham Commission Reports and their program of reforms (Kelling 2003, 4; Trojanowicz and Bucqueroux 1990, 55). Vollmer had earlier pushed for reforms in a series of articles wherein he advocated the application of "scientific principles to organization, deployment of personnel, criminal investigation, and crime prevention" (Kelling 2003, 4). In the commission reports, he listed ten measures necessary for the reform of American police departments (Trojanowicz and Bucqueroux 1990, 55). First and foremost, he demanded "the corrupting influence of politics should be removed from the police organization," thus echoing the sentiment expressed by Woodrow Wilson decades earlier (Trojanowicz and Bucqueroux 1990, 55). Like Wilson, Vollmer believed that leadership in government organizations was important and those seeking those posts should be competent, possessing the requisite education and experience (Trojanowicz and Bucqueroux 1990, 55). During the late 19th and early 20th century, it was not uncommon for aspiring politicians to hold top managerial posts in police departments (Trojanowicz and Bucqueroux 1990, 54). Both Theodore Roosevelt and Thomas Dewey held such police agency positions (Trojanowicz and Bucqueroux 1990, 54).

Other recommendations included raising the qualifications for employment, adopting a standard hiring process, devising a method for reporting and measuring crime, deploying personnel in a more reasoned manner, and the creative use of technology to respond to, and solve, crimes (Trojanowicz and Bucqueroux 1990, 55-56). All of this evidenced a faith in the ability of science to increase productivity of the police and provide better service to the public (Kelling 2003). Fredrick

The Idea of Community Policing 99

Taylor's thoughts on the philosophy and methods of "scientific management," previously embraced by the private sector, were starting to make their way into the public sector management of police departments (Kelling 2003, 5). The neutrality associated with the implementation of scientific methods in policing was considered valuable as it could be translated into political neutrality (Kelling 2003, 5). Administrative decision making now had an objective basis, with the goal of efficiency rather than in a subjective, politically-motivated rationale (Kelling 2003, 5).

Bruce Smith was another reformer, though he never served as a police officer (Kelling 2003, 5; Steverson 2008, 139). He was among the number of reformers who called for the end of using the police to perform a host of other duties that did not involve the enforcement of criminal law. In fact, one of the assigned duties he believed extraneous was police censorship of movie and theater performances (Smith 1929, 3). Smith examined municipal police administration in a 1929 article that outlined the application of scientific methods in the organization and administration of municipal police departments (Smith 1929; Goldstein 1977, 247-248). The article was among the first to call for a neutral police department led by an independent police chief that had the technical knowhow to run a public safety bureaucracy (Smith 1929). Smith was an associate of Vollmer, and with him was influential in the development of prominent police scholar and Police Chief O.W. Wilson (Walker 1999, 33; Steverson 2008, 139-140). Wilson, who at times in his career was chief executive at the Wichita, Kansas and Chicago police departments, was also a professor of criminology at the University of California (Walker 1999, 33). One of Wilson's most important contributions to the field of policing was the production of *Police Administration*, considered by many to be the most widely read and influential books used by police chiefs as a handbook for the administration of a professional police organization (Kelling 2003). The work, first produced in 1950, saw three editions in his lifetime and two more after his passing.

For decades, Wilson's *Police Administration* (1950) served as a blueprint for managers and executives seeking to professionalize their departments. The book built upon the earlier work by Smith (1929), giving detailed instructions on the ways in which to organize the department, deploy personnel, and conduct specialized tasks such as traffic enforcement and criminal investigations (Wilson 1950). New technologies were sought to increase effectiveness. The implementation of manual databases for the recording and retrieval of a variety of criminal information, eventually led to the use of computers for those purposes (Wilson 1950; Wilson and McLaren 1972). O.W. Wilson was among the first to advocate the use of the automobile and two-way radio in patrol work (Kelling 2003, 6). The system as envisioned had officers deployed in automobiles with two-way radios, who were then directed from a central dispatch center. These officers were to patrol certain geographically defined areas in accordance with a pre-established deployment plan. When citizens found themselves in need of police services, they need only make a telephone call to the police department and an officer in a radio-car would respond. If the citizen's needs were beyond the officer's expertise and training, a specialist with those skills was called. This was also another of Wilson's contributions; he furthered the efforts at increasing specialization in the areas of criminal investigations and criminalistics (Wilson 1950). Increasingly specialized training also became a requirement of the professional police officer as the division of responsibilities were thought important to the efficient operation of the department and the provision of public safety (Wilson 1950; Kelling 2003).

O.W. Wilson's mentorship and works were influential in the development of Los Angeles Police Chief William Parker, and Parker's efforts to reform and professionalize that department. Many regard that department under Chief Parker's leadership to be the quintessential model of a professional police department during the mid-20th century. The Sergeant Joe Friday, just-the-facts style of policing came to symbolize the new professionalism that was sweeping the nation's police departments by the mid-20th century. Those practicing this new professional style of policing perceived they were achieving a degree of effectiveness, efficiency, and – above all – enjoying a certain level of "autonomy" that comes from the absence of "political interference" (Goldstein 1977, 134-135).

THE (ALLEGED) DEMISE OF POLICING'S PROFESSIONAL MODEL

Thus far, we have seen how the adoption of the London model caused U.S. cities to convert their assortment of watches into a full-time police department. These agencies tended to gravitate toward doing a better job of maintaining social order rather than adopting a crime fighting mission (Lane 1980; Monkkonen 1992). That was still largely in the hands of constables and sheriffs (Bacon 1939; Lane 1980). This proved to be an opportunity for politicians, in that a standing police force in their employ could easily be converted to a tool by which the politician could help their friends and keep their enemies at bay. Often, the police were deployed in an oppressive manner against other ethnic or cultural groups in an effort to control their access to power (Levett 1975). While the tradition of citizens on the watch engaged in that kind of activity was disliked (and the subject of London-style reforms), the practice of a professional, organized, full-time, taxpayer funded body of men doing those same tasks was found repugnant to Progressives, and eventually internal reformers. There is general agreement (but not unanimity) that "the 1890s mark the transition to a crime-control model for the police" (Lane 1980, 19-20; Monkkonen 1992, 558). In many regards, the police had not realized that their presence in greater numbers and a round-the-clock deployment model made them more suitable to be the primary enforcer of criminal laws as opposed to the constables and sheriffs (Monkkonen 1992). As they were called upon increasingly to enforce criminal laws, order maintenance enforcement activities declined in their priority. Greater demand and "the narrowing focus of police on crime in turn came with a new set of external pressures, including demands for efficiency, honesty, and crime control" (Monkkonen 1992, 556).

We have also seen the demand for efficiency and honesty fit well with the Progressives and other reformers' calls for a professional and politically neutral police. Taylorism was useful in advancing a professional model of policing that was both scientifically informed and politically neutral (Swanson, Territo and Taylor 1993, 82-87; Kelling 2003, 5). Though "Taylorism" itself has "come and gone," its lasting legacy is that it has imbedded into policing the ideal of efficiency – that is, decision making in policing should be based on reasoned objective analysis irrespective of political influence (Swanson, Territo and Taylor 1993, 84). The professional model of policing made great strides in the middle part of the 20th century, adapting to changing thinking in the area of management and technology that each sought to achieve greater efficiency. Efficiency, as an ideal, has doggedly maintained its hold on policing, at times holding the status akin to a gold standard for police practices.

Furthermore, we have seen there is a close relationship between operational efficiency and political autonomy. In fact, as we see the value of efficiency ascend in policing, we also see the "emergence of police autonomy as a virtue" for local governments (Goldstein 1977, 134). It was considered a mark of a highly professional department to keep police matters outside the meddling hands and prying eyes of the public (Goldstein 1977, 134; Kelling 2003, 10). So important was the value of political neutrality that it was a frequent platform of local politicians to promise "autonomy to the police," and upon running for re-election "brag about the degree of independence they allowed the police" (Goldstein 1977, 135). Policing was increasing becoming something that was done *for* citizens rather than *with* citizens. Instead of citizens being seen as "active" subjects, as they were in the days of the citizen watch, they were increasingly viewed as "passive" objects and "consumers" of police services (Bayley and Shearing 1996, 588).

There are the "negative by-products of autonomy," the bulk of which manifested themselves during the 1960s (Goldstein 1977, 135-136). Professional police departments began zealously guarding the autonomy granted them (Kelling 2003). Any encroachment for any reason resulted in the police crying foul. In far too many instances, that autonomy – without much accountability – was conceded to the police. Increasingly, the professional police service was becoming accountable to no one other than itself and its own standard of efficiency (Goldstein 1977).

Autonomy led not only to a lack of accountability, but in separating themselves from the larger democratic mechanisms of accountability the police became unpalatably distant from the people they served (Goldstein 1977, 133-136). This adversarial "us versus them" dynamic is widely regarded as one of the most recalcitrant aspects of the professional model, leading to a "siege mentality" that is counterproductive (Crank 1994, 330; Kleinig 1996, 230; Bratton 1998, 244). This distancing of the police from the people flew in the face of the famous axiom of the reform movement widely attributed to Sir Robert Peel, that the "the police are the public and [...] the public are the police" (Trojanowicz and Bucqueroux 1990, 45). It is this troubling separation – the standing of this axiom on its head – that led Crank to observe, "[t]he latent consequences of such 'professionalized' organizational structures [...] was a fundamental separation of police from community [which] contributed to a 'we-them' siege mentality"

The Idea of Community Policing

(1994, 330). The nation's police were perfectly positioned to respond inappropriately to the civil disorder of the 1960s.

One of the by-products of police activities during the tumultuous 1960s was that it brought into question the value of efficiency as a guiding standard of police. For example, investigative practices in a variety of circumstances came under Supreme Court review because they fell outside constitutional authority (Kelling 2003). Though these tactics may have resulted in the perception of increased efficiency as reflected in arrest or case clearance rates, the Court nevertheless held them illegitimate as they failed to meet Constitutional standards. In fact, were it not for these and other standards, policing would be more efficient. Certainly one could cynically argue that quarantining all citizens in place and conducting house-to-house searches for illicit contraband would be an efficient method of removing prohibited items from society, but at what cost? Activities such as these, because they are beyond the pale of democratic norms, are not legitimate.

Increasingly, the issue of efficiency at the cost of legitimacy has gained the attention of those scholars researching the connection between democracy and policing (Manning 2010). The studies of the police responses to critical events in the 1960s in nearly every instance called for reforms that had legitimacy consistent with the rule of law and democratic norms in a place of priority over the value of efficiency. Evidence of this new direction can be seen in the difference between O.W. Wilson's first edition of *Police Administration* (1950) and his third edition. Recall that this work was considered the blueprint for building a professional police organization consistent with the scientific method. The first edition began with the orderly and logical construction of the bureaucracy that is the police department. The work was written as a technical manual, in the style of an engineering document. However, by the time the third edition was published in 1972, much change had taken place on the social and political landscape. The original work largely remained intact, but the first five chapters of that new edition consisted of an extended discussion about the relationship between the police and citizens, and reflected the recognition that "the relationship of police to government and politics" cannot be sidestepped and must be addressed (Wilson and McLaren 1972, 14). Goldstein similarly observed, it is a "common misconception accounting for present difficulties [...] that the police function is apolitical" (1977, 141). He goes on to say, "city government is political and [...] police functioning is political" (1977, 141).

The stage was set at the end of the 1960s and early 1970s for a new way of policing, one that is not only efficient but, more importantly, legitimate. The host of presidential commissions and recommendations issuing therefrom, gave rise to community policing. This development was best summed up by Trojanowicz and Bucqueroux when they observed that "history demonstrates, many factors set the stage for the birth of Community Policing [including] the isolation of officers in police cars[,] the narrowing of the police mission to crime fighting[, and] a scientific approach to management that stressed efficiency more than effectiveness" (1990, 67). Despite its best efforts to resist, politics again encroached on police affairs. Questions concerning the legitimate use of force against citizens – particularly in the case of disenfranchised minorities – brought the national conversation about policing in close proximity to the larger conversation about the nature of American democracy, and questions about its legitimacy.

CHAPTER 5

The Long Slide: A Return to Efficiency-Oriented Policing

Despite great strides in the preceding decades toward professionalization, rising crime and increasing conflict between the police and the policed in the 1960s left little to show in the way of progress. Seemingly forgotten in the race toward maximum efficiency was that citizens in a democracy have a voice and that politics is an inevitable part of "policing a free society" (Goldstein 1977, 14). The parade of presidential commissions and subsequent findings identified gaps between the police and citizens that were a fundamental part of the failure (Kelling 2003). None was more critical than the earliest of these reports – the 1967 report entitled *The Challenge of Crime in a Free Society*, issued by President Johnson's Commission on Law Enforcement and Administration of Justice (Kelling 2003, 14). The report identified the central problem – the relationship between the police and the policed – and recommended steps to improve that relationship (Goldstein, 1977; Kelling 2003).

Among the most important recommendations were those relating to the establishment of community relations units within local police departments (Trojanowicz and Bucqueroux 1990; Kelling 2003). In their implementation, these initiatives could go one of two ways; on the one hand, they could consist of honest efforts in a "serious attempt to identify and solve neighborhood problems" (Kelling 2003, 14). On the other, however, they could be largely empty gestures that could cause more harm than good. This was a concern of the commission, which cautioned against public relations initiatives that were cynically designed to "'sell the police image' to the people" (1967b, 100). The expectation was that these initiatives would have real substance in that they would serve to "acquaint the police and the community with each other's problems and to stimulate action aimed at solving those problems" (1967b, 100).

Still, in the power relationship that exists between the police and the public, there are not a lot of incentives for the police to do anything other than try to press their message. With little guidance or deep thought as to how to work in concert with the public, community relations units all too often were ineffective. In many instances, the message citizens heard from the public relations officer was not consistent with the reality they observed from the street officer (Kelling 2003). The purpose of the public relations enterprise was to begin the process of "collaboration" generally understood as "working together"; to "jointly" co-labor (Palmiotto 2011, 88-89). However, this presumes decisions have been made as to what should be done and how things should proceed. In other words, collaboration proceeds without genuine deliberation. This view exposes the assumption that consensus exists between the police and the policed as to the task to be performed and the manner in which it is to be performed. All that is lacking is a level of comfort on the part of the public as it pertains to policing methods. By presuming that the only need the public has of its police is the production of a public safety product, the role of the public's role is reduced to that of compliant consumer.

In many ways, the 1967 report represents a missed opportunity in that it did not go far enough in its critique. As Kelling summarizes:

> However strong the forces for change that were converging on the police, the 1967 report of President Johnson's crime commission reaffirmed the strategy associated with traditional police reform and professionalism. Aside from acknowledging that some police tactics were unpopular in minority communities and urging the development of community relations programs, the report endorsed the reform agenda: more police, better equipment, more education for officers, improved command and control, enhanced training of officers, expanded use of technology – in other words, continued implementation and refinement of the reform agenda. (Kelling 2003, 15)

In the end – despite a head nod toward community engagement – the 1967 report re-affirms the professional model of policing advocated by the progressives' reform. In this new era of policing programs that frequently use the term "oriented" in their name, the new professional model may be called *efficiency-oriented policing*.

Proceeding from the position that despite the turmoil of the 1960s and 1970s efficiency remains the dominant ideal in American policing, this chapter has several goals. The first is to identify the enduring features common to the multitude of practices falling under the "umbrella" of "community policing" (Goldstein 1987, 8). In the end, we observe the considerable effort expended in the direction of organizational change and development. Left woefully underdeveloped is a deeper understanding of the citizens' role in policing. Secondly, this chapter will analyze problems of community policing's implementation. These problems present significant opportunities for competing policing programs that are efficiency-oriented, driven by quantifiable methods and results. This chapter concludes with a look at developments outside of policing that have helped push traditional community policing efforts to the side, and moved competing programs to the fore. I include among these the responsiveness of the police bureaucracy to trends in government management philosophy, the manner in which crime became politicized in the 1990s, and the changing nature of the domestic public safety environment in the post-9/11 era.

COMMON FEATURES OF COMMUNITY POLICING PROGRAMS

Both of the 1967 reports issued by the *President's Commission on Law Enforcement and Administration of Justice* stopped short of calling for a radical rethinking of American policing with a new and enlightened view of the problem – namely, the problem of policing a democracy. Instead, attempts were made to shore up its existing operations by engaging in more public relations initiatives. Any substantial efforts in the direction of reform in the wake of the turbulent 1960s took the form of additional programs. These consisted of add-on duties or initiatives designed to ease tensions and foster better public relations, yet at the same time allowed the police to persist in its original law enforcement mission. Among the earliest of these was the *team policing* initiative (Goldstein 1979; Sherman 1986; Trojanowicz and Bucqueroux 1990).

The idea originated in Great Britain in the mid-20th century and found its way into the recommendations of the 1973 report by the *National Advisory Commission on Criminal Justice Standards and Goals* (National Advisory Commission 1973; Palmiotto 2011, 89-92). These efforts centered on the formation of limited partnerships for the purposes of resolving a problem in a fixed geographical area (Palmiotto 2011). The partnership included other organizations of government, the affected residents, and permanently designated personnel from the police department (National Advisory Commission 1973; Goldstein 1979; Palmiotto 2011). Among the difficulties with team policing was funding (Worrall and Zhao 2003). The strict dedication of personnel to such initiatives increased personnel costs (Swanson, Territo and Taylor 1993). Consequently, once these problems were resolved, the personnel were reallocated – if not to another team policing initiative – back to their original duties. The demands of efficiency and the reality of resource limitations were driving factors. Therefore, the initiative did not result in any long-term or fundamental change in the way policing was conducted, and as a consequence was largely abandoned (Walker 1999, 173-174). Even worse was the fact that partnerships forged with the community were left to founder.

The team policing concept was followed by the *problem-oriented policing* concept (Goldstein 1979; Walker 1999; Palmiotto 2011). Herman Goldstein designed this new approach to policing after assessing what he believed to be the failures of the team policing concept (1979). First, Goldstein saw team policing as still a reactive rather than proactive measure designed to prevent crime (1979; Walker 1999, 158). Secondly, he perceived that team policing was a temporary fix designed to treat the symptoms of a larger problem rather than address the root cause of crime directly (Goldstein 1979, 1987, 1990). Goldstein advocated advanced training in problem recognition and resolution (1979). He proposed that this work would be continuous in that it would require constant dialogue with the community and on-going maintenance and monitoring of the root causes (once properly identified) so that any recurrence might be immediately addressed (1990). These, and a host of locally-defined variants, were swept into a larger concept termed *community policing* (Goldstein 1987; Trojanowicz and Bucqueroux 1990).

However, broadening the concept into a sort of catchall has made defining community policing a somewhat elusive and moving target.

This difficulty has been a long-recognized and quite frequently discussed issue among both scholars and practitioners alike (Scheider, Chapman, and Schapiro 2009, 696). This is in large part due to the fact it emerged as a practice aimed at solving a real-world problem. Seen as a solution to address a wide array of crime-related social problems in a multitude of places and a myriad of contexts, community policing practice emerged primarily from the milieu of "human activities and commonsense knowledge," paying relatively little attention to theoretical grounding (Willis, Mastrofski, & Weisburd 2007, 151). If asked for the definition of community policing, it would not be unusual for a practitioner's response to consist of examples of community policing in practice. Furthermore, as Skolnick and Bayley observe, "[i]f one goes to police departments and says, 'Show me an example of community policing,' one will be shown different activities in different places" (1988, 4). The broad features and considerations of the practice enjoy a certain "plastic" quality, in that it is often adapted to fit the local context (Eck and Rosenbaum 1994, 1; National Research Council 2004, 85). As researchers from the National Institute of Justice aptly put it, the policing profession is rife with "locally defined versions of community policing" (National Institute of Justice 2000a, 20).

As multiple team policing and problem-oriented programs emerged across the country, so too did a number of local variants. Nonetheless, each seemed to share some common features. In the mid to late 1980s, the term *community policing* came into vogue, and in 1990 Trojanowicz and Bucqueroux argued that all similar programs should be subsumed under the heading of *community policing* (1990, 5-20). Though locally divergent, each variant shares common features, thus making community policing "a coherent concept [with] identifiable programmatic elements" (Skolnick and Bayley 1988, 4).

By the mid-1990s, nearly every major police department in the U.S. claimed to be practicing some sort of community policing (National Research Council 2004, 104-105). This is largely attributable to the thinking of Robert Trojanowicz and Bonnie Bucqueroux, who in 1990 proposed that prior problem focused initiatives could all be incorporated into a broader program that they called "community policing" (1990, ix, 8-11; National Research Council 2004, 233). They proposed that these new ways of policing constituted a new "philosophy" of policing that, regardless of varying programmatic specifics, shared some common features (1990, ix). It is this shared philosophy combined with organizational arrangements that constitute the core of each generally accepted example of community policing, and allows each variant to lay claim to the title of community policing by virtue of shared programmatic features (Skolnick and Bayley 1988, 4; National Research Council 2004, 233).

These features, summarized in an assessment produced by the National Research Council (2004), are important to this examination, though discussed in a different order herein. They include a "rethinking of the police function" as reflected in operational activities that are "problem-oriented" (Goldstein 1977, 11; National Research Council 2004, 85-90). Also included is a clear emphasis on organizational "decentralization" and "community engagement," (National Research Council 2004, 85-90). The extent to which they are inter-related cannot be overstated. Each of these require a change of thinking about policing ("philosophy") that is reflected in the changed manner in which policing is conducted ("organizational strategy") (National Research Council 2004, 85).

The first feature concerns community policing's requirement for a rethinking of "police functions" that looks beyond the important but narrow mandate to address crime in the community (National Research Council 2004, 85-88). This new way of thinking about the role and function of the police calls upon agencies to see their mission and activities as part of a larger goal of government to assist in the creation of community wellbeing. This is achieved in part through participation in both prevention and intervention initiatives. The goal of community policing in this regard is to assist in the provision of the highest quality of life for the citizens, which involves more than just addressing serious crime. Important in this regard is the police role in reducing the fear of crime by communicating accurate information as to the scope and scale of crime at the neighborhood level. This is a radical shift away from merely responding to emergency calls for service after a serious crime has been committed.

The 1973 report produced by the *National Advisory Commission on Criminal Justice Standards and Goals* records the beginnings of a shift in the way police thought about their function. At that time they noted the police have not only "improved their ability to deal with crime and disorder [...] they have also taken great strides in responding to the demands of their communities for greater service involvement and responsiveness" (11). They observe: "In less than 10 years, the nature of debate in the police service has changed. The question no longer is, 'Should we be involved in nonenforcement programs?' Now the question is, 'How should we be involved in them?'" (1973, 11) That, they note, was the difficult question of the times. The commission reports the difficulties of the era, stating:

> Inside and outside the service, there is little agreement on the role of the police. While one citizen group demands more nonenforcement programs, another demands that police devote all resources to direct protection and vigorous enforcement. Lack of manpower and fiscal resources has caused delay or abandonment of many programs to improve police-community relations, and the police have had to assign priorities to the delivery of direct protection services. (1973, 11)

The lack of funding and personnel to meet new expectations brought about by this rethinking of the police mission will be discussed in the subsequent section, but it is worth noting that this shortcoming is a persistent theme throughout the development of community policing era.

Among the pioneers in this rethinking of the police function was Herman Goldstein, who devoted a chapter in his famous *Policing a Free Society* to an in-depth examination of "The Police Function" (1977, 21-44). Building on the work of Egon Bittner, James Q. Wilson, and Jerome H. Skolnick concerning research into the daily activities of police officers, Goldstein concluded that much of it did not involve the enforcement of criminal law (Goldstein 1973, 24-29). Instead, it involved resolution of low-level order issues and general public safety services, such as directing traffic (Goldstein 1977, 25). Goldstein's analysis led him to conclude that "to analyze the *totality* of police functioning and the police *as an institution*, it is essential to break through the confining criminal justice framework, for it is now clear that it is not sufficiently comprehensive to encompass all that goes on in the daily operations of a police agency" (1977, 32). Therefore, to Goldstein's way of thinking, relegating the police to a component (albeit a large one) in the criminal justice system was a failure in the series of reports produced by the 1967 *President's Commission on Law Enforcement and Administration of Justice* (1977).

Goldstein's seminal paper, "Improving Policing: A Problem-Oriented Approach," introduced the concept of problem-oriented policing (1979; Palmiotto 2011, 180). In that piece, he observed that too much attention had been paid to the "means" of policing, and not enough to the "ends" of policing (1979, 238). In other words, in the era of professionalization, American policing was narrowly focused on a law enforcement mission that emphasized organizational capacity and capabilities; the agency's means. If any attention was given to the "ends" of policing, it was generally overshadowed by the goal of efficiency (1979, 239). As Goldstein put it, "those agencies that have succeeded in developing a high level of operating efficiency have not gone on to concern themselves with the end results of their efforts" (1979, 239). He contended that tasks do not define the ends of policing, rather it is the other way around; the task is supposed to further the ends of policing (Goldstein 1979, 241-242). Goldstein argues that the purpose of the police task is to "deal with a wide range of behavioral and social problems that arise in a community – [and] that the end product of policing consists of dealing with these *problems*" (1979, 242).

By 1990, this rethinking of the police function was evidenced in the "emergence of a new 'common wisdom' on the police" (Goldstein 1990, 10). In his 1990 work, *Problem-Oriented Policing*, Goldstein noted that "substantial progress has been made in our thinking about the police" (11). The "common wisdom on the police" that had emerged in "most quarters" included an understanding that "the police do much more than deal with crime," and in fact deal with a "wide range of functions" that do not involve crime (1990, 11). Many of the problems they are called upon to address – and *should* address – do not involve criminal acts (1990, 11). Furthermore, in many instances even where lawful, the better solution to some social problems may not involve criminal enforcement action at all (1990, 11). This line of thinking is reflected in another seminal work of 1990: Trojanowicz and Bucqueroux's *Community Policing: A Contemporary Perspective*. They also note this new way of thinking about policing, that "by broadening the police mandate beyond a narrow focus on crime" police should look beyond the symptoms of social illness that is crime and "find a way to address the broad underlying causes" (Trojanowicz and Bucqueroux 1990, 122).

The second feature is closely related to the first. Once a new perspective on the role and function of the police in the community is adopted, so too must a new view of the work to be accomplished. Instead of addressing crime as it appears in the form of a 911 call, agencies engaging in community policing activities must look beyond the criminal act to the root causes and attempt to address those. This "problem orientation" identified by the National Research Council is better understood as a re-orientation of the agency toward community problems, of which crime is just one symptom (2004, 90). A problem-oriented approach to the tasks of policing often involves outside non-police agencies with specialized skills (National Research Council 2004, 90). Imperative here is the third feature discussed below as it concerns changes to the organization that allows personnel to work in fixed geographical areas for an extended period in order to acquire a deep understanding of the problem and develop partnerships and network with stakeholders and other community agencies (National Research Council 2004).

This shift toward a new vision of the work to be performed took time to evolve, though it had its origins in the reports issued in 1967 by the *President's Commission on Law Enforcement and Administration of Justice*. However, one of the key faults of that 1967 presidential commission report identified by Kelling was that it essentially re-affirmed the crime fighting mission of the police (2003, 15). There was no radical rethinking of the work that constitute policing's tasks. Instead, they recommended better and more publicly acceptable ways to continue as before. This thinking informed the 1973 recommendations of the *National Advisory Commission on Criminal Justice Standards and Goals*, which proposed the "team policing" concept (154-161). The report recommended that police departments reorganize in a manner that allowed patrol officers, detectives, and other specialized units to work together to address crime in a fixed geographical area (1973). The idea was that if internal bureaucratic barriers were eliminated, the police would be better able to respond quickly and effectively to serious crime. The same group – a team of police officers – was responsible for working on a particular type of crime or serious criminal activities within a fixed location until some relief was realized. One serious problem with this initiative was that once an agency-defined goal was reached, the team was usually disbanded or moved to another crime problem. There was no sustained effort to maintain gains made (Trojanowicz and Bucqueroux 1990, 67).

Goldstein, in the development of problem-oriented policing, submitted that the entire way of viewing the task of policing needed to change. By focusing on the mission of crime fighting, he believed the police spent far too much effort addressing the symptoms and not enough effort on the illness. Goldstein contended that a crime-fighting view of "police business [...] subdivided by means of labels tied to the criminal code, such as robbery, burglary, and theft [is] not adequate" (Goldstein 1979, 244-245). There is no consideration given to the underlying causes of criminality, the true problem of which crime is just a symptom. Furthermore, when the police task is viewed as the enforcement of a body of statutes, there is a naturally built-in system of prioritization as organizational efficiency is enhanced when structuring work along the lines of the criminal code (1979, 244-245).

Instead, Goldstein suggested that several different kinds of crime may have originated from the same underlying social condition, and if that condition can be addressed crime across the spectrum could be reduced or prevented all together (1979, 245-247; 1990, 32-33). Goldstein submitted that criminal phenomena should be researched more deeply and common denominators identified as these problems should be the focus of police efforts (1979, 250-257). Thus, when the police make it their business to identify these hidden causes of crime, "a 'problem' becomes the unit of police work" and not the "incident" (Goldstein 1990, 32, 35). In many instances, creative solutions that do not involve criminal enforcement work to reduce crime, such as changes in municipal zoning ordinances, arise as workable solutions (1979, 255; 1990 139-140).

Though Goldstein warned that narrowly defining the police task along the structure of the criminal code was suboptimal, he thought broad generalizations were no better (1979). Even while arguing for an approach to policing that focused on broader issues that better evince underlying problems, he warned that "attacking police problems under a categorical heading – 'crime' or 'disorder,' 'delinquency,' or even 'violence' – is bound to be futile" (1979, 244). However, in a very influential and widely read article in *Atlantic Monthly*, Wilson and Kelling (1982) argued that "disorder" was precisely the problem upon which the task of policing ought to focus (Kelling and Coles 1996, 19; Kelling 2003, 19). They suggested that low-level civil disorder leads to a sense of unease in the community, which could rapidly turn to a level of fear that is disproportionate to the amount of crime actually present (Wilson and Kelling 1982). As this fear grew in the community, the normal bonds and interactions between individuals erode, which over time leads to the destruction of a cohesive sense of community. As apathy and indifference sets in, the ground is ripe for criminal elements to ply their trade without much community resistance. The result is an increase in incidents of criminal activity and an adversarial law enforcement presence. It follows that, the task of policing – the problem to which the police must orient – is the lower level disorder offenses that threaten the individual's sense of wellbeing. It is also important for the police to work with individuals and stakeholders to revive a sense of community, which necessitates citizen engagement (Wilson and Kelling 1982).

The third feature of community policing concerns the critical organizational shift that must be achieved for any measure of success to be realized. Optimally, success in this area is thought to affect the first two features. Agencies that have successfully adjusted to a new perspective on their role in the community and have changed their conception of the work to be accomplished have undergone an organizational transformation in the form of "decentralization" (National Research Council 2004, 88-89). The push for decentralized organizational structures was an effort to create an agile organization that was able to respond quickly to the constantly evolving operational reality and the ever-changing dynamic of the problem to be solved. Scholars and practitioners expended considerable effort to change the institution and organizational structures of policing to achieve this particular goal. However, one researcher's assessment of the literature finds, "community policing advocates have tended to be unsuccessful in implementing their structural reform agendas" (Maguire 1997, 572).

As noted, the team policing concept's greatest contribution to the development of community policing's features was its radical reorganization of operational components to achieve the crime fighting mission (*National Advisory Commission on Criminal Justice Standards and Goals* 1973). The existing orthodoxy on organizational structure reflected the norms of "the professional model [that] stresse[d] operational efficiency, to be achieved by centralized control, clean-cut lines of organization, fuller and more effective use of police personnel, greater mobility, improved training, and increased use of equipment and technology" Goldstein 1977, 2). Team policing programs broke with convention by including team policing personnel in the lowest levels and across the organization in the planning and execution of programs and projects (1973, 160-161). Police agencies were placed on the road to re-organization and decentralization by giving personnel in the lowest levels of the organization the authority and training to make decisions on important operational matters (1973, 161).

As the 1973 task force report noted, "police officers are decisionmakers" and entrusted with considerable authority to exercise discretion (*National Advisory Commission on Criminal Justice Standards and Goals* 1973, 9). These decisions are often made in the field and under difficult and pressing circumstances. However, the "quasi-military" manner in which police agencies were (and often are) organized is better suited to maximize a military-styled central command and control goal rather than support an independent decisionmaker in the field who possesses rather broad discretionary powers (Redlinger 1994, 36). This trend toward decentralization ran counter to the prevailing wisdom on the organizational structure of policing in the mid-20th century, which to that point had maintained "centralization of authority […] provided police organizations with autonomy from local political machines" (Crank 1994, 330). Goldstein observed a "paradox" in American policing (1977, 131-132). Of policing in the mid-20th century he noted that while "the most distinctive characteristic of policing in the United States is the extent to which the police function is decentralized," when it came to individual police departments, they were highly centralized internally in ways that "effectively shield the police from the communities they serve" (1977, 131-132). However, while a certain level of decentralization existed – has always existed – in the form of the "precinct or station-house," those "local commanders […] usually had limited ability to shape the character of police operations" (Skolnick and Bayley 1988, 13).

Organizational changes toward decentralized structures were considered important because they allowed officers with detailed knowledge of the problems and their local context the latitude to engage the issues and resolve problems creatively (Goldstein 1990, 159-161; Trojanowicz and Bucqueroux 1990, 5-6). However, more was at stake than the efficient resolution of problems, particularly those that constituted the new policing task. Organizational change was necessary in order to consolidate the gains toward community policing's institutional reform agenda (Greene, Bergman, and McLaughlin 1994, 93). As dissimilarities in each local circumstance led to different locally defined variants of community policing, it also led to diverse organizational structures. As Williams noted, "[a]bsent a general theory to guide organizational restructuring, police agencies adopting community policing have been challenged to discover, through a process of trial and error, the kind of organizational structure that will maximize the probability of institutionalizing the change" (2003, 122).

The final, and arguably most important, feature of community policing concerns the necessity of "community engagement" with individuals and groups within the community (National Research Council 2004, 89-90). This feature is the oldest of all the features, finding its roots in the Presidential Commission recommendations of the 1960s and 1970s. It is a constant, finding its way into each variant in the development of the community policing practice. It is the object of the hardest lesson learned in the 1960s. Yet it remains the least well developed and the one to which deliberative democratic theory has the most to offer.

Skolnick and Bayley accurately and succinctly highlighted the importance of community engagement, noting that "the central premise of community policing is that the public should play a more active part in enhancing public safety" (1988, 4-5). Furthermore, they observed that "community policing should be said to exist only when new programs are implemented that raise the level of public participation in the maintenance of public order" (1988, 4-5). The public's part in community policing has been discussed in varied and often imprecise ways. There was a call issued as early as 1967 in the *Task Force Report: The Police* for increased citizen involvement in policing affairs. However, the entities and processes recommended generally took the form of "advisory committees" that appeared predicated on an assumed obligation on the part of the public to cooperate with the police (1967a, 156-157).

Again in 1973, the *National Advisory Commission on Criminal Justice Standards and Goals* furthered this line of thinking by recommending steps to aid the "police understanding of their role" by soliciting input from line-level employees and middle managers (34). The next step was presumed to be developing and executing an effective communications strategy to convey a "public understanding of the police role" (1973, 38). Once established, the authors of the commission recommendations suggested that the police meet with individuals and groups to enlist "public cooperation" as a means of "developing community resources" (61-62).

However, this top-down approach did not go far enough for Goldstein and others. As early as 1977, in *Policing a Free Society*, Goldstein began calling for a broader view of the public's involvement in American policing; in his view democratic values demanded it (140). Under community policing, the police-community relationship must be deep and thoroughgoing, reflecting "a new philosophy of policing, based on the concept that police officers and private citizens working together in creative ways can help solve contemporary problems related to crime" (Trojanowicz and Bucqueroux 1990, 5). What was required was a "partnership [...] with the community" that "made the community a co-producer of police services" (Goldstein 1990, 23-24). Making the public a full partner in the provision of public safety also required "the citizenry to do more to police themselves" (Goldstein 1990, 24). These partnerships often included direct involvement activities such as neighborhood patrols, or indirect involvement such as participation in community meetings either to exchange information about criminal activity or acquire insight into general neighborhood conditions (National Research Council 2004).

Many of these important early thinkers realized comprehensive relationships of this type in a democracy should go further and include discussions about policy matters (Goldstein 1977, 140; 1987, 25). Trojanowicz and Bucqueroux agreed, and called for "sharing power" to such an extent that citizens and groups were afforded "an opportunity to have input into the police priorities;" a program goal that persists to this day (1990, 12; U.S. Department of Justice 2000, 20). The degree to which the "community engagement" feature exists in any given variant of community policing program varies from community to community (National Research Council 2004, 89). It can be said to exist on a continuum; an observation made by Goldstein (1987, 25). However, an August 2000 U.S. Department of Justice assessment found "true community partnerships, involving sharing power and decisionmaking, are rare at this time, found in only a few of the flagship departments" (2000a, 20).

Developing U.S. police departments' capacity in regards to these four features is the goal of the U.S. Department of Justice and the mission of the Office of Community Oriented Policing Services (COPS Office). In addition to providing funding for personnel and technology for community policing efforts, the Violent Crime Control Act of 1994 funded technical assistance programs that include training and publications designed to help agencies achieve the aims of their community policing programs (U.S. Department of Justice 2000b; Worrall 2010). In its technical assistance publications, the COPS Office effectively compresses these four features identified above into three, and incorporates them in their official definition of the term community policing. The official definition promulgated by the COPS Office states that, "community policing is a philosophy that promotes organizational strategies, which support the systematic use of partnerships and problem-solving techniques, to proactively address the immediate conditions that give rise to public safety issues such as crime, social disorder, and fear of crime" (U.S. Department of Justice 2009a, 5; 2009b, 3). In their publication containing the official definition, the COPS Office identifies these three important elements and goes to some effort to develop them. The three critical elements of this definition are identified as being "community partnerships," "organizational transformation," and "problem solving" (U.S. Department of Justice 2009a, 5; 2009b, 3-4).

PROBLEMS WITH COMMUNITY POLICING'S IMPLEMENTATION

If American policing's lack "of a clear commitment to any values other than operating efficiency" helped propel the profession toward community policing, difficulties with community policing's implementation provided (and continues to provide) competing practices an opportunity to push American policing back toward efficiency-oriented models (Goldstein 1977, 12). Problems of any kind are evidence of a certain degree of inefficiency. However, criticisms of community policing traceable to inefficiency ought to have been anticipated. If the community policing model is as a reaction to an overemphasis on efficiency as an organizational value, then efficiency would naturally be a lower organizational priority, thus opening the agency to inefficiency arguments.

In 1993, the team of Swanson, Territo and Taylor noted five "problems with community policing" which can generally be traced back to some form of failure in the design, implementation, or execution of community policing programs. The five problems they identified are just as valid today as they were nearly twenty years ago at their initial statement. Their work serves as an excellent structure for this section's discussion on the shortcomings of community policing. The problems identified include "lack of [a] definition," resulting in "role confusion and low morale" (Swanson, Territo and Taylor 1993, 29). Adding to the charges of inefficiency is the fact that "community policing is expensive," which is compounded by a "lack of credible evaluation" (Swanson, Territo and Taylor 1993, 31). Finally, the Swanson, Territo and Taylor team note a "failure to understand the change process" on the part of agencies implementing community policing reforms (1993, 33). These major shortcomings have opened the door to criticisms and alternatives that risk returning policing too far in the direction of the efficiency-oriented professional model.

To these five I add a sixth shortcoming stemming from more recent scholarship. Recent evaluations concerning community policing's failure – as currently practiced – to achieve the goal of power sharing evidences an under-emphasis on the "community engagement" feature (National Research Council 2004, 89). Failure in this regard constitutes the greatest threat to the community policing paradigm's attempt to move beyond the efficiency-oriented professional policing model, inspired by the Progressive Era. This *community engagement* element is the core feature of community policing, and at the same time is its largest vulnerability. Further adding to the distress is the fact that each of the other three previously discussed core features identified by the National Research Council is in some way addressed by community policing's competitors. It is to this sixth problem that this research is directed. Little of the research on community policing is explicitly oriented toward community engagement. Better work in this regard is conducted in other disciplines. It is to this feature that deliberative democratic theory has the most to offer. In deliberative democratic practice, legitimacy does not take a backseat to the ideal of efficiency. If applied to the practice of community policing we may find an increased concern for legitimacy counterbalances the drive for efficiency. A bit of irony in this regard cannot escape mention before proceeding. At around the same time that Swanson, Territo and Taylor (1993) identified the "problems with community policing" which serve as the structure for this discussion, scholars in deliberative democracy were just starting to articulate a theory (29).

The first problem – community policing's lack of a well specified definition – has been addressed in this study in some detail in the foregoing chapters. Although the practice of community policing has been in place for nearly thirty years, "the concept of community policing remains only loosely defined" (Swanson, Territo and Taylor 1993, 29). Eck and Rosenbaum (writing somewhat contemporaneously with Swanson, Territo and Taylor) note even earlier complaints issued by "Manning (1988), Mastrofski (1988), and Klockars (1988)" concerning "the lack of definition [and] vagueness of community policing" (1994, 5). This issue has received recognition and treatment at intervals, both by those in academia and those in the plicing profession (Oliver and Bartigis 1998; National Research Council 2004, 232-233; Scheider, Chapman, and Schapiro 2009, 696; Palmiotto 2011, 215). However, as noted earlier, this conceptual vagueness has given community policing its "plastic" quality that allows for "locally defined" variants that fit unique community contexts (Eck and Rosenbaum 1994, 3; National Institute of Justice 2000a, 20). Still, it is difficult to discuss the relevant underlying theory with any precision without a fixed definition of the core concept.

The second issue which bedevils community policing relates to problems of "role confusion and low morale" (Swanson, Territo and Taylor 1993, 29). Researchers and practitioners alike have identified the problem of "role confusion" in the earliest days of community policing (Findley and Taylor, 1990, 71). The recasting of the police function, so important to the community policing paradigm, often stands in opposition to the deeply ingrained cultural norms of the professional model of policing (Findley and Taylor 1990, 71; McCold and Wachtel 1996, 4; Dicker 1998, 68; Adams, RoHe and Arcury 2002, 403; Herbert 2006a, 499; Mastrofski, Willis and Kochel 2007, 226). In those earliest days, officers socialized into the police culture associated with the professional model found it difficult "to merge the traditional model of law enforcement and social work as prescribed in a relatively nebulous concept of neighborhood policing" (Findley and Taylor 1990, 71). Knowing exactly what tasks the community policing model required proved confusing to some. Mastrofski (1988) raised these concerns and asked some difficult questions of Goldstein's 1987 call for a rethinking of the police function. Goldstein called for the police to look past the obvious criminal activity to the underlying social conditions and address the disorder that leads to criminality (1987, 1990). This almost has the look of a bygone era of policing in the colonial era discussed by Bacon (1939). Mastrofski took issue with "using police to reinforce informal community norms" because it made the assumption of homogenous communities with virtually universally held values (1988, 50-51). Mastrofski predicted this role confusion (1988).

Furthermore, Goldstein's argument for the radical rethinking of the police role gives rise to a paradox that contributes to this confusion. One of the chief concerns identified in the presidential commission reports of 1967 and 1973 was the problem of officer discretion. However, the types of order maintenance efforts that take place under community policing – particularly the enforcement of informal community norms – require extensive use of discretion. Indeed, policing in this manner requires a considerable degree of organizational decentralization in order to allow the officer on the street sufficient latitude to make these types of decisions (Adams, RoHe and Arcury 2002, 402).

What might charitably be called "role confusion" in the early days of community policing described by Findley and Taylor (1990, 71), gave way to what more accurately might be described as role rejection. Throughout the rest of the 1990s and into the 2000s, considerable research was conducted into officer resistance to the community policing model, as well as ways to correct for this resistance (Mastrofski, Willis, and Kochel 2007, 231-232). The lack of role clarity appears to have slowed reforms to a crawl as resistance to community policing seems to have found a perpetual source of fuel in the enduring cultural strength of the professional model of policing (Mastrofski, Willis, and Kochel 2007, 226). Researchers report evidence of a cultural divide within policing between those who practice community-oriented, or problem-oriented, policing and those who cling to a romanticized "crime fighting" role (Mastrofski, Willis, and Kochel 2007, 226). In information obtained in field interviews, researchers reported that many times those professing adherence to the professional model of policing expressed obvious disdain for the practice of community policing and those officers who practiced community policing (Dicker 1998, 60, 65, 73; Herbert 2006a; 499-500).

Community policing requires changes in organizational structures and organizational operational processes (Maguire 1997). As a result, change associated with community policing has historically met with organizational resistance (Redlinger 1994). As stated, decentralization of the organizational structure is an important step in achieving the organization agility necessary to adapt quickly to address community problems. Some scholars argue that the military bureaucratic model is largely responsible for the ills of American policing and must be removed (Angell 1971). However, this move away from a military bureaucratic structure was also met with resistance (Maguire 1997). In multiple studies, the principal sources of resistance identified by researchers included the first line supervisors, and the officers themselves (Dicker 1998; Glaser and Denhardt 2010).

It may well be that the drive to decentralization has exacerbated the issue of officer resistance. As discussed a bit earlier, organizational decentralization was thought an indispensable element in that it enabled the line-officers' capacity to respond quickly and creatively to problems with fewer bureaucratic constraints. Williams (2003) discusses another noteworthy reason why organizational restructuring was employed to accomplish community policing reforms. She noted that, generally speaking, "20th century police reform efforts have almost universally focused on changing the behavior of line personnel," and that in doing so gravitated to organizational theory for solutions (2003, 121). The conventional wisdom argued that "the structure of organizations [are] a major determinant of employee behavior" (Williams 2003, 121). Moreover, decentralized organizational structures empowered employees, changed behaviors, and thereby reduced resistance (Williams 2003, 121).

However, in more recent research on the organizational aspects of community oriented policing it is suggested that decentralization may in fact contribute to officer resistance. Using organizational "innovations" research, Morabito observed that "for a radical innovation such as COP, centralization can increase the likelihood of adoption because concentration of power within the organization may be needed to overcome opposition to change" (2010, 571). "Innovations" researchers argue that "organizations that have a high degree of formalization [...] may be better suited to adopt radical innovations because dissent can be stifled" (Morabito 2010, 571). As will be seen later in this chapter, Chief Bill Bratton would likely be sympathetic to this argument as the deployment and success of his COMPSTAT model of policing seems to reflect this thinking. Morabito goes on to observe that this way of thinking about organizations contrasts with that of the [community oriented] policing literature," which leans toward empowering line level officers (2010, 571).

Organizational decentralization effectively entrusted community policing reform to line officers, who by the weight of the evidence in the research seem inexorably resistant to that change. In addition, resistance often extends beyond the line officer into middle management (Gaines 1994). This was part of the reason for the demise of the "team policing" concept. Research cited by Gaines (1994) found that middle management shared responsibility for the resistance as their actions (or inactions) "undermined the success of the programs in an effort to recover their lost organizational power and authority" (Gaines 1994, 21).

The third problem which Swanson, Territo and Taylor identify is that "community policing is expensive" (1993, 31). That the bulk of this expense manifests itself as some form of personnel costs is long recognized (Swanson, Territo and Taylor 1993, 31). Even before it recommended that agencies adopt the team policing concept, the 1967 presidential commission noted in *The Challenge of Crime in a Free Society* that "there is impressive evidence that in many cities there are too few policemen" (*President's Commission on Law Enforcement and Administration of Justice* 1967b, 106, 117). After admitting many local police departments needed additional personnel to do the job under the existing methods of policing, the president's commission further indicated that adopting a "team policing" strategy "means additional personnel" will be necessary (1967b, 107, 117). As the early variants of community policing began to emerge in the 1970s and 1980s, it became clear that the demand on staffing levels was going to be a permanent feature of community policing.

If the police were going to improve their relationship with the community and engage problems at a deeper level, success was going to "depend [...] on the commitment of the department to allow CPOs [community policing officers] the time and opportunity to interact directly with the greatest number of people in the beat area" (Trojanowicz and Bucqueroux 1990, 349). Efforts to facilitate this interaction included a realignment of beat boundaries to give officers smaller areas to cover (Swanson, Territo and Taylor 1993, 31). The re-emergence of obsolete tactics, such as the foot patrols, also added to personnel costs (Wilson 1950, 95; Wilson and Kelling 1982; Trojanowicz and Bucqueroux 1990, 222-223). Community policing would also mean encumbering an officer's time to engage in proactive problem solving activities; this is a service status that often rendered them unavailable for emergency calls for service (Goldstein 1990, 151).

This was not without social significance inside the police culture as doing so exposed the officer to criticism by peers (Dicker 1998, 60, 73). An inefficiency and expense argument was at the root of these criticisms as well. As Herbert noted, detractors "dismiss community policing as an ineffectual waste of resources, as a refuge for peers who seek to avoid the rough and tumble of 'real police work'" (2006b 499). Added to the hard costs of more personnel to conduct community policing activities are the soft costs associated with the specialized training normally accompanying such COPS programs and additional training was often needed to overcome resistance to the adoption of community policing (Goldstein 1990, 167-168; Dicker 1998, 78-79; Morabito 2010, 572).

In sum, the operational demands for the proper execution of community policing programs has led to the conventional wisdom that these efforts are personnel-intensive and most often require additional resources. The demand for additional personnel entails fiscal considerations. The importance of this concern cannot be overstated as "[t]ypically, 80 percent to 90 percent or more of police department budgets are allocated to salaries and benefits" (Cordner 1992, 227). This figure is somewhat stable, as evidenced in police administration texts published over the last 40 years. For example, in 1972 Wilson and McLaren present an example of an actual police department budget that places personnel costs at approximately 90 percent of the overall budget (180). In a more recent example, Swanson, Territo and Taylor (2012) indicate, "personnel and personnel support costs may consume 80 or more percent of the budget" (519). However, it cannot escape observation that what issued from the presidential commissions were effectively findings by the federal government, the correctives for which would have to be paid by local governments. This is another example of the unique problems that arise out of the highly decentralized structure of American policing and the fact that the bulk of police service is provided, funded and controlled by local governments. The finding that there were not enough police officers on

America's streets, and a call for new methods that would require even more, placed a heavy fiscal burden on local governments.

Beginning in the 1970s and continuing to the present, the federal government responded with monetary assistance in the form of grants (Pate 2003, 515). The level of federal support has varied since 1965, with the "lowest levels of support" occurring in "the early to mid-1980s" (Pate 2003, 515). The first of these funding sources came from "the Law Enforcement Assistance Act of 1965, [wherein] US $7 million was appropriated for funding of local criminal justice programs" (Worrall 2010, 460). The Act "established an Office of Law Enforcement Assistance in the Department of Justice and charged it with funding demonstration projects for the development of new methods of crime control and law enforcement (U.S. Library of Congress 2002, CRS-2).

In response to the commission report's (*The Challenge of Crime in a Free Society*) call for increased assistance to local governments, Congress passed the Omnibus Crime Control and Safe Streets Act in 1968. The Act created the *Law Enforcement Assistance Administration* (LEAA), which over the course of its twelve years of existence spent approximately $7.5 billion, largely on "grants to state and local governments" (U.S. Library of Congress 2002, CRS-2 – CRS-3). The "LEAA's history is controversial" (U.S. Library of Congress 2001, CRS-3). First, because it awarded funding as a block grant to the states, which passed the funding through to police agencies, there was rather little control of its use (U.S. Library of Congress 2002, CRS-3). Secondly, "LEAA funds at the state, regional, and local levels […] funded many projects which [had] little to do with serious crime" (Goldstein 1977, 322). One of the lasting aspects of LEAA funding was a program under which many police officers received tuition assistance for college degrees (Goldstein 1977, 285).

Federal assistance waned in the 1980s, but reemerged in the later part of the decade with the Edward Bryne Memorial State and Local Law Enforcement Assistance program, which was passed into law as the Crime Control Act of 1990 (U.S. Library of Congress 2002, CRS-3). The statute authorized $900 million in assistance funding to local governments for "improving the function of their criminal justice system, preventing crime, and enforcing drug laws" (U.S. Library of Congress 2002, CRS-3). The program continues to this day, though consolidated with another grant program in 2005. This speaks to the legacy power the term *community policing* brings to discussions concerning the continuation of funding. In the end, while the funding structure was modified, funding continued nonetheless.

Figure 4.1. COPS Grant Funding and Inflation Adjustment

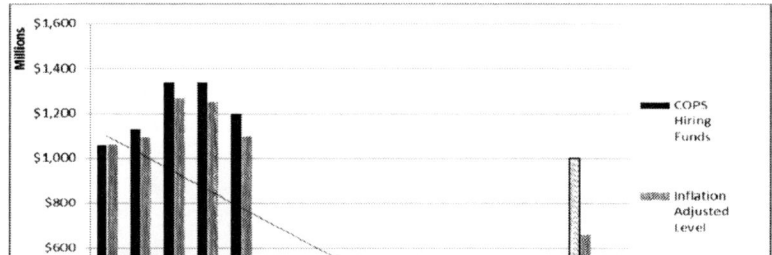

Violent Crime Control and Law Enforcement Act of 1994 created the most significant source of funding available for community policing programs. The law authorized $30.2 billion for a variety of "law enforcement and crime prevention programs under the Violent Crime Reduction Trust Fund," including "$8.8 billion for the Community Oriented Policing Service (COPS) programs" (U.S. Library of Congress 2002, CRS-3). The COPS program is still in existence to this day, but at much lower funding level (Worrall 2010, 460). The COPS programs generally provided performance-based multi-year grant funds "to local law enforcement agencies for the purposes of improving their community policing capabilities" (Worrall 2010, 460). At the outset, considerable funding was made available for the purposes of hiring the additional police officers required to give full effect to the practice of community policing. It should be noted that while the funding levels for hiring were significant at the outset, the levels dwindled over time. Particularly when adjusted for inflation, the levels of support have never returned to that seen in the mid-1990s (see Fig. 4.1). The only exception to this trend was the provision of one-time funding in 2009 from the American Recovery and Reinvestment Act.

However, as stated earlier, funding for additional personnel is extremely difficult on local governments. Moreover, with the position retention requirements extending several years after COPS grants expired, some agencies shied away from this funding stream. Another more creative way of putting more officers into community policing roles was the COPS MORE grants (Making Officer Redeployment Effective). The MORE program grants were for technology enhancements, and were predicated on the idea that if an agency were to use technology to operate more efficiently, it could redeploy police officers, freeing them up to engage in community policing activities (U.S. Department of Justice 2000a, 163-171). Though never enjoying funding levels like that seen with the hiring grants, these "grants were estimated to actually be cost-effective" (U.S. Library of Congress 2010, 13).

The fourth persistent problem of community policing is the "lack of credible evaluation" (Swanson, Territo and Taylor 1993, 31). The practice of community policing evolved over a period of years in response to the perceived shortcomings of the traditional-professional model of policing prominent in the mid-20th century. In the decades since its inception, scholars and practitioners have sought to measure the effectiveness of community policing. No clear consensus has emerged as to what those measures should be. Demonstrating the difficulty, Swanson, Territo and Taylor observed that while "[i]n reality, the empirical evidence that traditional policing methods have failed is at best mixed [...] traditional quantitative measures [...] are inappropriate for evaluating the success or failure of community policing" (1993, 31).

Community policing advocates rely heavily on the important Presidential Commission reports and findings to buttress their claim that policing needed to go in a new direction. Not only did it need to go in a new direction, but also the new direction could not be evaluated in the same manner as conventional policing (Swanson, Territo and Taylor 1993, 31; Kelling 1988, 6).

Probably the most important problem faced in assessing COPS programs and practices concerned the high value placed on efficiency. This was identified early on by Goldstein, who using the words of Phillip Selznick, accused police administration of falling into the "cult of efficiency" (1977, 227). Relying on a quote from fellow researcher Mark Moore, Kelling (1988) echoed the same sentiment, stating, "[t]he overwhelming danger, is that, in the name of efficiency, police and city officials will be tempted to maintain old patterns" (6).

More recently Braga called for improving community policing research, but stipulated that "external validity" and "generalizability" would be a constant problem in community policing research (2010, 175). Speaking to the imperfect conditions under which community policing research is conducted and its effect, Braga states:

> When a police department is willing to engage a more rigorous design, the external validity of the findings are called into question because the host departments and their contexts are described as not representative of all agencies or contexts that use the intervention. [...] Although the point is legitimate, all problem-oriented policing evaluations suffer from external validity concerns regardless of the degree of internal rigor in the evaluation research design. Problem-oriented policing is primarily an analytic approach to crime prevention that requires customizing interventions to highly localized crime and disorder problems. What works in preventing a street robbery problem in the public areas of Harvard Square in Cambridge, Massachusetts, might not work when applied to repeated robberies occurring in the London Underground Subway system. [...] Problem-oriented policing evaluations of many forms provide valuable guidance to police officers struggling with real-world problems. However, given the highly customized nature of effective problem-oriented policing interventions, it is important to recognize that the generalizability of specific crime prevention practices identified in an effective application of the approach might be limited, regardless of the evaluation approached used. (2010, 175)

Much of the evaluative research on community policing focuses on the effectiveness of the COPS program and therefore speaks indirectly to the effectiveness of community policing. COPS program grants came with the requirement that agencies adopt community policing methods. As a condition of funding, COPS required the recipients to engage in evaluations to determine the effectiveness of the particular program. Consequently, the U. S. Department of Justice and other federal entities seized upon the data and produced evaluations that have been used as an indirect evaluation of this method of policing. A report by the National Research Council summarized, stating, "[d]espite the large investment in research on community policing, outcome evaluations and other research still cannot comprehensively and definitively provide a guide to the usefulness of this strategy" (2004, 33). Braga, also noting the poor state of evaluative research on community policing, warned "[a]s 'evidenced based' approaches, with their premium on rigorous evaluation designs, gain currency in policy circles, funding for continued expansion of the problem-oriented policing agenda might be threatened" (2010, 175).

The fifth and final problem identified by Swanson, Territo and Taylor concerns a "failure to understand the change process" on the part of the police and the general public (1993, 33). Swanson, Territo and Taylor identified the scale and scope of the problem, which extended in a multitude of directions. Discussions about change had to include public expectations, as well as consider the limitations of the police culture. Methods of organization and new practices had to be integrated. In their estimation, "[f]ailing to understand the change process as long term, ongoing, and somewhat chaotic will doom community policing" (Swanson, Territo and Taylor 1993, 33). Their solution of a more thoroughgoing understanding of the change process centers primarily on the organization and its leadership (Swanson, Territo and Taylor 1993, 655-682).

More recent research has noted isomorphic tendencies in American police agencies (Zhao, He and Lovrich 2006; Giblin and Burruss 2009; Burruss and Giblin 2009). This research brings to bear the more recent work in institutional change theory. This should not be confused with organizational change theory the likes of which Swanson, Territo and Taylor relied upon (1993). Instead, it refers to theories of institutional change – particularly the historical institutionalism of Paul Pierson – that emerged in the late 1990s. The distinction between organizations and institutions is one made by Selznick who explains, "an organization [...] becomes an institution [by] the taking on of values, ways of acting and beliefs that are deemed important for their own sake" ([1957] 1984, 21). Institutions conceived as such transcend specific organizations. The phenomenon of isomorphism occurs when discrete organizations adopt the same values and practices. As multiple organizations begin adopting the same outlook in the form of values, practices, and structures, an institution is created.

Research is beginning to demonstrate that the institution of American policing is comprised of discrete police agencies coalescing around a basic framework that includes values, practices and institutional structures, for reasons not clearly understood (Zhao, He and Lovrich 2006; Willis, Mastrofski, & Weisburd 2007, 151). However, if this were not the case, transient citizens and professional police officers would have difficulty accessing police services or transitioning employment from one agency to another. In other words, the institution of American policing is made up of a host of discrete organizations exhibiting a significant degree of isomorphism. This being the case, it is important to understand that the organizational change component of community policing was pitted against the inertia supplied by the weighty institution of American policing as it had come to exist in the mid-20th century. Research and theory on historical institutionalism may have much to offer in the way of explaining why community policing has not enjoyed the results hoped for. More commentary will be offered in this regard in the closing chapter.

The sixth implementation problem proposed herein is the lack of effective methods and training for engaging the public. It is to this problem that this work is addressed. I contend that the community engagement component is the single most important, unique, and distinguishing feature of this practice. However, it nonetheless remains the most underdeveloped. It has been noted that "community policing should be said to exist only when new programs are implemented that raise the level of public participation" (Skolnick and Bayley 1988, 5). This feature was identified early on in the development of community policing when questions of police legitimacy were thrust into the debate in the 1960s. Evidence of this can be found in the earliest efforts in the president's commission reports that call for the formation of a variety of advisory councils and boards (1967a, 156-159). When advisory councils did not go far enough, there was a call for greater consideration of the will of citizens. Goldstein recognized early on that a "greater citizen voice in determining police operating policies" was what was required (1977, 142).

As community policing initiatives took flight throughout the 1980s, community participation played a role in widely varying degrees

(Goldstein 1987, 25). The goal, however, was to "engage the community as an equal partner in solving local crime and disorder problems" (Morabito 2008, 564-565). This meant in practice allowing the "community [to] participate in making some of the important decisions" (Goldstein 1987, 25). Doing so requires the police to share power with the public, thus giving effect to Peel's axiom "the police are the public and [...] the public are the police" (Trojanowicz and Bucqueroux 1990, 12, 45). In light of the history recounted in the third chapter of this work, this appears to have always been the case to some degree.

If it is accepted that "[t]he central premise of community policing is that the public should play a more active part in enhancing public safety," then failure in this regard is particularly distressing for the enterprise (Skolnick and Bayley 1988, 4-5). An August 2000 report from the U.S. Department of Justice suggests just that. In its *National Evaluation of the COPS Program – Title I of the 1994 Crime Act*, the National Institute of Justice determined that COPS grants recipients were generally found lacking in the area of forging community partnerships (2000a). The assessment is confined to grant recipients as partnership activities are part of the grant requirements (2000a, 189-190). Though there are many agencies that claim to be engaged in community policing practices, not all partake of COPS funding. Consequently the NIJ assessment might best be characterized as a convenient sample group from which to draw inferences about the state of community partnerships in community policing agencies.

Nevertheless, in that study the National Institute of Justice argued that the level of community involvement across all community policing agencies could "be placed on a continuum with two distinct endpoints. On the one end was "true *collaboration* in all phases of the work" and the other, "mere *involvement*" (U.S. Department of Justice 2000a, 1994). Researchers found "[t]emporary problem-solving partnerships [...] abundant" but "[t]rue community partnerships, involving power sharing and decisionmaking, are rare" (2000a, 199, 237). Stressing its importance to community policing, they note, "[t]he bottom line in this discussion of community partnerships comes down to power sharing" (2000a, 199).

At stake is more than effectiveness, but rather the legitimacy of the enterprise of policing in a democracy (Ponsaers 2001). Ponsaers notes: "The legitimacy of the police in community policing is strongly linked to the concept of democracy. [...] Thus, the legitimation comes from continuing processes of consultation and interaction with different communities within the society" (2001, 482). If "in a democratic society the legitimacy and power of police is given by citizens," and the enterprise of policing is dependent on such "partnerships [...] to solve problems through community engagement and collaboration," then more thought needs to go into the mechanisms of engagement (Scheider, Chapman, and Schapiro 2009, 700). It is to precisely this point that deliberative democratic theory has much to offer. Deliberation must precede collaboration, for it is in the deliberative process that power is shared. It is ironic to note that at the same time community policing was foundering in this regard, deliberative democratic theory was on its upward trajectory in political science and political philosophy.

THE ASSAILABLE PRACTICE: UNSTRUCTURED AND AMBIGUOUS

Increasingly over the last decade community policing has come under pressure, with criticism coming from several quarters. One quarter is the problem of measuring the effectiveness of community policing. This is made even more troubling by the fact that the concept of community policing has no clear definition. Compounding the problem further is the lack of clarity expressed by some scholars as to what we mean by the elemental term "community" (Trojanowicz and Bucqueroux 1990; Harcourt 2001). An associated criticism suggests that there are limits to community involvement. Identifying what those limits are is the subject of normative debate. Still others suggest the impossibility of the enterprise, and questions of the validity of input. Some researchers have addressed the problems of consensus in an ambiguous and amorphous notion of community, finding in the end this time-consuming process is a wasted effort if you cannot measure it (Herbert 2006b).

Though the police of the current era enjoy a degree of latitude not known in the 19th century, they still cannot completely escape the influence of trends in local government. As Moore states, "[t]he police also understand that they are creatures of municipal governments, and are, to some degree, accountable to them and through them to the citizenry at large" (Moore 1992, 109). In that regard, two issues of significance have arisen to complicate the advancement of community policing. These issues include the emergence of crime as a governance issue, and the issue of the effects of new public administration practices by local governments. These two issues in combination have given rise to a new direction in American policing, one that threatens to eclipse community policing entirely.

The Emergence of Crime as a Governance Issue

As the police began paying increased attention to the concerns of the community, the content of that dialogue became significant in a number of significant ways. First, as issues arose the police were not the only ones paying attention. Politicians and other governmental and non-governmental actors were listening as well (Simon 2007). As Simon notes, "crime has now become a significant strategic issue" (2007, 4). Citizens expected action. Politicians seized the opportunity, promising action that in time took the form of a "war on crime" (Simon 2007, 33-74). As citizen's expectations of resolution were being raised, and responsibility for public safety was being shared with a number of state and non-state actors, crime became a matter of increasing political and policy importance (Garland 2001; Simon 2007). Secondly, since the earliest days of community policing, we have seen the rise of victim advocacy (Simon 2007, 75-110). In response to pressure, legislation was adopted that enhanced penalties, mandated minimum sentences, and in some instances created new classes of crime (Simon 2007). With this new victim advocacy came political advocacy and, many times, funding to support new initiatives.

However, many of the concerns voiced by citizens did not necessarily involve serious crimes. Scholars and practitioners noticed that many times it was not crime itself that drove citizen concerns, but rather the fear of crime; the result of minor incivilities that give the impression of crime (Wilson and Kelling 1982; Hinkle and Weisburd 2008, 504). As Garland observes, this too became a "self-standing policy goal" (2001, 122). Moreover, scholars begin noting the emergence of crime as a political issue and a matter of governance. Identified "quality of life" issues became the focus of a variety of public agencies, not just the police (Harcourt 2001, 90-104; Garland 2001, 122).

This trend is the subject of Garland and Simon's work. Increasingly since the commission reports of the 1960s and 1970s, political actors have seized on the public's fear of crime – particularly violent crime – to advance a political agenda (Garland 2001, 13). The use of crime phenomenon as a governance issue is seen in the observation made by Simon that crime is no longer just a problem for government to manage, but is instead a tool or asset for governance (2007, 4-5). To summarize his position, crime is not merely an object of governance, but one through which the people are governed (Simon 2007, 4-5). This is effective when citizens, motivated by the fear of crime, make demands for security and other related services through their elected officials, who in turn respond with policy initiatives (Garland 2001, 10-11; Simon 2007, 75-78). This effect can extend to policy initiatives that, on the surface, may seem unrelated to crime. For example, Simons notes that arguments for changes in education policy may be proffered with the justification that a well-educated populace is less likely to commit crime (2007).

These initiatives not only require the government to take a policy stance, but commit funds in support of that policy. Garland notes a trend in the thinking on crime policy has transitioned "from a 'social' to an 'economic' style of reasoning" (2001, 188). The citizen demand for costly security services effectively creates a market, and the fluctuating levels of its availability suggests publicly-funded security services have the qualities of a commodity (Krahmann 2008, 4). The effect of this trend can be seen in the fiscal policy of some states. The use of Crime Control and Prevention Districts (CCPD) in Texas is one example.

Chapter 363 of the Texas Local Government Code authorizes certain cities and counties to create special districts (CCPD) within the jurisdiction – or encompassing the entire jurisdiction – for focused attention and programs aimed at reducing or preventing crime (State of Texas 1997). City councils or county commissioners courts may receive a request to form one of these districts from dissatisfied residents or move to create one on their own initiative. The law also makes allowances for a referendum to be held on the formation of a CCPD through the petition process, which bypasses the city council or commissioners court. The districts are created by a special election held in the territory they are proposed to encompass. If the referendum passes, the results are ratified by the city council or commissioners court. The creation of these districts has important implications for tax policy. These local governments ordinarily fund public safety for the entire community through either sale tax, property tax, or a combination of the two. The broader tax rates are set by the city council or commissioners court in a manner intended to achieve a level of uniformity across the entire community.

However, in the case of these special districts the voters elect to dedicate a portion of the sales tax collected in that district to CCPD activities. In some circumstances, the arrangement could involve the payment of additional taxes in the form of a higher sales tax rate. The determination of this rate is part of the referendum to establish the special district. Once approved, businesses within the Crime Control and Prevention District then collect the sales tax for the local government. These are dedicated funds for use only to support crime prevention and support enforcement operations within the district. Approved programs must fall within parameters set by the statute authorizing the district's creation.

The Effects of Public Administration Practice

The way in which public administration practice developed in the 1990s facilitated the return toward an efficiency-oriented model of policing, as police administrators – creatures of local government bureaucracy – were incentivized to pursue efficiency-oriented management strategies. In their effects, advances in public administration theory and practice have influenced the practice of community policing in several ways.

First, the idea of a depoliticized police was an outgrowth of the philosophy of a depoliticized public administration advocated by the Progressives of the late 19th century. The softening in the late 20th century of Woodrow Wilson's admonition that politics be separated from the enterprise of public administration lasted longer in policing than in the practice of public administration (Starling 1993, 34-36). Whereas Peel's reforms were aimed at depoliticizing criminal law enforcement, the adoption of English-style policing in the U.S. was anything but apolitical (Manning 1977; Lane 1980, 12). In large part, the English-styled uniformed police service was adapted in the U.S. to serve the aims of local politicians, with many police agencies engaging in social service work at the behest of ward politicians (Manning 1977; Lane 1980; Monkkomen 1992, 553-561). It would not be until the Progressive Era – Woodrow Wilson's era – that any move to depoliticize the police would take effect and that a narrowing of focus to crime fighting would occur (Lane 1980; Kelling and Moore 1988; Monkkomen 1992). This was the beginning of the professional era of policing and public administration, which had theoretical roots in the dominant science-based administrative theories of the time (Manning 1977; Goldstein 1979; Kelling 2003, Rosenbloom and Kravchuk 2005). This change toward independence, now so deeply embedded in the police culture, has become a major point of resistance to community policing. The weight of the research and the associeted scholarship seems to support the conclusion that this resistance has staved off the full implementation of community policing thus far, and the lack of institutional change has made more quantitatively-based programs (such as intelligence-led policing and COMPSTAT discussed below) more attractive and relatively easily assimilated (Weisburd *et al.* 2003; Walsh and Vito 2004; Dabney 2010).

Secondly, advances in public administration theory and practice during twentieth century had an effect on police administration and subsequently community policing reform. In the first half of the twentieth century, these "scientific management" theories and related budget practices sought to remove politics from public administration by running government more in the manner of a business (Kelling 2003; Rosenbloom and Kravchuk 2005). This style of management placed a premium on tangible and quantifiable results. Indeed, policing exhibited a "preoccupation with [...] methods, process, and efficiency over effectiveness" (Goldstein 1990, 15). This theme was reflected in the police administration literature of the time, which heavily stressed traditional scientific and bureaucratic management theories (Sheehan and Cordner 1979; Swanson, Territo and Taylor 1993). Modifications made to public administration thought arising out of the "New Public Management" (NPM) in the 1990s continued to emphasize quantifiable evidence as the primary measure of success (Rosenbloom and Kravchuk 2005, 20-26). As with scientific management before it, NPM also had its origins in the private sector and was broadly thought to be a major part of the answer to the shortcomings of government at all levels (Rosenbloom and Kravchuk 2005, 20; Swanson, Territo and Taylor 2012, 183). The NPM strategy has several important tenets, but two in particular deserve mention here (Rosenbloom and Kravchuk 2005, 20-21).

First, NPM holds that "[p]ublic administration should focus on achieving results rather than primarily on conforming to procedures" (Rosenbloom and Kravchuk 2005, 20). Knowing what passes for satisfactory results is a major preoccupation of public administrators under NPM, and the selection of key indicators of success is an important policy judgment (Rosenbloom and Kravchuk 2005, 22-23). Knowing the exact measure of these indicators is also important and the principal purpose of the benchmarking process (Ammons 1996). The selection of these key indicators should reflect the goals and values of NPM, which include "efficiency, cost effectiveness, and customer satisfaction" (Moon and DeLeon 2001, 328). Benchmarks are performance measures that allow organizations to measure the progress made toward its goals, and compare its performance with other similarly-situated organizations (Ammons 1996, 2-3).

Consequently, entities that adhere to NPM and employ benchmarking rely on quantitative data to gauge effectiveness and efficiency. In recommending benchmarks for police departments, Ammons identifies three analytical categories: "inputs," "outputs," and "outcomes" (1996, 186). Within each, he further specifies three to five indicators. Only one indicator concerns community policing, and is placed under the category of outputs rather than outcomes. Here Ammons suggests agencies count the number of "persons participating in crime prevention activities" (1996, 186). The remaining measures focused on a variety of quantifiable data that police agencies have been keeping for decades, such as crime statistics and officer deployment patterns (Ammons 1996, 186). This type of data is relied upon heavily in the COMPSTAT program discussed below.

The second NPM value requiring mention is the importance placed on "customer satisfaction" (Moon and DeLeon 2001, 328). An important goal of public administration under NPM was to "make it customer-driven [...] treating the public and clients like customers [to] enhance public administration's service ethic and efficiency" (Rosenbloom and Kravchuk 2005, 21). Satisfaction, or happiness, appears to supply a modicum of legitimacy. One would think this form of public management would improve the chances of community policing success in that NPM boasts that it is "citizen" or "customer focused" (Rosenbloom and Kravchuk 2005, 22). However, measures of citizen satisfaction, though valuable, are ultimately subjective measures. Other measures, such as crime data are thought to be more objective and less susceptible to bias. The continued focus on traditional performance measures, and the speed with which new technology makes this data useful (even in the field) has proved problematic for the community policing model (Alpert and Moore [1993] 2000; McDonald 2000). In the last two decades, order maintenance policing, intelligence-led policing, and particularly COMPSTAT-style programs, arose in large part due to their compatibility with NPM (Weisburd *et al.* 2003; Walsh and Vito 2004; Dabney 2010).

POST 9/11 POLICING: COMPSTAT, EVIDENCE-BASED, AND INTELLIGENCE

Faced with conflicting assessments of the effectiveness of community policing and renewed political pressure to address crime problems efficiently, the ground was ripe for a useful alternative. The development of evidenced-based and intelligence-led policing methods began to take shape to address community policing's problem orientation, but not necessarily its community engagement component. The earliest steps toward the development of these initiatives involved the use of "computer" produced crime "statistics" (hence the term COMPSTAT) in a creative way to address crime problems in New York City. William Bratton – largely credited for its development – indicates that he advanced COMPSTAT to make up for what he came to believe to be the weaknesses of community policing (Weisburd *et al.* 2003). Before proceeding, it is important to note that Bratton does not abandon community engagement, but instead personally utilizes the practice in a manner that realizes its full potential (Bratton 1998). His personal use of community policing practice is a template for power sharing that can be used – that has been used to good effect – by other police administrators.

However, in Bratton's estimation, decentralization placed many of the most important decisions in the hands of individuals in the lowest levels of the organization, officers who were too junior to know what to do. In addition to placing a tremendous amount of responsibility on the agency's least experienced or qualified personnel, it relieved the experienced and qualified staff in middle management positions of much of their responsibility. Bratton, and others like him, did not stop practicing community policing upon promotion. Instead, they took the task with them and continued engaging citizens while holding command rank (Bratton 1998; Maple 1999). While this works against the concept of decentralization, it does advance community policing's ideal of shared power advanced by the likes of Trojanowicz and Bucqueroux, as well as the COPS Office. Decentralization and power sharing are often at odds. A lot is expected of less tenured officers under the community policing model. Ironically, while they are empowered to make life and death decisions, they generally do not have the authority to make policy commitments on behalf of the department (Bratton 1998, 199). Speaking to them about power sharing is a pointless endeavor because they do not have power to share. Bratton discusses this as he describes the status of community policing upon his arrival in New York, stating:

> The community-policing plan that had been put into practice when I arrived focused on the beat cop. [...] In theory, that's fine; beat cops are important in maintaining contact with the public and offering them a sense of security. [...] Giving cops more individual power to make decisions is a good idea. [...] But the community-policing plan as it was originally focused was not going to work because there was no focus on crime. [...] The new beat cop was a kid. No twenty-two-year-old kid from Long Island was going to come to Harlem, Hollis, the Upper East Side, or East New York and solve that neighborhood's problems. The city's problems were complex and difficult for the most experienced police and social service experts; these kids were unprepared and ill equipped to handle them, and it was unrealistic to expect that they could. (Bratton 1998, 198-199)

The onus for achieving reductions in crime and improvement in the quality of life under COMPSTAT shifts from the beat officer to the area commander (Bratton 1998; Maple 1999; Swanson, Territo and Taylor 2012, 53). This change in locus of responsibility calls for a shift in organizational thinking. Specifically with regard to organizational orientation, "[w]hereas community and problem-oriented policing is a bottom-up philosophy [...] Compstat and intelligence-led policing is much more hierarchical and emphasizes the top-down approach" (Swanson, Territo and Taylor 2012, 226). To that end, agencies

The Long Slide   141

practicing COMPSTAT have standing meetings wherein mid-level and senior police commanders are called to account for the crime in and disorder statistics their area of responsibility, reporting situational status, strides made toward improving the situation (if not resolution) and future steps to meet assigned goals (Bratton 1998; Maple 1999).

Bratton, COMPSTAT's principal champion, credits Jack Maple with solidifying the practice into a coherent method (Bratton 1998, 223-224). Fundamental to COMPSTAT are four key elements (Maple 1999, 32):

1. Accurate and timely intelligence
2. Rapid deployment [of assets]
3. [Use of] effective tactics
4. Relentless follow-up and assessment

The first element requires taking the most up-to-date crime data available and turning it into usable intelligence – usually in a geographical format – that identifies the times and places criminal phenomena are occurring. These usually take the form of pin maps (Swanson, Territo and Taylor 2012, 53). Aided by such criminal intelligence tools, the second element calls for police commanders to direct personnel and resources to priority problem areas. This was (and is) affectionately referred to as "cops on dots" (Maple 199, 128). This method of using geographical information systems to identify these problem areas is also referred to as "hot-spot policing" (Maple 1999, 32; Swanson, Territo and Taylor 2012, 64). Addressing these areas is an important part of a police commander's duties; they are held accountable for the "dots." The goal, as Maple puts it, is to have mid-level commanders "stop being territorial to their functions and become more territorial to actual territories" (1999, 32). The third element is directly related to evidenced-based policing in that it requires that the resources deployed to the problem areas need to use "effective tactics [...] that reduce crime or improve the quality of life" (Maple 1999, 32). Agencies seek out and use the "best practices" available, and "encourage innovation" in the development of new methods (Maple 1999, 32). Finally, there are regularly scheduled meetings – most often weekly – to report progress to the department's senior administration. Interestingly, this accountability mechanism tends to breed competition and synergy (Bratton 1998).

The COMPSTAT model expanded across the nation rather quickly and threatened to eclipse traditional community policing practice (Weisburd *et al.* 2003). However, to the thinking of many, this represents a return to an earlier model of policing (Magers 2004). It is widely regarded and embraced in the post 9/11 era. In its implementation, it is heavy on law and order, as evidenced by the frequent use of zero-tolerance campaigns designed to rid a problem area of a specific type of crime or disorder offense (Maple 1999; Swanson, Territo and Taylor 2012, 50, 55). While not overtly antithetical to community policing, in practice it is low on citizen involvement in the manner traditionally understood by community policing advocates. The concern is that distance may be starting to grow between the police and the policed once again.

In the mid-1990s, a few scholars began advocating for an "evidenced-based" model of policing that used the medical model (evidence-based medicine) as its primary template (Trojanowicz and Bucqueroux 1990; Sherman 1998). The goal was to use more robust research methods for determining what practices had the best results and implement those practices as widely as possible (Sherman 1998). Over a decade later, Braga would echo this call for better methods and "more rigorous designs" in the "evaluation of problem-oriented policing initiatives," with the caveat that "all problem-oriented policing evaluations suffer from external validity concerns" that reduce "the generalizability of specific crime prevention practices" (2010, 173-175). In addition to identifying potential best practices, rigorous analytical methods might be useful to assess individual officer and agency performance (Sherman 1998). For this reason, evidence-based policing fits neatly with NPM as it also advocates the creation and periodic revalidation of performance benchmarks (Sherman 1999).

In the decade since the 9/11 attacks, a new model of policing has gained considerable attention. Called "intelligence-led policing," (ILP) the model emerged after those terrorist attacks in response to the realization that the largest force immediately available to respond to such incidents – if not prevent them – is the same force that patrols the city streets on a daily basis (McGarrell, Freilich and Chermak 2007). Therefore, in addition to addressing crime and disorder, the police added a major new dimension it their mission – that being homeland security (Carter and Carter 2009, 310).

The adoption of intelligence-led policing in the U.S. in the first decade of this millennium has something in common with the American policing reforms of the 19th century in that they both originated in Britain (Carter and Carter 2009, 310-312). Called the British National Intelligence Model (NIM), the system was developed in the 1990s to "deal with organized crime, drugs, and other complex crimes unique to [...] the changing political environment associated with the European Union (EU), where, among other factors, immigration and customs checkpoints were eliminated for persons travelling between the EU member countries" (Carter and Carter 2009, 310-311). All British police agencies were required to adopt the model in 2002, which uses intelligence processes to address everything from "local recurring crime problems" to "transnational organized crime, terrorism, and other criminal threats to Britain" (Carter and Carter 2009, 311).

Intelligence-led policing has several attractive qualities that fit well with the emerging trends. For one, it seems rather closely related to COMPSTAT, though the two approaches have their differences. Whereas COMPSTAT is a "crime management tool," intelligence-led policing "is concerned with all crimes and all threats [and] not just terrorism" (Carter and Carter 2009, 320). Another important difference is that COMPSTAT is "incident" driven, focusing on the detailed analysis of crime events that have passed (Carter and Carter 2009, 320). In contrast, intelligence-led policing produces assessments or estimates that "focuses on threats rather than crimes that have occurred" (Carter and Carter 2009, 320). One might say that COMPSTAT helped blaze the trail for intelligence-led policing (Carter and Carter 2009, 320). The goal in intelligence-led policing is to produce an accurate assessment that is actionable by decisionmakers and field personnel (Carter and Carter 2009; U.S. Department of Justice 2005).

Secondly, some thought intelligence-led policing could be combined with community policing, thereby making the later more effective (U.S. Department of Justice 2005, 10-12; U.S. Department of Justice 2009c, 86-87; Swanson, Territo and Taylor 2012, 68-69). This combination also seemed to promise relief to community policing in that the methods of intelligence-led policing allowed for an efficient use of resources and information sharing. In particular, the model's reliance on technology and methods similar to COMPSTAT meant that agencies could get by on existing personnel (Swanson, Territo and

Taylor 2012, 69). In fact, recent scholarship on COMPSTAT examines its "co-implementation" with community policing (Willis, Mastrofski, and Kochel 2010).

Moreover, community policing's community engagement component had much to offer intelligence-led policing as well. Advocates of intelligence-led policing seized upon the networks of community partnerships, seeing in them an information collection infrastructure that intelligence-led policing requires to meets its mission. For that reason, the U.S. Department of Justice guidance document suggests a policing model that "blends intelligence-led and problem-oriented policing" (U.S. Department of Justice 2005, 10).

An important distinction must be made before proceeding. There is a difference between information and intelligence. Information is the basic data that, upon analysis by a qualified individual, becomes infused with meaning that can be used by decisionmakers and officers in the field (U.S. Department of Justice 2005, 3). Once this is accomplished, information becomes intelligence. Intelligence consists of processed data, which is information acquired from a wide array of sources. Community policing partnerships are natural sources for information; they are indeed a pre-existing information collection mechanism. This asset was identified in the recommendations resulting from a March 2002 Intelligence Summit held in Alexandria, Virginia, just months after the 9/11 attacks. Carter and Carter (2009) effectively capture the participants' observations in a compression quote, stating:

> Over the past decade, simultaneous to federally led initiatives to improve intelligence gathering, thousands of community-policing officers have been building close and productive relationships with the citizens they serve. The benefits of these relationships are directly related to information and intelligence sharing: COP officers have immediate and unfettered access to local, neighborhood information as it develops. Citizens are aware of, and seek out COP officers to provide them with new information that may be useful to criminal interdiction or long-term problem solving. The positive nature of COP/citizen relationships promotes a continuous and reliable transfer of information from one to the other. It is time to maximize the potential for community-policing efforts to serve as a gateway of locally based

information to prevent terrorism, and all other crimes. (Carter and Carter 2009, 319)

Moreover, the fruits of community policing efforts are an easy source for someone wishing to identify and locate groups of people with special characteristics or interests. As part of basic beat knowledge developed through continuous interaction, most officers "know the community – i.e., its makeup, its ties to other countries or particular belief structures" (U.S. Department of Justice 2005, 11). In its assessment of threats and targets, intelligence-led policing appears poised to fall prey to the problems inherent in a view of society informed by pluralism.

Indeed, viewing the citizen as an informant brings an old dynamic back to the forefront. The use of informants in policing has a history on both sides of the Atlantic that stretches back to the pre-colonial and colonial historical periods (Levett 1975; Lane 1980). Policing's extreme dependence on informants made the practice ripe for corruption and abuse (Lane 1980). It was not uncommon in those early days for informants to make false claims against innocent people that materially benefited the police and the informant (Lane 1980, 10). Though the practice has been subjected to a greater degree of control through judicial decisions and agency policies, the practice continued to be a concern into the 1960s (International Association of Chiefs of Police 1990). Though consideration was given to this concern, there remained an expectant tone in the early presidential commission reports of the 1960s that the citizens would willingly cooperate with the police and provide information when asked as it was thought to be to their benefit (1967a, 159).

For the police, the use of the term *informant* automatically generates an orientation toward the individual that is framed by policy if not experience. Informants are to be "managed" and "controlled," and personal relationships are forbidden; they are to be viewed as "tools" (International Association of Chiefs of Police 1990, 1). Moreover, enterprising officers are expected to cultivate informants from a multiple sources in a variety of social contexts. Targeting groups for police infiltration is an effective means of gathering information for intelligence analysis. However, the idea of targeting and infiltrating is not without risk as it pertains to the perception of legitimacy from the perspective of the targeted group (Harris 2010).

Viewed cynically, one could argue there does not appear to be much room for power sharing in this type of arrangement. Community partnerships under a blended community-oriented, intelligence-led policing model could be viewed as mechanisms to develop informants rather than co-equal citizen partners engaged in the provision of public safety services and order. The conversion of community partnerships to an information collection infrastructure for intelligence-led policing is certainly an efficient use of an asset paid for in part with federal dollars. But to what end? Does American policing practiced in this way risk a crisis of legitimacy the likes of which have not been seen since the 1960s?

CHAPTER 6
Reflections

The connection between the practice of community policing and deliberative democratic theory suggested herein is not solely an exercise in academic abstraction, but rather supported in no small measure by decades of professional experience. As demonstrated in this work, community policing was promoted for its potential crime control capabilities early in its development. Over time, the increased emphasis on community policing's supposed capacity to control crime resulted in a shift in focus away from community policing's central practice – namely, community engagement that results in shared power. The emergence over the last two decades of policing models better suited to the crime control mission has caused community policing's cache to wane. These competitors' claims of effectiveness in this regard were not without substantial merit. However, these new models pay but scant attention to community policing's *raison d'etre*. At the very heart of the community policing movement – it's mostly forgotten genesis – is the quest for a new kind of legitimacy for the police in a democratic society.

Fortunately, for reasons not clearly understood, the legacy of community policing is proving difficult to leave behind. Increasingly, there are calls for some sort of amalgam. For example, some prominent scholars call for "co-implementation" initiatives that allow community policing and newer models to work side-by-side with varying levels of integration (Willis, Mastrofski, and Kochel 2010). Others argue for a full "unification" strategy that integrates COMPSTAT or intelligence-led policing initiatives with community policing (Scheider, Chapman, and Schapiro 2009, 694). These developments have significant merit. Evaluations conducted thus far seem favorable, indicating they are efficient and effective, thus advancing two important public service goals. However, without careful reflection as to what happened to community policing followed by a re-specification and contemporary restatement prior to integration efforts, the net effect of such efforts may well spell the end of the original core emphasis of community policing.

It has been argued here that the community engagement component is the central feature of community policing, but the one least well developed. Lacking has been a clear way for the police to access and actualize the central truth about community policing – that is, the concept at its core entails a different kind of legitimacy that goes to the heart of democracy. Though this is changing in some quarters, by and large these are notions the police are not as familiar with as they could be. Deliberative democratic theory provides a better grounding for the community engagement component of community policing and a practical method for realizing its potential. Therefore, in closing I will offer some considerations for a way forward that salvages the important aspect of community policing that any unification or co-implementation initiative should include. A brief summary of this chapter follows.

First, the issue of legitimacy deserves revisiting. Historically, the thinking on police legitimacy has been seen in one of two ways. On the one hand, police legitimacy rests on the notion of the rule of law. If, to paraphrase John Adams, *ours is a nation of laws and not men*, then there is little room for the subjective whims of rulers. Unfortunately, as Simon's contribution discussed early suggests, the politically motivated "war on crime" coupled with a thoroughly efficient neo-professional model of policing gives rise to notion of rule *by* law enforcement (Simon 2007, 33-74). On the other hand, the capacity and effectiveness of the police to affect the ends to which laws are directed is a second source of legitimacy. This type of legitimacy is most often directed to the methods of policing. Both of these types of legitimacy have an objective quality. However, as will be discussed below, when one form of legitimacy is called into question, there is a tendency to seek refuge in the other. Moreover, with both sharing an objective quality, they both seem viable. Community policing adds a third way of looking at legitimacy. Moore, contrasting with the other two forms of legitimacy, articulated this third way when he wrote:

> The concept of community policing also changes thinking about the bases of police legitimacy. In community policing, the justification for policing is not only its capacity to reduce crime and violence at a low cost while preserving constitutionally guaranteed rights but also its ability to meet the needs and desires of the community. Community satisfaction and harmony become important bases of legitimacy along with crime fighting competence and compliance with the law. Politics, in the sense of community responsiveness and accountability, re-emerges as a virtue and an explicit basis of police legitimacy. (Moore 1992, 123)

This form of legitimacy has democratic roots and is more difficult for the police because of its subjective nature and deficiencies in knowledge of ways of realizing it. Deliberative democratic practices hold promise in this specific regard.

Secondly, I note important points of similarity between deliberative democratic thinking and community policing. Conceptualizing community policing's community engagement component as an exercise in deliberative democracy may be the best way to realize the promise of community policing as originally conceived. Practical aspects of deliberative democracy offer a template to guide citizen-police interaction. If the ideal result of the community engagement component of community policing is a greater degree of shared power, then any legitimate collaboration must be preceded by meaningful deliberation. There is much to build on as some changes in police training over the past twenty years may serve to ease the transition to a better-developed community engagement model based on deliberative democratic theory. These changes over the past two decades include an increased emphasis on police ethics training, as well as cultural diversity training (Kleinig 1996, Kleinig and Smith 1997; Shusta, Levine, Wong, and Harris 2005). Additionally, increasing attention has been given to the principles of democracy and civics in law enforcement basic and leadership training curriculum in the U.S. and abroad (Bayley 2001, U.S. Department of Justice 2003).

Third, in using deliberative democratic methods to actualize this third conception of police legitimacy, community policing becomes more than a model of policing. It has the potential to transcend its status as a method of policing and become the embodiment of democratic policing itself. Historically, the connection between American policing and democratic principles was largely inferred through institutional arrangements. While it is true that institutional arrangements place considerable constraints on the police, the manner in which vested authority was exercised in the 1960s served to call into question the role of the police in a democratic society. Heretofore, the strength of this connection was largely assumed by virtue of the geographical fact that American policing takes place in the United States and was therefore presumed democratic. However, this geographical fact was not enough to insulate the police from forceful allegations of authoritarianism and even totalitarianism in the 1960s. The solution proposed by presidential commission findings was for the police to improve their relationship with the public through a variety of practices designed to engage the citizenry. The practices that resulted ultimately evolved into community policing. Community policing's central practice – engagement with citizens to share power in achieving public safety goals – had the goal of restoring democratic legitimacy through democratic means that start with some form of discourse. Furthermore, the history of American policing and its evolution through the community policing era serves to substantiate Whitehead's point that democratization – even in an advanced democracy – is an ongoing process (2002).

In closing, these conclusions offer several avenues for further research. The first concerns the need to update the sociologically-based research so popular in the 1960s. As discussed earlier in this work, the 1960s and 1970s witnessed a boon in social research of multiple segments of society. Researchers such as Jerome Skolnick, James Q. Wilson, Albert J. Reiss, Jr., and Peter K. Manning all contributed to this body of work, focusing on the social aspects of the police and police work. The findings of these scholars have been formative to administrative and training practices ever since. However, an entire generation of police officers has since entered (and departed) the profession. It would be interesting to determine if there are social differences between the police officers of the 1960s and those of today to see if the change in the police culture those studies hoped for has been actualized.

A second area of needed research concerns change management. Specifically, I argue there are lessons to be learned from the difficult history of community policing that speak to the management of change.

By all accounts, the tremendous turmoil and impact on large segments of society should have resulted in much more comprehensive change in policing practice. The methods employed by scholars of historical institutionalism appear effective at explaining why – looking over long periods – changes either does or does not occur. A second closely related area for research is the long-term effect of police history on American political development. As discussed in this work, crime has become increasingly viewed as a governance issue. This is largely attributable to the commodification of security, its availability from diverse sources, and policies concerning its distribution discussed earlier. Now more than ever, it may be quite worthwhile for researchers to investigate the impact of crime and crime management's effect on American political development. In sum, a substantially better understanding of the experiment that was community policing might aid other initiatives of this type avoid the pitfalls of failed attempts to initiate and sustain adaptive change.

THE LEGITIMACY QUESTION REVISITED

Community policing's enduring contribution is that it forced a presumptively democratic institution – American policing – to think about its legitimacy in a new way. In earlier eras, "[l]aw, especially criminal law, and police professionalism were established as the principal bases of police legitimacy" (Kelling and Moore 1988, 5). The community policing model and the associated practices which emerged from the tumult of the 1960s led to a timely "renewed emphasis on community, or political, authorization for many police tasks, along with law and professionalism" (Kelling and Moore 1988, 11). This third way of thinking about legitimacy found its earliest expressions in the series of presidential commission reports of the 1960s and 1970s. In the years that followed, this new way of conceptualizing police legitimacy gained increasing attention in the policing literature and was discussed in terms more commonly used by political theorists in their treatment of the larger concept of democratic legitimacy (Moore 1992, 123; Ponsaers 2001, 482; National Research Council 2004, 291; Murphy, Hinds, and Fleming 2008, 136; Gau and Brunson 2010, 258, 275).

However, moving from concept to practice has proven difficult for policing (Herbert 2006b, 484). Deliberative democratic theorists speak of democratic legitimacy in these same terms, but to a greater and more comprehensive extent. As deliberative democratic scholar Joshua Cohen points out, "deliberative democracy is primarily a theory of 'democratic legitimacy'" ([1996] 1997, 407). The practices emerging for deliberative democratic thinkers have the advantage of a more clearly specified conception of democratic legitimacy. It is to this deliberative democratic scholarship that community policing scholars should look for a more robust understanding of legitimacy and a better set of methods of actualizing it. Moreover, legitimacy generated through deliberative democratic means offers better footing for authoritative action, having a transformative effect on both the police and the policed.

The research on community policing portends an uncertain future. Increasingly, models and methods of policing that have emerged in response to community policing's failings appear rooted in the more traditional ideas of police legitimacy so clearly summarized by Kelling and Moore. They warrant some attention in this closing chapter, and to be contrasted even further with the more democratic view of police legitimacy.

The first source of legitimacy resorted to by the police is *law*. It is argued by some that around the turn of the 20th century "criminal law became the primary source of police authorization" (Kelling 2003, 7). However, the discussion of early American policing presented herein describes an even longer history of such activity that goes back as far as the enforcement action taken by the watch in support of locally promulgated standards of conduct constituting ordinances. Respect for the rule of law is held in high regard by democratic societies in that it presumes to remove the element of capriciousness from government action. Moreover, it preserves civil society by removing the threat of vigilante justice and placing jurisdiction over such matters in the hands of a third party. The police thus "entrusted with provision of services with a high potential for violence, noncompliance, and conflict, view and claim the law as the fount of legitimacy" (Manning 1977, 100). Manning asserts that particularly where it concerns violence and serious disorder, "the law serves as a mystification device or canopy to […], legitimate, and rationalize police conduct" (1977, 101).

This leads to the second source of legitimacy on which the police began to rely in the 20th century. In additional to the law itself, legitimacy is derived from the character of its enforcement. Specifically, I refer to the character of the manner and method of the law's enforcement. This source of legitimacy is described by Kelling and Moore as "police professionalism" (1988, 5). The turn toward professionalism as a source of police legitimacy cannot be understood absent the history of American policing. As indicated earlier in this work, the movement toward professionalism in policing was a reaction against the domination of police agencies by political bosses. As Crank aptly observed, "[t]he police professionalism movement" holds a "narrow view of police legitimacy" that is rooted in its ability to achieve its mission in a manner of its choosing – i.e., the scientific method, with its emphasis on efficiency (1994, 329).

Whereas the argument for a type of police legitimacy based on the rule of law focuses on the authority to take action against prohibited conduct, an argument for police legitimacy based on policing's professional character focuses on the method and manner in which those actions are taken. The two are quite complementary and self-reinforcing; any deficiency or threat to one of these forms of legitimacy is corrected or compensated for with the other. The police point to the rule of law as a source of legitimacy, until legal constraints begin to interfere with police effectiveness toward achieving the law's underlying goal. Included in these constraints are court decisions and any resultant policy that creates limits on police methods. Decisions that change police practices to add safeguards arguably complicate police work and make it less efficient. The Miranda decision is an example of a case that added steps to various stages of the criminal justice process. Initially it was decried as a threat to the values underlying the law and that it favored the criminal to the detriment of the victim by making the investigative process inefficient. Conversely, this drive toward efficie.icy is rooted in a sort of political mandate for law and order, until pushed to the point it is interpreted as political interference, at which point the police revert to the rule of law argument.

Missing from the discussion on American policing before the 1960s was any real consideration for the larger source of legitimacy. The crisis of legitimacy extended to all areas of government (Rumbaut and Bittner 1979, 241; Crank 1994, 325-331; Ponsaers 2001, 482). Writing in the wake of the tumult of the 1960s, Rumbaut and Bitter observed that the "conceptions of the police and of the problems of policing have been shaped by the crisis of legitimacy that faced all institutions of government in the 1960s" (1979, 241). Lacking was a sense of trust between the people and the government and "trust in policing cannot be examined separately from trust in government" (Goldsmith 2005, 446). The expression of the people reacting to the loss of trust was seen in the many conflicts – large and small – that occurred throughout the 1960s. Pushed to action, government was forced into a period of official public self-examination in search of its lost legitimacy. The police were not exempt from this critique. On the matter of lost legitimacy and its relevance to problems in policing in the 1960s Crank observes:

> [The] loss of legitimacy is a ceremonial process marked by rituals of public degradation and absolution through the adoption of a new legitimating mandate. [...] For the police, public degradation and revocation of legitimacy occurred ceremonially through the two blue-ribbon panels [...] issuing reports in 1967. (1994, 328)

The official critique was truly comprehensive as the "Crime Commission (1967) [...] criticism struck at the heart of the professionalism movement" (Crank 1994, 329). Lacking in the police profession was the recognition that in a democracy, the much broader conception of legitimacy – "the process by which authority wins acceptance from the governed" – applied narrowly and specifically to policing as well (Lane 1980, 18).

Central to the movement that spawned the community policing era was the belief that policing a democratic people should be different; that "[i]n a democracy [...] state power must be seen as an exercise of the community and not an action against it" (National Research Council 2004, 291). This new conception of legitimacy important to community policing acknowledges "[t]he legitimacy of the police in community policing is strongly linked to the concept of democracy [as] legitimation comes from the continuing processes of consultation and interaction" (Ponsaers 2001, 482).

Increasingly we have seen concepts and definitions associated with democratic theory receiving attention in the policing literature. For example, in the National Research Council's *Fairness and Effectiveness in Policing*, the researchers note that "[b]y legitimacy we mean the judgments that ordinary citizens make about the rightfulness of police conduct and the organizations that employ and supervise them" (2004, 291). This new conception of legitimacy has proved to be somewhat problematic for policing as "perceptions of legitimacy are, by definition, subjective" (National Research Council 2004, 291). The historically relied upon sources of legitimacy were considerably more objective; they were more fixed in nature. This new form of democratically-based legitimacy is more fluid, transient, and sometimes chaotic.

The imagery of the democratization process is captured well by the scholar Lawrence Whitehead. He explained the changing conceptions of, and practices in, a democracy in a manner that seems applicable to the idea of police legitimacy in a democracy. He uses the imagery of a ship that is "anchored" but "floating" (2002, 7). In some regards, democratic legitimacy – and by clear extension police legitimacy – never stray too far from some core ideals. However, there is enough flex (within tolerances) to permit adjustment to new circumstances. This adjustment has proven to be difficult for American policing in that it still relies on the seemingly firmer, more objective sources of legitimacy – namely, that laws need enforcing and this enforcement must be done efficiently. A point missed by many police practitioners is that this preoccupation with the rule of (or *by*) law, and its accompanying premium on efficiency, was precisely what was being called into question in the 1960s.

DELIBERATIVE DEMOCRATIC THEORY AND THE PRACTICE OF COMMUNITY ORIENTED POLICING

In addition to the recognition that the larger notion of government's democratic legitimacy applied equally to its police was the realization that somehow the police needed to develop methods for accessing this higher form of police legitimacy. That was what the community relations initiatives, and eventually community policing, were supposed to do. The early community relations efforts largely failed because they tried to sell the public on the standard notions of police legitimacy based on law and professionalism (Kelling and Moore 1988; Kelling 2003). This clinging to the traditional sources of legitimacy demonstrated a lack of awareness on the part of the police that in a democracy "the environment provides legitimacy," and is not imposed by the police on the environment (Giblin and Burruss 2009, 352). The historical facts of American policing reflected in Whitehead's metaphor illustrate the notion that legitimacy does come from the societal environment (Giblin and Burruss 2009). In a democracy, objective forms of legitimacy first require subjective forms of support.

By comparison, legitimacy based in *law* and *procedural* efficiency is a rather simple matter. It is objective, rational, and often scientific. However, one of the problems of the 1960s was that these very forms of legitimacy came under attack from a variety of sources, including the U.S. Supreme Court (Kelling 2003). Laws thought to maintain public order, as well as efficiency-oriented police practices aimed at achieving those goals, were being struck down as un-constitutional by the U.S. courts. For example, while the *procedure* of denying suspects access to counsel may have been efficient, it was not in keeping with the core values expressed by the Constitution (Kelling 2003, 12-13). Similarly, a *law* governing who could sit where on a bus based on their race was equally invalid (Swanson, Territo and Taylor 2012, 27-28).

The search for subjective forms of legitimacy is much more problematic for governmental agencies, including the police. While it was clear a new conception of legitimacy was needed, what was lacking was a method for determining what was legitimate. It was argued earlier that when these deficiencies were recognized in the turmoil of the 1960s and 1970s, pluralist thinkers in vogue at the time supplied the dominant theory concerning accessing and understanding the public. Pluralism represented the best-developed and ready-to-hand method available for assessing citizen's beliefs about what government – and by extension the police – should do. The theory of pluralism was believed to supply an explanation as to how legitimacy could be generated in the political and societal environment through social groups (Giblin and Burruss 2009, 352-353). However, in the end, legitimacy becomes tied to notions of individual happiness – notions that can be quite transient and vulnerable to manipulation.

Pluralism clearly has its limits. It can give insight and understanding into social phenomena that exists at a given point in time. The problem is that pluralist thinking generally regards people's interest as being largely fixed, resistant to change, and deeply rooted in some aspect of their social identity (Held 2006). Therefore, when it comes to intentionally effecting social change, pluralist theory is of little use. This reflects a division within sociological studies that exists to this day. Some hold to a pure empirically based sociological theory that seeks to understand and explain social phenomena, while others advance arguments that seek to create social change (Sanderson 2005). Stephen K. Sanderson, in a criticism on the state of sociological theory, suggests that a bright-line be drawn between sociological theory and social theory (2005, 2-3). Sociological theory, in his view, should be oriented toward understanding and explaining social phenomena through empirical testing. He complained that the field of sociology has been taken over in larger part by what he calls "social commentators and critics" who seek to create social and political change (Sanderson 2005, 2). These individuals he refers to as "social theorists" and he includes among them noted "social thinkers" like Foucault, Derrida, and Habermas (Sanderson 2005, 1-2).

Nevertheless, as pluralism was the most developed theory for understanding society at the time of the crises of the 1960s, it became uncritically – but firmly – embedded in the police understanding of the community. Pluralist assumptions are found in the subsequent development of community policing and its evaluation. In many ways, pluralist thought still informs how the police tend to see the community. Because pluralist thinking holds that the individual's interests are generally fixed and discernible through some aspect of their identification with a group, which in many instances is in opposition to another social group, the incidence of conflict is a permanent feature of societal life in the pluralist conception of the polity. Many times, the police associate this type of conflict, or its potential, with inefficiency.

Yet elsewhere, the dominance of pluralist thinking began to wane. In noting the decline of pluralism's sway, Sklansky (quoting Carol Pateman) concluded, "[p]luralism had lost favor […] in part because of its 'preoccupation with the stability of the political system'" (2008, 68). In other words, pluralist thinking was not thought to be the best mechanism to affect adaptive change. What pluralism does is allow generalizations through the grouping of individuals by some social aspect believed to be a clue to their interests. Once this is determined, the result is often some sort of tailored appeasement. As Sklansky observes, "[m]ollification always serves the interest of stability" (2008, 68). The community relations initiatives of the 1960s and 1970s can be characterized this way, which may explain their failure. Pluralism is limiting in that its bias toward achieving some state of equilibrium between groups appears to preclude the possibility for inspired individual and social transformation. However, in other arenas the turmoil of the 1960s and 1970s was to lead to new ways of thinking about legitimacy.

At about the same time American policing was developing reforms built around a pluralist understanding of the community in an attempt to regain legitimacy, deliberative democratic scholarship was just in the beginning of its development into a major presence. As we have seen, deliberative democratic theory emerged in part as a reaction against a pluralist understanding of interest formation (Held 2006; Sklansky 2008, 67). Deliberative democrats maintain interests can and do change, and reason plays an important role in the adaptation to change process. Deliberative democratic theory offers an alternative path toward legitimacy. It also offers American policing an appropriate comprehensive process for achieving legitimacy. The history of community policing has proven consistent with Sklansky's observation that "concerns about actual, objective 'legitimacy' prove hard to separate from concerns about *perceived* legitimacy" (Sklansky 2008, 68). However, deliberative democratic theory's edge is that it places an "emphasis on legitimacy, both actual and perceived" (Sklansky 2008, 93). In fact, "[d]eliberative democracy, […] is first and foremost a theory about legitimacy: that is to say, about what makes democracy both worthy of respect (actual legitimacy) and likely to achieve respect (perceived legitimacy)" (Sklansky 2008, 93). For this precise reason, deliberative democratic theory places a premium on the procedure for determining what is deserving of citizen and governmental support.

A point of commonality between deliberative democracy and community policing is the emphasis both place on *procedural justice*. Generally speaking, "[p]rocedural justice refers to the perceived fairness of the procedures involved in decision-making and implementation, and the treatment people receive from the authority" (Murphy, Hinds and Fleming 2008, 139). In no small way are the concepts of "procedural justice and legitimacy" related as "people will defer to decisions because those decisions are made through fair processes" (National Research Council 2004, 301). In fact, the "key antecedent of legitimacy is procedural justice" (Murphy, Hinds and Fleming 2008, 136). What was lacking was a coherent and comprehensive procedure to guide citizen-police interaction in the community policing model; one that was capable of realizing the goal of legitimacy by first meeting the requirements of procedural justice. In a democracy, this is achieved principally through genuine discourse. As

Gau and Brunson observe, the "[f]eeling that one's voice has been heard and taken seriously is [...] integral to procedural justice and police legitimacy" (2010, 275). Furthermore, it "is a necessary component of any policing paradigm," including those of COMPSTAT and intelligence-led policing (Gau and Brunson 2010, 258).

The procedures for discourse in deliberative democratic theory have much to offer community policing practice. Particularly of value are the rules for discourse offered by Habermas. While I earlier conceded that the deliberative democratic scholars Gutmann and Thompson are largely correct on the limits of Habermas's thought (Gutmann and Thompson 1996; 2004), nonetheless, his rules governing argumentation are very much viable. The weight of history and research show that the role of citizen input and involvement as originally conceived is clearly important in the community policing model. The manner in which that discourse takes place is of great importance to the public and the police alike. However, little research has been conducted that applies this theory to practice. If there is one weakness identified, it is the lack of training in how to initiate and facilitate these dialogues. It has been asserted that the reforms of community policing were "aimed at reinvolving the police in the life of the community" (Crank 1994, 331). However, I would submit that comprehensive change requires the community to be reinvolved in the life of their police, and deliberative democratic methods represent the best hope at achieving this. Again, it must be stressed that in order to realize the goal of power sharing in community policing, deliberation must precede collaboration.

The similarities between the concerns of community policing and deliberative democracy are uncanny. Just as "community policing has been plagued by definitional ambiguity," (Scheider, Chapman, and Shapiro 2009, 696), deliberative democratic theory has been criticized for some conceptual imprecision (Chambers 1996). While not unified, certain strains of thought emerge that have special relevance to the preservation of community policing. Chambers (1996) argues the applicability of the theory to a wide array of governance practices. She contends, "deliberative democratic theory has moved beyond the 'theoretical statement' stage and into the 'working theory' stage" (1996, 307). As such, she contends that deliberative democratic theory is eminently applicable to the practice of public policy formulation, and that in practice this has been occurring with greater frequency, starting in the late 1980s and early 1990s (Chambers 1996, 315). Again, I note this theory was just coalescing into its practically useful form at about the same time as community policing practice was at its zenith.

While a review of the literature on police administration and community policing yielded no clear evidence of a frank discussion of deliberative democratic theory, examination of public administration literature did reflect considerable activity in this area. Deliberative democratic themes and theory are being researched and applied to a variety of planning enterprises, to include environmental, land use, and economic development (Forester 1999). Public administration scholars show evidence of developing deliberative practices in a variety of ways. For instance, Kathi and Cooper (2005) discuss the enhancement of policy efficacy through the engagement of neighborhood councils in the municipal planning process. Strains of early thought in community policing can be seen in their work as they argue that the citizen should be viewed not simply as a "passive consumer" of agency services, but as a citizen with whom the agency should collaborate for the greater good (Bayley and Shearing 1996, 588).

Cooper, Bryer and Meek (2006) further argued for a more comprehensive model of citizen involvement, indicating that a "citizen-centered collaborative public management" model is, in fact, a quite productive model of "civic engagement" (76, 80). While public meetings are the most common venues of dialogues between those that govern and the governed, Adams (2004) questions the value of these exchanges in the highly structured format in which they normally occur. He concludes that though many times the rules governing public meetings seem to prevent the type of dialogue one would expect to precede formal action, they nevertheless provide an opportunity for citizens to connect with policymakers and other interested parties and construct a network connection with them. These connections forge relationships around which political movements can coalesce.

Still another example of public administration research involving deliberative democratic themes is found in the 2004 research of Irvin and Stansbury, who question whether collaboration is "worth the effort" (55). They observe that if citizens were involved in every aspect of policy formation, little would get done. In addition, the cost of protracted citizen involvement is high to the agency. They offer a useful model to explain the varied level of attention by citizens.

Conversely, their model serves as a decision tool, suggesting when an agency ought to involve citizens and an estimate of the political costs involved.

A new revitalized model of community policing should blend David Bayley's "principles of democratic policing" (responsiveness, accountability, transparency) with deliberative practices recommended by scholars. Particular attention ought to be paid to deliberative democratic theory's reliance on Habermas's "discourse ethics" (1983). Habermas's thought is pivotal. If the dialogue is less than open and honest, the enterprise of deliberation is undermined. If the police are not open in their discussions – share accurate and complete information – the public may "exit" from the exercise (Hirschman 1970).

An arrangement such as this is not without precedent. Some federally funded programs have formal structures of shared governance. For instance, program requirements for Head Start funds mandate the formation of a parents' advisory council to advise the governing board. This body, made up of member-participants, is required to approve local policies through mechanisms of shared governance (U.S. Department of Health and Human Services 2008). Additionally, in this age of technology, there appears to be no good reason why agencies cannot post policy proposals online and receive comments; this would constitute a virtual citizen jury such as that proposed by Fishkin or Beetham. Moreover, the sophisticated methods of analyzing and reviewing crime data in the COMPSTAT model could be directed toward the examination of citizen comments and input to get at the root causes of community problems. The intelligence analysis component will need to look at more than crime data; social data could have an important role too.

The issue of decentralization continues to pose problems for community policing (Gaines 1994; Bratton 1998). As identified by proponents of COMPSTAT, community policing decentralizes important community decisions to the lowest level of the organization (Weisburd et al. 2003; 2010). As Weisburd and others reported, many times these are the organization's least experienced people. While decentralization in theory made the individual officers more accessible to the people, it does not necessarily make the organization – or the institution of policing – more accessible to the citizens. However, to date I have found nothing in the literature that suggests structural changes to increase officer empowerment through decentralization necessarily requires police commanders and senior administrators to vacate an active role in community engagement or surrender responsibility for outcomes. I submit that what is often missing in community policing programs is sustained community engagement by the department's most senior administrators – that is, at the level at which power sharing can actually be realized. Incidentally, the research examined in preparing this work concerning levels of commitment to community policing's community engagement element held by senior police administrators consists almost exclusively of self-reported data.

COMMUNITY POLICING AS DEMOCRATIC POLICING: DEMOCRATIZATION IN PROGRESS

Several democratization scholars have noted the need for research into the relationship between the police and their role in the democratization process. For example, Larry Diamond has identified the role and relationship of the police in the development of democratic regimes as "a crucial and commonly overlooked arena" in studies of democratization (1999, 94). Similarly, Whitehead observes that ideas about "the nature of citizen security" have important implications for "processes of democratization" (2001, 171). The recognition that democratization processes are ongoing has important consequences when it comes to matters of governance and public administration. Because domestic security is an important goal of governance and public policy, and because coercive force is the key resource possessed by government to achieve that goal (and one that must be accounted for to the people), the manner in which this public good is provided becomes of critical concern to the citizens (Diamond 1999; Bayley 2006).

As previously observed in this work, many criminal justice scholars write about democracy and democratic policing as if it is a known quantity and definitively reified (Berkley 1969). It is difficult to gain a clear idea what democratic policing is while democratic theorists are still arguing about the nature of democracy. However, this is not to suggest that we abandon the examination. Democratization scholarship is most helpful in this regard. Allowing for a dynamic conceptualization of democracy, this arena of research points out that democratization is a "process" that no regime can claim to have completed entirely (Whitehead 2002, 6-7, 30-32). This approach seems to have borne itself out in the treatment of the idea of democracy and of a democratic police in the policing literature. Recall the metaphor used by Whitehead of the "anchored" but "floating" understanding of democracy (2002, 7). By "anchored" Whitehead means a "core of meaning" comprised of "ineliminable components" (2002, 7, 31). These consist of principles that constitute a democratic society's core values. These core principles embody prevailing norms and practices, which are in the near-term subject to a limited degree of "contestation" (Whitehead 2002, 7). However, over the long-term, changes in social "context" can create periods of conflict wherein practices believed consistent with these "ineliminable components" are challenged and change demanded (Whitehead 2002, 19).

Beyond this somewhat settled core are a host of issues to be decided before action is taken. It is here that Whitehead's "floating" conception of democracy "expresses ideals and values that are at least partially subjective and variable across time and space" (2002, 31). Over a long period, this can change conceptions of democracy on the periphery. Thus, "[d]eliberation arises not because of reasoning from first principles, or due to the creation of artificial institutions, but because it becomes necessary in order to tackle social needs" (Whitehead 2002, 24-25). Continuous and ongoing dialogue within a society that includes its government is fundamental to democracy and part of the democratization process. As Whitehead notes:

> [T]here is never any definite 'cut off point' beyond which the matter is settled beyond all further reconsiderations. On the contrary, even when the social consensus over a particular policy or a particular political discourse seems at its most overwhelming, the separate consciousness of individual citizens continue to engage in critical deliberation, rechecking, interrogating, and reinterpreting what seems to have been agreed. (Whitehead 2002, 18)

This is a view consistent with Gutmann and Thompson's position that deliberative democracy never considers matters closed forever, but fit subjects for ongoing dialogue (1996; 2004).

Not only is it important to study the treatment of ideas of democracy in the policing literature, but it will be important to continue doing so. Recent scholarship is beginning to reflect increased attention to the idea of democratic policing. While David H. Bayley's works are the earliest examples of this type of research, David Alan Sklansky's *Democracy and the Police* (2008) and longtime policing scholar Peter K. Manning's *Democratic Policing in a Changing World* (2010) are two recent examples well worth noting.

In the mid-1980s, a task force of law enforcement professionals and administrators began working with the U.S. Department of Justice's Community Relations Service to produce a generally acceptable set of "principles of good policing" (U.S. Department of Justice 2003). The idea was to reduce violence between citizens and the police and restore police credibity in the eyes of disaffected citizens. In 1993, the body produced a statement of seven principles of good policing (U.S. Department of Justice 2003). In 2003, a follow-up committee reiterated those seven principles (U.S. Department of Justice 2003).

The first principle of good policing holds that "[t]he police department must preserve and advance the principles of democracy" (U.S. Department of Justice 2003, 5). The body warned that American police officers "must" act consistent with "precious American values" in order to be considered democratic (2003, 5). Beyond that, they offered few details on the character of these values, other than to say the police should lead through right actions to "become the living expression of the meaning and potential of a democratic form of government;" this is particularly important in regard to "respecting" and "protecting" the Constitutional rights of citizens (2003, 5). That was the extent of the discussion on what democratic principles were. The fourth principle did call on police departments to "involve the community in the delivery of its services" (2003, 5). They direct the police to take concrete steps for "providing a mechanism for the community to collaborate with the police" (2003, 5). These mechanisms were what community policing was intended to be. Nevertheless, the specific "principles of democracy" that police departments are expected to "preserve and advance" as mandated by this first principle remains unspecified (U.S. Department of Justice 2003, 5).

Bayley's previously discussed work on police democratization is helpful in this regard, and suggests a specific rubric which is useful in assessing democratic performance (2001). In an effort to assist with the process of the democratization of foreign police forces, Bayley identified three key principles of democracy that represent the hallmark of a democratic police force. These concepts, summarized as the principles of *responsiveness, accountability,* and *transparency* are consistent with (and critical to) both community policing and deliberative democratic theory alike. It is critical to recognize that the people judge whether the police have met these standards to a satisfactory level, and they form opinions as to their legitimacy accordingly. These principles call for responsiveness to the people, accountability to the people, and transparency before the people. They may serve well as American policing's "ineliminable components" constituting "a core of meaning that is 'anchored'" (Whitehead 2002, 7, 31).

These principles have an enduring quality, and if deeply imbibed in the police culture may produce a degree of flexibility that allows the institution to recognize the need for and accommodate timely change. Community policing's community engagement component should be informed by these core values. These principles are actualized in the deliberative democratic process through the practice of authentic and ethical discourse (Chambers 1996; Held 2006). I submit that the promise of community policing as originally conceived will receive its highest expression through the adoption of deliberative democratic practices, transforming community policing from a tentative model of policing to a well-grounded theory of democratic policing.

STEPS IN THE RIGHT DIRECTION

A number of initiatives and efforts are underway that appear to align police practices with the recommendations of deliberative democratic thinkers. Included among those originating and leading these efforts are scholars, policymakers and practitioners. Many involve combinations of each. The International City/County Management Association (ICMA) has an official sub-group of its membership dedicated to increasing and improving citizen engagement in a variety of areas of local government. This emphasis is reflected in their journal *Public Management* where practitioners can routinely find articles that suggest ways to increase citizen engagement and public participation. In fact, that journal's March 2014 edition was dedicated thematically to the issues of "public participation [...] public engagement [and] civic discourse" (Vogel, Moulder, and Huggins 2014, 7). Not only did the edition report the findings of an ICMA sponsored survey on the topic (Vogel, Moulder, and Huggins 2014), a separate article offered citizen inclusion strategies useful in "community-based strategic planning" efforts (Novak 2014, 13).

Professional policing journals focusing on law enforcement practice and administration regularly address the issues of community engagement and public participation. The October 2013 issue of *The Police Chief*, a journal published by the International Association of Chiefs of Police (IACP), contained a series of thematically related articles on the issues of community engagement and public participation. Noteworthy pieces include an article by Georjean Trinkle and Todd A. Miller on ways to develop "comprehensive partnerships" and "collaborations" to "solve community issues" (2013, 26-27). They suggest a strategy that includes a carefully created coalition of diverse community partners to address problems. In another article, Hassan Aden describes the success he has enjoyed by including the community in the department's strategic planning process. This allows key groups and individuals to help set agency priorities and fosters support for their implementation (2013, 28-31). In yet another article, Jo Vitek suggests that such collaborative efforts should not be viewed solely as a means to decrease crime, but a way to increase "community capacity building" (2013, 50). In this piece, she recognizes that the activities of a police agency can be important to the economic health and viability of the community.

Each of these articles, without explicitly stating so, references an activity wholly in keeping the deliberative democratic practices. These likely emerged as commonsense responses on the part of practitioners to real-world situations. Clearly, they have enjoyed results. However, I believe there are two other particularly well structured initiatives gaining the attention of practitioners and scholars that merit detailed discussion.

The first concerns work in the area of procedural justice and police legitimacy. Tom R. Tyler, a leading scholar in this area, began his inquiries in the early 1990s. Numerous other scholars have since taken up these issues and extended the discussion to other related important subjects. The Police Executive Research Forum (PERF) and U.S. Department of Justice support this work, which focuses on the quality of the interaction between the police and the policed. Recently, the Office of Community Oriented Policing Services (COPS), an agency within the U.S. Department of Justice, announced the availability of grant funds for the purposes of furthering procedural justice efforts (U.S. Department of Justice – Office of Community Oriented Policing Services 2014).

The second involves the work of David M. Kennedy on what is popularly known as the High Point Strategy. This strategy for reducing violent and drug-related crime is also supported through technical assistance and funding by the U.S. Department of Justice (Kennedy and Wong [2009] 2012). What is interesting about these initiatives is that, while they have fundamentally different perspectives on criminological theory, they both provide an opportunity to engage in community policing in keeping with the deliberative methods suggested in this work.

Police Legitimacy and Procedural Justice

The seemly axiomatic observation that people are more likely to observe limits on their behavior when they believe those in authority have treated them fairly and justly demonstrates the importance of *legitimacy* in achieving compliance with the law. This is one of the important conclusions Tom R. Tyler reached when studying what motivates individuals to comply with legal constraints on their behavior ([1990] 2006; 2014). The findings of his research have received wide attention for their potential to improve the quality of the interaction between the police and the public (Tyler and Huo 2002; Sunshine and Tyler 2003; Tyler and Fagan 2008). Many law enforcement agencies and other organizations, such as the Police Executive Research Forum (PERF) and the U.S. Department of Justice, have seized on this to create and fund initiatives focused narrowly on this interaction (Tyler 2014). Because this interaction contains potential for deliberative dialog advocated by this work, further exploration of Tyler's work is warranted.

The path to Tyler's important findings originated in a study in which he questioned the role *deterrence* plays in achieving compliance with the law ([1990] 2006, 3-4, 269). The threat of sanction as a device to obtain compliance with the law has long propelled criminological theory and criminal justice policy (Tyler [1990] 2006, 269). However, as a compliance mechanism, *deterrence* requires a fundamentally utilitarian view of the individual, meaning basic human motivation centers on the enjoyment of pleasure and avoidance of pain. Tyler questions the health of societies that are heavily – or exclusively – dependent on a system of punishment to obtain compliance with the law. The "exercise [of] coercion" upon which punitive systems depend "consume[s] large amounts of public resources," risking serious deleterious side-effects in liberal societies (Tyler [1990] 2006, 23). Specifically he offers: "[I]n democratic societies the legal system cannot function if it can influence people only by manipulating rewards and costs" (Tyler [1990] 2006, 22). To that end, Tyler concluded that a self-regulating individual motivated by an "internalized obligation" to comport with the law was healthier for society because such voluntary behavior positively reinforce societal norms ([1990] 2006, 24-26).

Tyler argues that the individual's motivation to voluntarily comply with the law is heavily dependent on the perceived validity of the law, and by extension the authorities charged with ensuring compliance ([1990] 2006, 26). Tyler uses the term *legitimacy* to describe this perception. Relying on the thought of comparative political theorist David Easton, Tyler observes: "Legitimacy exists when the members of a society see adequate reason for feeling that they should voluntarily obey the commands of authorities" ([1990] 2006, 26). In his earliest works, Tyler indicates he is most concerned with discerning the factors that influence the individual's perceptions of legitimacy. Tyler suggests that, when it comes to the police, this perception is influenced by "three judgments" individuals make (2014, 9). First, it reflects a "belief that the police are honest" and worthy of the public's "trust and confidence" (Tyler 2014, 9). Secondly, the presence of legitimacy suggests a measure of "defer[ence] to the law and to police authority" (Tyler 2014, 9). Thirdly, the situational subjective validation of legitimacy reflects a belief that the decisions and activities of the police are "justified and appropriate to the circumstances" (Tyler 2014, 9).

Before proceeding, it is important to recognize Tyler's thought and research focuses on the transactional level. His goal was the empirical study of contributors to those feelings of legitimacy. Therefore, as his unit of analysis was the individual, he intentionally avoids political and institutional theory ([1990] 2006, 27-30). This has important implications for his findings concerning the ways in which legitimacy is perceived and reinforced in individuals. In more recent literature, greater attention has been paid to political theory as it pertains to the concept of legitimacy, and particularly the dialogical approach (Bottoms and Tankebe 2012; Tankebe and Liebling 2013).

In his earliest study and in those conducted since, Tyler finds that the perception of legitimacy was dependent on how the individual felt they were treated when conflict arose. In fact, he found the ultimate outcome – or decision – made by the authorities was less important than the process that was used to arrive at that conclusion ([1990] 2006; 2014). Tyler uses the term *procedural justice* to describe the process by which authoritative decisions are made, which serve to engender feelings of legitimacy. Particularly, four key features of the transaction with the police tend to support perceptions of legitimacy. First, people want to have an opportunity to "tell their side of the story" (Tyler 2014, 9). Being fully and fairly heard is only part of the individual's expectation. An unbiased neutral hearing by the decision maker is the second element of the process. Included in this is the importance of "transparency" on the part of decision makers concerning the rules and principles by which arguments will be judged (Tyler 2014, 10). Thirdly, the manner in which the individual is treated during the process is important. When decision makers treat people with dignity and respect, it communicates to the individual that the authority values them as a person and does not view them as merely a problem to be dealt with or an opportunity for the exercise of official power. This is related to the final element of procedural justice. When treated fairly and justly in the manner described above, trust is fostered between the individual and the authority. This trust grows "when they believe the authorities with whom they are interacting are benevolent and caring, and are sincerely trying to do what is best for the people with whom they are dealing" (Tyler 2014, 10).

The linkage between legitimacy and procedural justice underpins much of Tyler's efforts and is useful in explaining and understanding multiple aspects of support for the law and the authorities. In addition to explaining why people voluntarily comply with the law ([1990] 2006), this template has been used to explain how the police can ease acceptance of authoritative decisions (Tyler and Huo 2002). In other studies conducted since, the foundation laid by Tyler is used to provide insight into why individuals are willing to cooperate with the police and how best to foster that cooperation (Tyler and Fagan 2008). This has important implications for projects and initiatives such as community policing and encouraging individuals to report crime. In still another study, the framework is used to explain how the police can enhance institutional support (Sunshine and Tyler 2003). In all of these studies, the focus is on the quality of the interaction between the individual and those in authority. Recent scholarship is now paying attention to the important role dialogue plays in achieving legitimacy (Bottoms and Tankabe 2012). Deliberative democratic theory may have much to offer in this regard.

The High Point Strategy

Where Tyler questions the validity of deterrence based models of criminological theory and policy, David M. Kennedy takes the opposite approach (Kennedy 2009a). The High Point Strategy for reducing violent and drug related crime has as its central feature the strategic and aggressive use of deterrence to target and dissuade likely offenders (Kennedy 2009a). The program calls for extensive meetings and group interactions between various community stakeholders before and during the operational phases (Kennedy 2009a). An occasion exists here for the type of deliberative dialogue suggested by this work. A brief discussion of the High Point Strategy offers insight into the opportunities it presents.

The High Point Strategy, as it is commonly known, is a Drug Market Intervention Initiative (DMI) that takes its name from the first city in which it was implemented – High Point, North Carolina (Chambers 2010). This initiative is a multi-step strategy designed to reduce crime – particularly violent crime – associated with "overt drug markets" (Kennedy and Wong [2009] 2012, 4; Chambers 2010). It was the identification of the "overt market" as the problem's key feature rather than the drugs themselves that represented the first departure from the standard understanding of the issue of drug related violent crime (Kennedy and Wong [2009] 2012, 7). This starting point would lead to the discovery of other misunderstandings about criminogenic factors surrounding drug related crime (Kennedy 2009a).

The "overt market" itself was found to exist in a social context that led to its perpetuation and toleration. First, these markets are generally known and easily accessible to those wishing to purchase illicit drugs. "Overt markets" are generally found "in poor, minority communities and have clearly defined geographical boundaries" (Kennedy and Wong [2009] 2012, 7). They possess "strong self-sustaining dynamics [in that] [b]uyers know that they can buy in a particular area and sellers know that they can sell there" (Kennedy and Wong [2009] 2012, 7). These geographical areas are commonly known by consumers and law enforcement officials alike, as they are routinely the subject of intensive enforcement efforts – intense to the point of seeming oppressive to area residents (Kennedy and Wong [2009] 2012). Traditional efforts include "high levels of street stops, vehicle stops, and warrants served on residents, and frequently leads to high levels of arrest, conviction, probation, incarceration, and parole, especially for younger men" (Kennedy and Wong [2009] 2012, 8).

Probably most damaging to the fabric of the neighborhood are "zero-tolerance" initiatives, designed to make arrests for all observed violations regardless of their severity (Chambers 2010, 25). The hope of this strategy is to displace the criminal element. It is not unusual for these initiatives to deploy high numbers of police officers, concentrating them in a given geographical area. This increases the probability of a citizen encounter with the authorities. A consequence of such enforcement effort's intensity is that "law abiding members of the community often had hostile encounters with the police" (Chambers 2010, 25). Moreover, the net effect of these efforts was to work at the edges of the problem without getting to the heart of the issue.

The heart of the issue, in Kennedy's estimation, was not that deterrence did not work, but that it had been inadvertently – yet systematically – destroyed through "intensive [...] enforcement efforts" and "ineffective [...] sanctions" (2009a, 63). Moreover, as the subjects of these enforcement efforts trend toward minority groups in disproportionate numbers, understandings of what constitutes normal can change over time. This is what Kennedy refers to as "the erosion of stigma" (2009a, 63). That is to say, once a significant portion of a group bears the stigma, it can "become normative, taking on the status of a 'rite of passage'" (Kennedy 2009a, 63). In this way is "stigma [...] converted to standing" and a seemingly new societal norm gradually evolves that stands in contrast to other sectors of the community (Kennedy 2009a, 65). Once generalized, this *standing* is perceived as tolerance if not outright acceptance of drug dealing by those who are in some manner associated with the offenders. When objections are not registered through informal social mechanisms, silence is interpreted as assent and a counter-culture evolves. The assumption is often made by those outside the neighborhood that those closest to the offender support criminality and do not support the law or enforcement efforts. As Kennedy finds through the High Point initiative, this is very often not true (Kennedy and Wong [2009] 2012; Kennedy 2009a; Kennedy 2009b). This became clear during a series of meetings between the community and law enforcement officials as part of the initiative. It should be noted that these meetings provide an extraordinary opportunity for deliberative democratic thinkers wishing to work in the public safety context.

David M. Kennedy, architect of the High Point Strategy, maintained the key to addressing the central issue was to "create" and then "mobilize deterrence" (Kennedy and Wong [2009] 2012, 22; Kennedy 2009a, 131). In the multi-stage process of the High Point Strategy, the most serious and violent offenders – which are usually relatively few – are arrested and adjudicated swiftly. This effectively removes them from the overt drug market environment. Next, the lower-level offenders are identified. These offenders are targeted through normal methods and cases produced through the usual methods all the way to the point where they would normally be filed for prosecution (Kennedy and Wong [2009] 2012).

However, prior to prosecution the targeted offenders are sent letters advising them that they have been caught and that a criminal charge could be filed. Instead of filing the case, the offender and key "influentials" – those previously identified individuals believed to be in a position to help the offender rehabilitate without incarceration – are invited to a meeting where they are told the case will be placed in a suspended status ("banked") unless the offender reoffends (Kennedy and Wong [2009] 2012, 22-24). Rather than relying on the individual to rationally refrain from contemplated criminal conduct because of the possibility of incurring sanctions, this form of deterrence dissuades future offenses because the individual knows "ahead of time" – practically "certain" – they will face sanctions (Kennedy and Wong [2009] 2012, 23).

The Bureau of Justice Assistance appropriately named the High Point Strategy a Drug Market *Intervention* Initiative (my emphasis added). The *intervention* is critical to the outcome. Indeed, it could be argued that the success of the initiative turns entirely upon the success of this one element. The intervention, termed "the call-in," is where "law enforcement, community members, and services providers deliver a unified message" (Kennedy and Wong [2009] 2012, 25). However, the process of creating this unified message calls for another type of intervention. Indeed, it is in creating the process through which the community prepares for this encounter that deliberative democratic theorists may have much to offer.

In preparing for High Point's call-in, several meetings were held with key community members, residents of the affected area, social service providers, and law enforcement officials. It was during the preparation for these meetings that Kennedy uncovered what he termed the "norms and narratives" of each group (Kennedy and Wong [2009] 2012, 8). These consist of the beliefs and assumptions each group holds about the other groups, including their assumptions as to how they are viewed by other groups (Kennedy and Wong [2009] 2012, 8-11). Moreover, Kennedy determined that the assumptions each group held for the other "were wrong" and that compounding "the problem was that none of the [...] groups told the other groups how they saw the other" (Chambers 2010, 26). Frank discussions were held, facilitated by Kennedy, wherein each group disclosed these views. Myths were dispelled and common ground found and articulated. This became the basis of the unified message delivered to offenders during the call-in and reinforced in a multitude of venues, public and private.

Sustaining the initiative's positive gains requires the re-writing of old and aberrant norms with explicitly stated and informally reinforced social norms consistent with the goals of the strategy (Kennedy 2009a, 130-134). This evidences a belief that the best source of deterrence comes from a society that will self-mobilize to condemn behavior that deviates from the norm and is not depend solely on authoritative action or official sanction. Kennedy observes this in his reflections on the High Point initiative, stating, "[t]he community is infinitely tougher than anyone else could ever be" (2009b, 16). This transfer from formal control by authorities to the more effective informal social control brings to mind an observation made by George Orwell, who wrote:

> In a society in which there is no law, and in theory no compulsion, the only arbiter of behavior is public opinion. But public opinion, because of the tremendous urge to conformity in gregarious animals, is less tolerant than any system of law. (Orwell [1946] 2008, 305)

The success of the High Point Strategy is widely acknowledged. It is one of the most promising initiatives ever instituted to combat drug related violence and crime, and its success has been largely replicated in other jurisdictions (Kennedy and Wong [2009] 2012, 43; Kennedy 2009b, 17). Kennedy, buoyed by the success of his model, asserted the following in a 2009 meeting of the National Network for Safe Communities: "This is no longer a strategy. It is a movement" (Chambers 2010, 23). This movement has much in common with community policing as previously practiced. It also presents many opportunities for a new community policing model through the employment of ethical discourse in the service of deliberative dialogue as recommended in this work.

AVENUES FOR FUTURE RESEARCH

In the 1960s and 1970s, scholars such as Jerome Skolnick (1966), James Q. Wilson (1968) and Albert Reiss (1971) studied the social aspects of the police culture. It would be worthwhile to revisit this type of work, not for the purpose of replication but rather to take a fresh look at the social and psychological aspects of police officers and the police culture. There is a limited amount of research in this area. An example of interesting research in this vein is offered by the Center for the Application of Personality Types. This organization conducts original research and analysis of data from other studies using the Myers-Briggs Type Indicator (MBTI) results for police officers (Hennessy 1999). This research uses the MBTI to dispel the myth that police officers are "cold, condescending, matter-of-fact, and without compassion" (Hennessy 1999, x). This line of research is of use in the recruiting, retention, and training of police officers (Hennessy 1999, x-xi). It is also helpful to the leadership and administration of police organizations (Hennessy 1999; Lynch and Lynch 2005). An example of research findings that offer insight useful in this regard is presented by Lynch and Lynch (2005), who report MBTI analysis findings that detected "introverts" were over-represented in the police ranks when compared with the general population (2005, 146). If this is the case, this cannot help but have ramifications for the community engagement component of community policing, and may go a long way toward explaining the phenomenon observed by so much of the research and the commission findings that officers are too often rather disconnected from the communities they serve (Kelling 2003).

The second and arguably most important avenue of research concerns the contribution an analysis of community policing's history would provide to change management scholarship. The practice of community policing emerged from a decade marked by social strife that was at times violent. The 1960s and early 1970s was a "crucible" in which the police dealt with the effects of riots, assassinations of major leaders, and an increase in crime (Rumbaut and Bittner 1979, 241). In the wake of pervasive social discord, changes in police practices should have had the best chances of taking hold. The call for change appears to have enjoyed wide support from the citizens, the media, politicians, and even within policing itself. So how did a promising initiative enjoying such widespread support falter and in due course fade?

The methods of historical institutionalism are useful in this regard. Scholarship in American Political Development and the history of ideas makes use of the historical institutional method. Using this framework, one could examine the treatment of citizen involvement in American policing as reflected in theory and practice (Pierson 2000a, 2000b, 2004). This approach holds that historical sequencing is critical to understanding political and social phenomena and is useful for illuminating why one historical trajectory was chosen over another (Pierson and Skocpol 2002). Once that path is chosen, it tends to replicate and reinforce itself over time. This is referred to as "path dependence" (Pierson 2000a; 2000b; 2004). Additionally, changes to that trajectory may be difficult to achieve because gains may reinforce the current path, making it economically irrational to change course (Pierson 2000b). Pierson refers to this as "increasing returns" (2000b).

Historical institutionalism takes particular issue with other social change theories which hold that large changes have, at their root, large causes (Pierson 2000b, 251). Historical institutionalism maintains that significant and lasting change does not necessarily arise from some event of great magnitude; rather, the reverse is often the case (Pierson 2000b). Social changes take place over time – often from small origins – and the sequence of events plays a large role in the outcome (Tilly 1984; Pierson 2000a, 2004; Pierson and Skocpol 2002). In Pierson's words, "history matters" (2000b, 252). Opportunity for change presents itself at key moments in history, points in time which are referred to as "critical junctures" (Pierson 2000b, 263; Capoccia and Kelemen 2007, 348).

Critical junctures are "qualitatively different from the 'normal' historical development of the institutional setting" and uniformly consist of *"relatively* short periods of time during which there is a *substantially* heightened probability that agents' choices will affect the outcome" (Capoccia and Kelemen 2007, 348). In the social and political setting critical junctures can appear when "authorities collide and standards of legitimacy abrade" (Orren and Skowronek 2002, 748). However, "a tipping point is not a critical juncture," nor is "change [...] a necessary element of a critical juncture" (Capoccia and Kelemen 2007, 351, 352). Indeed, although all the conditions may be present for change, that change may not actually materialize. This is a condition Capoccia and Kelemen refer to as "near misses" (2007, 352).

Historical institutional analysis may help explain the case of American policing's *near miss* encounter with the change that community policing was supposed to bring. One hypothesis is that at the point American policing was weakened to the point where it was ripe for change, complementary institutions stepped in to prop up the existing arrangements. Pierson refers to this as an "institutional density" argument (2000b, 259). These may be "[b]oth formal institutions [...] and public policies [that] place extensive, legally binding constraints on behavior" (2000b 259). Local governments and the courts represent two such entities that place weighty (possibly unwitting) demands on policing that can serve as a countervailing force against change. If local governments encourage community policing efforts, but punish inefficiency, the net policy effect may be to move away from the conflict-ridden din community engagement can be. At the same time, court cases have increased procedural safeguards to protect against wrongful convictions. These extend from the technical and scientific aspects of evidentiary matters to the addition of procedural requirements on the investigative process. In sum, there is an increased reliance on the technical aspects of policing, which generally calls for greater training and professionalism. These complementary institutions – local governments and the courts – may well have served as crutches, allowing the weakened institution of American policing to weather the storm until it could regain its strength and continue on its path.

Reflections

The change that appeared so promising in American policing may represent a "near miss" as defined by Capoccia and Kelemen (2007, 352). Unfortunately, deliberative democratic theory had not sufficiently developed to the point it was available to shore up community policing practice. They have much in common in their connection to democracy. Community policing and democratic theory share a similar problem in that they are often discussed with imprecision and can both be difficult to measure (Alpert and Moore [1993] 2000; Thurman and Reisig 1996; Whitehead 2002). This appears to be a clue to a relationship between the two. Community policing and deliberative democracy are both broadly used practices, but the latter practice is grounded in theory. It demonstrates that on matters of theory, the scholarship in deliberative democracy has a better foundation upon which to build and critically diagnose problems.

Deliberative democratic theory has much to offer scholars intent on salvaging the idea of community policing, provided policing is ready to jettison a single counterproductive ideal – namely, an overemphasis on the ideal of efficiency when it comes to community engagement. By reviewing the history of community policing subsequent to a deep discussion on deliberative democratic theory, I believe the reader sees what is missing and how deliberative democratic theory fills the void.

This *near miss* is terribly disappointing when considering how close deliberative democracy and community policing came early on. For example, in the 1967 Task Force Report, the committee reports on the positive effects of "neighborhood committees," (1967a, 157) stating:

> Neighborhood committees also allow the police and public to consider the enforcement of minor crimes statutes in the area. There is a measure of discretion in the way these ordinances are enforced that allows the police to take account of community mores, cultural patterns, poverty, and housing conditions. Open discussion with neighborhood residents as to what their tolerance is for noise, for drunks on the streets, or for youths congregating on hot summer nights will help to produce law enforcement which protects rather than harasses the residents and induces citizens to aid and respect, rather than harass, the police. Where police discretion is involved, an

accurate reading of community sentiments is an invaluable guide to the law enforcement officer. [...] This lesson is brought home by an incident in 1966 in Perth Amboy, N.J. A newly enacted antiloitering ordinance was applied to Puerto Rican slum dwellers whose leisure time was often spent in street socializing. After disturbances occurred and large numbers of police had to be assigned to that area every night, city officials finally agreed to redraft the ordinance and submit it to Puerto Rican representatives for their comments. (1967a, 157)

In the post 9/11 era a balance is lacking, as the concern for justice and subjective legitimacy in American policing are gradually taking a back seat to a demand for efficiency. I argue that this replacement represents a return to an earlier model of policing, and therefore puts us at some avoidable risk should tumultuous times return. The community engagement component of community policing represented American policing's closest encounter with a more democratic and less technocratic form of policing. Trojanowicz and Bucqueroux made essentially the same point when they offered, "community policing is a [...] philosophy" and "not a technique" (1990, 5, 20). I offer, and have argued, that recent works concerning the democratization of foreign police agencies are relevant to American policing because they apply in equal measure to community policing and deliberative democratic practices (Bayley 2001, 2006). Deliberative democratic practices offer mechanisms to actualize the core democratic principles of responsiveness, accountability and transparency identified by Bayley (2001), thereby fulfilling the promise of community policing. The idea of "discourse ethics," fundamental to Habermas's idea of deliberative democratic theory, is equally vital to achieving the goals of community policing ([1983] 1990). Less than forthright engagement in discourse and deliberations with the community many again threaten to undermine American policing's legitimacy. Through the systemic application of more mature deliberative democratic practices, community policing can become much more than a model of policing. It can become the central force behind of a new vision of democratic policing.

References

Ackerman, Bruce and James S. Fishkin. [2002] 2003. Deliberation day. In *Debating Deliberative Democracy*, ed. James S. Fishkin and Peter Laslett, 7-30. Malden, MA: Blackwell Publishing.

Adams, Brian. 2004. Public meetings and the democratic process. *Public Administration Review* 64, no. 1 (January/February): 43-54.

Adams, Richard E., William M. Rohe and Thomas A. Arcury. 2002. Implementing community-oriented policing: Organizational change and street officer attitudes. *Crime & Delinquency* 48: 399-430.

Aden, Hassan. 2013. Inviting the community into the police strategic planning process. *The Police Chief* 80, no. 10 (October 2013): 28-31.

Almond, Gabriel A. 1990. *A Discipline Divided: Schools and Sects in Political Science*. Newbury Park, CA: Sage Publications.

Almond, Gabriel A., G. Bingham Powell, Jr., Kaare Strom and Russell J. Dalton. 2001. *Comparative Politics: A Theoretical Framework*. 3rd ed. New York: Longman.

Alpert, Geoffrey P. and Mark H. Moore. [1993] 2000. Measuring police performance in the new paradigm of policing. In *Community Policing: Contemporary Readings*, eds. Geoffery P. Alpert and Alex R. Piquero, 2nd ed., 215-232. Prospect Heights, IL: Waveland Press.

Alterman, Eric. 2002. Rawls and us. *The Nation* 275, no. 22 (December 23, 2002): 10-10.

Amir, Menachem and Stanley Einstein. 2001. Introduction. In *Policing, Security and Democracy: Theory and Practice*, eds. Menachem Amir and Stanley Einstein, 13-16. Huntsville, TX: Office of International Criminal Justice.

Ammons, David N. 1996. *Municipal Benchmarks: Assessing Local Performance and Establishing Community Standards*. Thousand Oaks, CA: Sage Publications, Inc.

Angell, John E. 1971. Toward an alternative to the classic police organizational arrangements. *Criminology* 9, no. 2-3 (August-November): 185-206.

Bacon, Seldon D. 1939. *The Early Development of American Municipal Police: A Study of the Evolution of Formal Controls in a Changing Society (Volumes I and II)*. PhD diss., Yale University. In ProQuest Dissertations and Theses, http://proquest.umi.com. libproxy. utdallas.edu/pqdweb?index=6&did=756595031& Srch Mode=1&sid=1&Fmt=6&VInst=PROD&VType=PQD&RQT=30 9&VName=PQD&TS=1339117785&clientId=10361 (accessed June 7, 2012).

Bailey, Kenneth D. 1994. *Methods of Social Research*. 4th ed. New York: The Free Press.

Barany, Zoltan. 1997. Democratic consolidation and the military: The East European experience. *Comparative Politics* 30, no.1 (October): 21-43.

Barlow, Hugh D. 1984. Theories of crime I: Foundations of modern criminology. In *Introduction to Criminology*, 3rd ed., 23-60. Boston: Little, Brown and Company

Bayley, David H. 1979. Police function, structure and control in Western Europe and North America: Comparative and historical studies. *Crime & Justice* 1: 109-143.

──────. 2001. *Democratizing the Police Abroad: What to Do and How to Do It*. Washington, D.C.: National Institute of Justice.

──────. 2006. *Changing the Guard: Developing Democratic Police Abroad*. New York: Oxford University Press.

Bayley, David H. and Clifford D. Shearing. 1996. The future of policing. *Law & Society Review* 30, no. 3: 585-606.

Berkley, George E. 1969. *The Democratic Policeman*. Boston, MA: Beacon Press.

Beetham, David. 2005. *Democracy*. Oxford: Oneworld.

Bessette, Joseph M. 1980. Deliberative democracy: The majority principle in republican government. In *How Democratic is the Constitution?* ed. Robert A. Goldwin and William A. Schambra, 102-116. Washington, D.C.: American Enterprise Institute for Public Policy Research.

———. 1994. *The Mild Voice of Reason: Deliberative Democracy and American National Government*. Chicago: University of Chicago Press.

Bohman, James. 1998. Survey article: The coming of age of deliberative democracy. *Journal of Political Philosophy* 6, no. 4: 400-425.

———. 2003. Deliberative toleration. *Political Theory* 31, no. 6 (December): 757-779.

Bohman, James and William Rehg. 1997. Introduction. In *Deliberative Democracy: Essays on Reason and Politics*, eds. James Bohman and William Rehg, ix-xxx. Cambridge, MA: The MIT Press.

———. 2011. Jürgen Habermas. *Stanford Encyclopedia of Philosophy*. September 6, 2011. http://plato.standford.edu/archives/win2011/entries /habermas/. (accessed May 1, 2012).

Bottoms, Anthony and Justice Tankebe. 2012. Beyond procedural justice: A dialogic approach to legitimacy in criminal justice. *The Journal of Criminal Law & Criminology* 102, no. 1: 119-170.

Braga, Anthony A. 2010. Setting a higher standard for the evaluation of problem-oriented policing initiatives. *Criminology & Public Policy* 9, no. 1: 173-182.

Bratton, William. 1998. *Turnaround: How America's Top Cop Reversed the Crime Epidemic*. New York: Random House.

Burruss, George W. and Matthew J. Gilbin. 2009. Modeling isomorphism on policing innovation: The role of institutional pressures in adopting community-oriented policing. *Crime & Delinquency*, (14 July 2009): 1-25.

Capoccia, Giovanni and R. Daniel Kelemen. 2007. The study of critical junctures: Theory, narrative, and counterfactuals in historical institutionalism. *World Politics* 59, no. 3 (April): 341-369.

Carter, David L. and James S. Albritton. 1999. Community policing: A more efficacious police response or simply inflated promises. In *Controversial Issues in Policing*, ed. James D. Sewell, 206-223. Needham Heights, MA: Allyn and Bacon.

Carter, David L. and Jeremy G. Carter. 2009. Intelligence-led policing: Conceptual and functional considerations for public policy. *Criminal Justice Policy Review* 20, no. 3 (September): 310-325.

Celador, Gemma Collantes. 2005. Police reform: Peacebuilding through 'Democratic Policing'? *International Peacekeeping* 12, no.3 (Autumn): 364-376.

Chambers, Simone. 1996. *Reasonable Democracy: Jürgen Habermas and the Politics of Discourse*. Ithaca, NY: Cornell University Press.

――――――. 2003. Deliberative democratic theory. *Annual Review of Political Science* 6: 307-326.

Chambers, Tate. 2010. The High Point strategy: Its creation, implementation, and future. *The United States Attorneys' Bulletin* 58, no. 2 (March 2010): 23-36.

Cohen, Joshua. [1989] 1997. Deliberation and democratic legitimacy. In *Deliberative Democracy: Essays on Reason and Politics*, ed. James Bohman and William Relig, 67-92. Cambridge, MA: MIT Press.

――――――. [1996] 1997. Procedure and substance in deliberative democracy. In *Deliberative Democracy: Essays on Reason and Politics*, ed. James Bohman and William Relig, 407-437. Cambridge, MA: MIT Press.

Cooper, Terry L., Thomas A. Bryer and Hack W. Meek. 2006. Citizen-centered collaborative public management. *Public Administration Review* 66, Special Issue (December): 76-88.

Cordner, Gary W. 1992. Human resource issues. In *Police Management: Issues & Perspectives*, ed. Larry T. Hoover, 227-249. Washington, DC: Police Executive Research Forum.

Cordner, Gary and Elizabeth Perkins Biebel. 2005. Problem-oriented policing in practice. *Criminology & Public Policy* 4, no. 2 (May): 155-180.

Crank, John P. 1994. Watchman and community: Myth and institutionalization in policing. *Law & Society Review* 28, no. 2: 325-351.

Dabney, Dean. 2010. Observations regarding key operational realities in a compstat model of policing. *Justice Quarterly* 27, no. 1 (February): 28-51.

Dahl, Robert A. 1998. *On Democracy*. New Haven: Yale University Press.

Dai, Mengyan and Richard R. Johnson. 2009. Is neighborhood context a confounder? Exploring the effects of citizen race and neighborhood context on satisfaction with the police. *Policing: An International Journal of Police Strategy & Management* 32, no. 4: 595-612.

Davis, Diane E. 2006. Undermining the rule of law: Democratization and the dark side of police reform in Mexico. *Latin American Politics & Society* 48, no.1 (Spring): 55-86.

Diamond, Larry. 1997. Consolidating democracy in the Americas. *Annuals of the American Academy of Political and Social Science* 550, (March): 12-41.

———. 1999. *Developing Democracy: Toward Consolidation.* Baltimore: Johns Hopkins University Press.

———. 2002. Advancing Democratic Governance: A Global Perspective on the Status of Democracy and Directions for International Assistance March 2002. http://www.stanford.edu/~ldiamond/papers/advancing_democ_governance.pdf (accessed November 26, 2007).

———. 2005. Lessons from Iraq. *Journal of Democracy* 16, no.1 (January): 9-23.

Diamond, Larry, Seymour Martin Lipset and Juan Linz. 1987. Building and sustaining democratic government in developing countries: Some tentative findings. *World Affairs* 150, no.1 (Summer): 5-19.

Dicker, Todd J. 1998. Tension on the thin blue line: Police officer resistance to community-oriented policing. *American Journal of Criminal Justice* 23, no. 1: 59-82.

Dodsworth, Francis M. 2004. 'Civic' police and the condition of liberty: The rationality of governance in eighteenth-century England. *Social History* 29, no. 2 (May): 199-216.

Downing, Brian M. 1992. *The Military Revolution and Political Change: Origins of Democracy and Autocracy in Early Modern Europe.* Princeton, NJ: Princeton University Press.

Doyle, Michael W. and Nicholas Sambanis. 2000. International peacebuilding: A theoretical and quantitative analysis. *American Political Science Review* 94, no.4 (December): 779-801.

Dryzek, John S. 1987. Discursive designs: Critical theory and political institutions. *American Journal of Political Science* 31, no. 3 (August): 656-679.

———. 2000. *Deliberative Democracy: Liberals, Critics, Contestations.* Oxford: Oxford University Press.

———. 2001. Legitimacy and economy in deliberative democracy. *Political Theory* 29, no. 5: 651-669.

———. 2010. Mini-publics and their macro consequences. In *Foundations and Frontiers of Deliberative Governance*, ed. John Dryzek with Simon Neimeyer, 155-176. Oxford: Oxford University Press.

Dryzek, John S. and Simon Neimeyer. 2010. Representation. In *Foundations and Frontiers of Deliberative Governance*, ed. John Dryzek with Simon Neimeyer, 42-65. Oxford: Oxford University Press.

Eck, John E. and Dennis P. Rosenbaum. 1994. The new police order: Effectiveness, equity, and efficiency in community policing. In *The Challenges of Community Policing*, ed. Dennis P. Rosenbaum, 3-23. Thousand Oaks, CA: Sage Publications.

Elster, Jon. [1986] 1997. The market and the forum: Three varieties of political theory. In *Deliberative Democracy*, eds. James Bohman and William Rehg, 3-34. Cambridge, MA: MIT Press.

———. 1998. Introduction. In *Deliberative Democracy*, ed. Jon Elster, 1-18. Cambridge: Cambridge University Press.

Fearon, James. 1998. Deliberation as discussion. In *Deliberative Democracy*, ed. Jon Elster, 44-68. Cambridge: Cambridge University Press.

Ferguson, Kristin M. and Charles H. Mindel. 2007. Modeling fear of crime in Dallas neighborhoods: A test of social capital theory. *Crime & Delinquency* 23, no. 2 (April): 322-349.

Findley, Kenneth W. and Robert W. Taylor. 1990. Re-thinking neighborhood policing. *Journal of Contemporary Criminal Justice* 6, no. 2 (May): 70-78.

Fishkin, James S. 1991. *Democracy and Deliberation: New Directions for Democratic Reform*. New Haven: Yale University Press.

Forester, John. 1999. *The Deliberative Practitioner: Encouraging Participatory Planning Processes*. Cambridge, MA: MIT Press.

Freeman, Samuel. 2000. Deliberative democracy: A sympathetic comment. *Philosophy and Public Affairs* 29, no.4 (Autumn): 371-418.

Gaines, Larry. 1994. Community-oriented policing: Management issues, concerns, and problems. *Journal of Contemporary Criminal Justice* 10, no. 1 (February): 17-35.

Garland, David. 2001. *The Culture of Control: Crime and Social Order in Contemporary Society*. Chicago: University of Chicago Press.

Gau, Jacinta M. and Rod K. Brunson. 2010. Procedural justice and order maintenance policing: A study of inner-city young men's perceptions of police legitimacy. *Justice Quarterly* 27, no. 2 (April): 255-279.

Germann, A.C. 1969. Community policing: An assessment. *Journal of Criminal Law* 60, no. 1 (March): 89-96.

Giblin, Matthew J. and George W. Burruss. 2009. Developing a measurement model of institutional processes in policing. *Policing: An International Journal of Police Strategies & Management* 32. no. 2: 351-376.

Giliomee, Hermann. 1995. Democratization in South Africa. *Political Science Quarterly* 110, no.1 (Spring): 83-104.

Glaser, Mark A. and Janet Denhardt. 2010. Community policing and community building: A case study of officer perceptions. *American Review of Public Administration* 40, no. 3 (May): 309-325.

Goldsmith, Andrew. 2005. Police reform and the problem of trust. *Theoretical Criminology* 9, no. 4: 443-470.

Goldstein, Herman. 1977. *Policing a Free Society*. Cambridge, MA: Ballinger Publishing.

——. 1979. Improving policing: A problem-oriented approach. *Crime & Delinquency* 25, no. 2 (April): 236-258.

——. 1987. Toward community-oriented policing: Potential, basic requirements, and threshold questions. *Crime & Delinquency* 33, no. 1 (January): 6-30.

——. 1990. *Problem-Oriented Policing*. New York: McGraw-Hill.

——. 2008. How I got here. *Gargoyle* 33, no. 2 (Winter/Spring): 16-21.

Greene, Jack R., William T. Bergman and Edward J. McLaughlin. 1994. Implementing community policing. In *The Challenge of Community Policing: Testing the Promises*, ed. Dennis P. Rosenbaum, 92-109. Thousand Oaks, CA: Sage Publications.

Gutmann, Amy and Dennis Thompson. 1996. *Democracy and Disagreement: Why Moral Conflict Cannot be Avoided in Politics, and What Should be Done About It*. Cambridge: Belknap Press.

——. 2004. *Why Deliberative Democracy?* Princeton: Princeton University Press.

Habermas, Jürgen. [1962] 1991. *The Structural Transformation of the Public Sphere: An Inquiry into a Category of Bourgeois Society.* trans. Thomas Burger with assistance of Frederick Lawrence. Cambridge, MA: The MIT Press.
———. [1971] 1973. *Legitimation Crisis.* trans. Thomas McCarthy. Boston: Beacon Press.
———. [1983] 1990. *Moral Consciousness and Communicative Action.* trans. Christian Lenhardt and Sherry Weber Nicholsen. Cambridge, MA: MIT Press.
———. [1990] 1993. *Justification and Application: Remarks on Discourse Ethics.* trans. Ciaran P. Cronin. Cambridge, MA: MIT Press.
———. [1992] 1996. *Between Facts and Norms: Contributions to a Discourse Theory of Law and Democracy,* trans. William Rehg. Cambridge, MA: MIT Press.
Hampton, Jean. 1997. *Political Philosophy.* Boulder, CO: Westview Publishing.
Harcourt, Bernard E. 2001. *Illusion of Order: The False Promise of Broken Windows Policing.* Cambridge, MA: Harvard University Press.
Harris, David A. 2010. Law enforcement and intelligence gathering in Muslim and immigrant communities after 9/11. *New York University Review of Law & Social Change* 34: 123-190.
Hawdon, James and John Ryan. 2003. Police-resident interactions and satisfaction with police: An empirical test of community policing assertions. *Criminal Justice Policy Review* 14, no. 1 (March): 55-74.
Held, David. 2006. *Models of Democracy,* 3rd ed. Stanford, CA: Stanford University Press.
Hennessy, Stephen M. 1999. *Thinking Cop Feeling Cop: A Study of Police Personalities.* 3rd ed. Gainsville, FL: Center for Applications of Psychological Types, Inc.
Herbert, Steve. 2006a. *Citizens, Cops, and Power: Recognizing the Limits of Community.* Chicago: University of Chicago Press.
———. 2006b. Tangled up in blue: Conflicting paths to police legitimacy. *Theoretical Criminology* 10, no. 4: 481-504.

Hinkle, Joshua C. and David Weisburd. 2008. The irony of broken windows policing: A micro-place study of the relationship between disorder, focused police crackdowns and fear of crime. *Journal of Criminal Justice* 36, no. 6 (November): 503-512.

Hirschman, Albert O. 1970. *Exit, Voice, and Loyalty: Responses to Decline in Forms, Organizations, and States*. Cambridge, MA: Harvard University Press.

Hiskey, Jonathan T. and Shaun Bowler. 2005. Local context and democratization in Mexico. *American Journal of Political Science* 49, no.1 (January): 57-71.

Hume, Lisa and Michael Miklaucic. 2005. Exorcising Demons of the Past: Seizing New Opportunities to Promote Democratic Policing. July 7, 2005. http://www.usaid.gov/ policy/cdie/7-07-05_final.pdf (accessed November 26, 2007).

Huntington, Samuel P. 1991. How countries democratize. *Political Science Quarterly* 106, no.4: 579-616.

International Association of Chiefs of Police. 1990. Confidential informants: Concepts and issues paper (whitepaper). June 1990. IACP National Law Enforcement Policy Center. Alexandria, VA: International Association of Chiefs of Police.

Irvin, Renee A. and John Stansbury. 2004. Citizen participation in decision making: Is it worth the effort? *Public Administration Review* 64, no. 1 (January/February): 55-65.

Kathi, Pradeep and Terry L. Cooper. 2005. Democratizing the administrative state: Connecting neighborhood councils and city agencies. *Public Administration Review* 65, no. 5 (September/October): 559-567.

Kelling, George L. 2003. The evolution of contemporary policing. In *Local Government Police Management*, eds. William A. Geller and Darrel W. Stephens. 4th ed., 3-26. Washington, D.C.: International City/County Management Association.

Kelling, George L. and Catherine M. Coles. 1996. *Fixing Broken Windows: Restoring Order and Reducing Crime in Our Communities*. New York: Touchstone.

Kelling, George L. and Mark H. Moore. 1988. *The Evolving Strategy of Policing*. Washington, D.C.: National Institute of Justice.

Kennedy, David M. 2009a. *Deterrence and Crime Prevention: Reconsidering the Prospect of Sanction*. New York: Routledge.

———. 2009b. Drugs, race and common ground: Reflections on the High Point intervention. *The NIJ Journal*, no. 292 (March 2009): 12-17.

Kennedy, David M. and Sue-Lin Wong. [2009] 2012. *The High Point Drug Market Intervention Strategy*. Washington, D.C.: Community Oriented Policing Services. http://www.cops.usdoj.gov/Publications/e08097226-HighPoint.pdf (accessed April 5, 2014).

King, Martin Luther, Jr. [1963] 1999. Letter from Birmingham Jail. In *Ideas and Ideology: A Reader*, eds. Terence Ball and Richard Dagger, 360-370. New York: Longman.

Kleinig, John. 1996. *The Ethics of Policing*. Cambridge: Cambridge University Press.

Kleinig, John and Margaret Leland Smith. 1997. The development of criminal justice ethics training. In *Teaching Criminal Justice Ethics: Strategic Issues*, eds. John Kleinig and Margaret Leland Smith. vii-xix. Cincinnati, OH: Anderson Publishing Company.

Klockars, Carl B. 1985. *The Idea of Police*. Beverly Hills, CA: Sage Publications.

Kohn, Richard H. 1997. How democracies control the military. *Journal of Democracy* 8, no.4: 140-153.

Krahmann, Elke. 2008. Security: Collective good or commodity? *European Journal of International Relations* 14, no. 3 (September): 379-404.

Kubrin, Charis. 2008. Making order of disorder: A call for conceptual clarity. *Criminology & Public Policy* 7, no. 2 (June): 203-214.

Lane, Roger. 1980. Urban police and crime in nineteenth-century America. *Crime & Justice* 2: 1-43.

Leighton, Barry N. 1991. Visions of community policing: Rhetoric and reality in Canada. *Canadian Journal of Criminology*, 33: 485-522.

Levett, Allan E. 1975. Centralization of City Police in the Nineteenth Century United States. PhD diss., University of Michigan. In ProQuest Dissertations and Theses, http://proquest.umi.com.libproxy.utdallas.edu/pqdweb?index=1&did=760418901&SrchMode=1&sid=3&Fmt=6&VInst=PROD&VType=PQD&RQT=309&VName=PQD&TS=1339118212&clientId=10361 (accessed June 6, 2012).

Liederbach, John, Eric J. Fritsch, David L. Carter and Andra Bannister. 2008. Exploring the limits of collaboration in community policing: A direct comparison of police and citizen views. *Policing: An International Journal of Police Strategy & Management* 31, no. 2: 271-291.

Loader, Ian. 2006. Policing, recognition, and belonging. *Annuals of the American Academy of Political and Social Science* 605, (September): 202-21.

Locke, John. [1690] 1980. *Second Treatise of Government.* Indianapolis: Hackett Publishing.

Lord, Vivian B., Joseph B. Kuhns and Paul C. Friday. 2009. Small city community policing and citizen satisfaction. *Policing: An International Journal of Police Strategy & Management* 32, no. 4: 574-594.

Lynch, Ronald G. and Scott R. Lynch. 2005. *The Police Manager*, 6th ed. Newark, NJ: Matthew Bender & Company, Inc.

MacNamara, Donal E. J. 1972. Review of *The Police and the Public*, by Albert J. Reiss, Jr. *The Journal of Criminal Law, Criminology, and Police Science* 63, no. 3 (September): 409-411.

Magers, Jeffery. 2004. COMPSTAT: A new paradigm for policing or a repudiation of community policing? *Journal of Contemporary Criminal Justice* 20, no. 1 (February): 70-79.

Maguire, Edward R. 1997. Structural change in large municipal police organizations during the community policing era. *Justice Quarterly* 14, no. 3 (September): 547-576.

Manin, Bernard. 1987. On legitimacy and political deliberation. trans. Elly Stein and Jane Mansbridge. *Political Theory* 15, no. 3 (August): 338-368.

Manning, Peter K. 1977. *Police Work: The Social Organization of Policing.* Cambridge, MA: MIT Press.

————. [1984] 2000. Community-based policing. In *Community Policing: Contemporary Readings*, eds. Geoffery P. Alpert and Alex R. Piquero, 2nd ed., 23-34. Prospect Heights, IL: Waveland Press.

————. 2010. *Democratic Policing in a Changing World.* Boulder, CO: Paradigm Publishing.

Mansbridge, Jane. 1999. Everyday talk in the deliberative system. In *Deliberative Politics: Essays on Democracy and Disagreement*, ed. Stephen Macedo, 211-239. New York: Oxford University Press.

Maple, Jack. 1999. *The Crime Fighter: How You Can Make Your Community Crime Free*. New York: Doubleday.

Marenin, Otwin. 2004. Police training for democracy. *Police Practice & Research* 5, no. 2 (May): 107-123.

Martin, David. 2002. Spatial patterns in residential burglary: Assessing the effect of neighborhood social capital. *Journal of Contemporary Criminal Justice* 18, no. 2 (May): 132-146.

Marx, Gary T. 2001. Police and democracy. In *Policing, Security and Democracy: Theory and Practice*, eds. Menachem Amir and Stanley Einstein, 35-45. Huntsville, TX: Office of International Criminal Justice.

Mastrofski, Stephen D. 1988. Community policing as reform: A cautionary tale. In *Community Policing: Rhetoric or Reality?* eds. Jack R. Greene and Stephen D. Mastrofski, 47-68. New York: Praeger Publishers.

Mastrofski, Stephen D., James J. Willis and Tammy Rinehart Kochel. 2007. The challenges of implementing community policing in the United States. *Policing: A Journal of Policy and Practice* 1, no. 2: 223-234.

McCarthy, Thomas. 1975. Translator's introduction. In *Legitimation Crisis*. trans. Thomas McCarthy, vii-xxiv. Boston: Beacon Press.
———. 1994. Kantian constructivisim and reconstructivism: Rawls and Habermas in Dialogue. *Ethics* 105 (October): 44-63.

McCold, Paul and Ben Wachtel. 1996. Police officer orientation and resistance to implementation of community policing. Paper presented at the annual meeting of the American Society of Criminology, Chicago, Illinois. November 20-23. https://www.ncjrs.gov/pdffiles1/Digitization/165617NCJRS.pdf (accessed August 6, 2012).

McDonald, Phyllis. 2000. COP, COMPSTAT, and the New Professionalism: Mutual support or counter productivity. In *Community Policing: Contemporary Readings*, eds. Geoffery P. Alpert and Alex R. Piquero, 2nd ed., 233-256. Prospect Heights, IL: Waveland Press.

McGarrell, Edmond F., Joshua D. Freilich and Steven Chermak. 2007. Intelligence-led policing as a framework for responding to terrorism. *Journal of Contemporary Criminal Justice* 23, no. 2 (May): 142-158.

Mill, John Stuart. [1861] 2001. *On Representative Government*. Kitchener, Ontario: Batoche Books.

Monkkonen, Eric H. 1992. History of urban police. *Crime & Justice* 15: 547-580.

Moon, M. Jae and Peter DeLeon. 2001. Municipal reinventions: Managerial values and diffusion among municipalities. *Journal of Public Administrations Research & Theory* 11, no. 3 (July): 327-351.

Moore, Mark H. 1992. Problem-solving and community policing. *Crime & Justice* 15: 99-158.

———. 1994. Research synthesis and policy implications. In *The Challenges of Community Policing*, ed. Dennis P. Rosenbaum, 285-299. Thousand Oaks, CA: Sage Publications.

Morabito, Melissa Schaefer. 2010. Understanding community policing as innovation: Patterns of adoption. *Crime & Delinquency* 56, no. 4: 564-587.

Murphy, Kristina, Lyn Hinds and Jenny Fleming. 2008. Encouraging public cooperation and support for police. *Policing & Society* 18, no. 2 (June): 136-155.

National Advisory Commission on Civil Disorders. 1968. *Report of the National Advisory Commission on Civil Disorders*. Washington, D.C.: U.S. Government Printing Office.

National Advisory Commission on Criminal Justice Standards and Goals. 1973. *Report on Police*. Washington, D.C.: U.S. Government Printing Office.

National Commission on the Causes and Prevention of Violence. 1969. *To Establish Justice, to Insure Domestic Tranquility: Final Report*. Washington, D.C.: U.S. Government Printing Office.

National Research Council. 2004. *Fairness and Effectiveness in Policing: The Evidence*. Eds. Wesley Skogan and Kathleen Frydl. Washington D.C.: The National Academies Press.

Novak, Julia. 2014. Dreams that make a difference: The value of community-based strategic planning. *Public Management* 96, no. 2 (March 2014): 12-15.

Novak, Kenneth J., Leanne Fiftal Alarid and Wayne L. Lucas. 2003. Exploring officers' acceptance of community policing: Implications for policy implementation. *Journal of Criminal Justice* 31, no. 1 (January-February): 57-71.

O'Neill, Tip. 1994. *All Politics is Local and Other Rules of the Game.* New York: Times Books.

Oettmeier, Timothy N. and Mary Ann Wycoff. [1997] 2000. Personnel performance evaluations in the community policing context. In *Community Policing: Contemporary Readings*, eds. Geoffery P. Alpert and Alex R. Piquero, 2nd ed., 373-404. Prospect Heights, IL: Waveland Press.

Offe, Claus and Ulrich K. Preuss. 1991. Democratic institutions and moral resources. In *Political Theory Today*, ed. David Held, 143-171. Stanford, CA: Stanford University Press.

Oliver, Willard M. and Elaine Bartigis. 1998. Community policing: A conceptual framework. *Policing: An International Journal of Police Strategies & Management* 21, no.3: 490-509.

Orren, Karen and Stephen Skowronek. 2002. The study of American Political Development. In *Political Science: State of the Discipline*, eds. Ira Katznelson and Helen V. Milner, 722-754. New York: W.W. Norton & Company.

Orwell, George. [1946] 2008. Politics and literature: An examination of Gulliver's Travels. In *All Art is Propaganda: Critical Essay*, 292-315. New York: Houghton Mifflin Harcourt.

Palmer, Donald. 1996. *Does the Center Hold?: An Introduction to Western Philosophy.* Mountain View, CA: Mayfield Publishing.

Palmiotto, Michael J. 2011. *Community Policing: A Police-Citizen Partnership.* New York: Routledge.

Parkinson, John. 2006. *Deliberating in the Real World: Problems of Legitimacy in Deliberative Democracy.* New York: Oxford University Press.

Pate, Anthony M. 2003. External resources. In *Local Government Police Management*, eds. William A. Geller and Darrel W. Stephens. 4th ed., 515-558. Washington, D.C.: International City/County Management Association.

Pattavina, April, James M. Byrne and Luis Garcia. 2006. An examination of citizen involvement in crime prevention in high-risk versus low-to-moderate-risk neighborhoods. *Crime & Delinquency* 52, no. 2 (April): 203-231.

Pelfrey, William V. Jr. 2000. Precipitating factors of paradigmatic shift in policing: The origin of the community policing era. In *Community Policing: Contemporary Readings*, eds. Geoffery P. Alpert and Alex R. Piquero, 2nd ed., 79-92. Prospect Heights, IL: Waveland Press.

Pierson, Paul. 2000a. Not just what, but when: Timing and sequence in political process. *Studies in American Political Development* 14, (Spring): 72-92.

———. 2000b. Increasing returns, path dependence, and the study of politics. *American Political Science Review* 94, no. 2 (June): 251-267.

———. 2004. *Politics in Time: History, Institutions, and Social Analysis*. Princeton: Princeton University Press.

Pierson, Paul and Theda Skocpol. 2002. Historical institutionalism in contemporary political science. In *Political Science: State of the Discipline*, eds. Ira Katznelson and Helen V. Milner, 693-721. New York: W.W. Norton & Company.

Pino, Nathan W. 2001. Community policing and social capital. *Policing: An International Journal of Police Strategies & Management* 24, no. 2: 200-215.

Pino, Nathan W. and Michael D. Wiatrowski. 2006a. Policing and police reform in the US: Adequate for export? In *Democratic Policing in Transitional and Developing Countries*, eds. Nathan W. Pino and Michael D. Wiatrowski 43-68. Burlington, VT: Ashgate Publishing.

———. 2006b. The principles of democratic policing. In *Democratic Policing in Transitional and Developing Countries*, eds. Nathan W. Pino and Michael D. Wiatrowski, 69-97. Burlington, VT: Ashgate Publishing.

Pogge, Thomas. 2007. *John Rawls: His Life and Theory of Justice*. Oxford: Oxford University Press.

Ponsaers, Paul. 2001. Reading about "community (oriented) policing" and police models. *Policing: An International Journal of Police Strategy & Management* 24, no. 4: 470-496.

President's Commission on Campus Unrest. 1970. *Report of the President's Commission on Campus Unrest*. Washington, D.C.: U.S. Government Printing Office.

President's Commission on Law Enforcement and Administration of Justice. 1967a. *Task Force Report: The Police*. Washington D.C.: U.S. Government Printing Office.

——————. 1967b. *The Challenge of Crime in a Free Society*. Washington D.C.: U.S. Government Printing Office.

Rawls, John. 1951. Outline of a decision procedure for ethics. *The Philosophical Review* 60, no. 2 (April): 177-197.

——————. [1971] 1999. *A Theory of Justice*, revised edition. Cambridge: Belknap Press.

——————. 1985. Justice as fairness: Political not metaphysical. *Philosophy & Public Affairs* 14, no. 3 (Summer): 223-251.

——————. 1989. The domain of the political and overlapping consensus. *New York University Law Review* 64, (May): 233-55.

——————. [1993] 1997. The idea of public reason. In *Deliberative Democracy: Essays on Reason and Politics*, ed. James Bohman and William Relig, 93-141. Cambridge, MA: MIT Press.

——————. [1993] 2005. *Political Liberalism*, expanded edition. New York: Columbia University Press.

Redlinger, Lawrence J. 1994. Community policing and changes in the organizational structure. *Journal of Contemporary Criminal Justice* 10, no. 1 (March): 36-58.

Rehg, William. 1996. Translator's introduction. In *Between Facts and Norms: Contributions to a Discourse Theory of Law and Democracy*, trans. William Rehg, ix-xxxvii. Cambridge, MA: MIT Press.

Reiss, Albert J. Jr. 1971. *The Police and the Public*. New Haven, CT: Yale University Press.

Remington, Frank J. 1965. The role of police in a democratic society. *Journal of Criminal Law, Criminology, and Police Science* 56, no. 3 (September): 361-365.

Rosenbaum, Dennis, Sandy Yeh and Deanna L. Wilkinson. 1994. Impact of community policing on police personnel: A quasi-experimental test. *Crime & Delinquency* 40, no. 3 (July): 331-353.

Rosenbloom, David H. and Robert S. Kravchuk. 2005. The practice and discipline of public administration: Competing concerns. In *Public Administration: Understanding Management, Politics, and the Law in the Public Sector*, 6th ed. 2-41. New York: McGraw Hill.

References

Rousseau, Jean-Jacques. [1762] 1987. *On the Social Contract.* Indianapolis: Hackett Publishing.

Ruddell, Rick and Matthew O. Thomas. 2009. Does politics matter?: Cross-national correlates of police strength. *Policing: An International Journal of Police Strategy & Management* 32, no. 4: 654-674.

Ruhl, J. Mark. 2004. Curbing Central America's militaries. *Journal of Democracy* 15, no.3 (July): 137-151.

Rumbaut, Ruben G. and Egon Bittner. 1979. Changing conception of the police role: A sociological review. *Crime & Justice* 1: 239-288.

Sanderson, Stephen K. 2005. Reforming theoretical work in sociology: A modest proposal. *Perspectives* 28, no. 2 (August 2005): 1-4.

Scheider, Matthew C., Robert Chapman and Amy Schapiro. 2009. Towards the unification of policing innovations under community policing. *Policing: An International Journal of Police Strategy & Management* 32, no. 4: 694-718.

Scott, Jason D. 2002. Assessing the relationship between police-community coproduction and neighborhood-level social capital. *Journal of Contemporary Criminal Justice* 18, no. 2 (May): 147-166.

Selznick, Philip. [1957] 1984. *Leadership in Administration: A Sociological Interpretation.* Los Angeles, CA: University of California Press.

Shafritz, Jay M. and Albert C. Hyde. 2007. Part one: Early voices and the first quarter century (1880s to 1920s). In *Classics of Public Administration*, eds. Jay M. Shafritz and Albert C. Hyde, 6th ed., 2-17. Boston: Thomson Wadsworth.

Shanahan, Donald T. 1975. *Patrol Administration: Management by Objectives.* Boston: Holbrook Press.

Sheehan, Robert and Gary W. Cordner. 1979. *Introduction to Police Administration: A Systems/Behavioral Approach with Case Studies.* Reading, MA: Addison-Wesley Publishing Company.

Sherman, Lawrence W. 1986. Policing communities: What works? *Crime & Justice* 8 (Communities and Crime): 343-386.

———. 1998. Evidence-based policing. *Ideas in American Policing.* (July 1998). Police Foundation. http://www.policefoundation.org/pdf/Sherman.pdf. (accessed August 14, 2012).

———. 2001. Consent of the governed: Police, democracy, and diversity. In *Policing, Security and Democracy: Theory and Practice*, eds. Menachem Amir and Stanley Einstein, 17-33. Huntsville, TX: Office of International Criminal Justice.

Shusta, Robert M., Deena R. Levine, Herbert Z. Wong and Phillip R. Harris. 2005. *Multicultural Law Enforcement: Strategies for Peacekeeping in a Diverse Society*, 3rd ed. Upper Saddle River, NJ: Pearson Prentice Hall.

Simon, Jonathan. 2007. *Governing Through Crime: How the War on Crime Transformed American Democracy and Created a Culture of Fear*. Oxford: Oxford University Press.

Sklansky, David Alan. 2008. *Democracy and the Police*. Stanford, CA: Stanford University Press.

Skolnick, Jerome H. 1966. *Justice without Trial: Law Enforcement in Democratic Society*. New York: John Wiley & Sons, Inc.

Skolnick, Jerome H. [1966] 2011. *Justice without Trial: Law Enforcement in Democratic Society*. 4th ed. New Orleans, LA: Quid Pro, LLC.

Skolnick, Jerome H. and David H. Bayley. 1988. Them and variation in community policing. *Crime & Justice* 10: 1-37.

Smith, Bruce. 1929. Municipal police administration. *Annals of the American Academy of Political and Social Science* vol. 146, (November): 1-27.

Starling, Gover. 1993. *Managing the Public Sector*, 4th ed. Belmont, CA: Wadsworth Publishing.

State of Texas. 1997. Texas Local Government Code. Acts of the 75th Legislature, chapter 165. Title 11, Chapter 363: Crime Control and Prevention Districts. http://www.statutes. legis.state.tx.us /Docs/LG/htm/LG.363.htm. (accessed September 30, 2012).

Stenton, Doris. 1926. England: Henry II. In *The Cambridge Medieval History: Contest of Empire and Papacy*, vol. 5. 554-591. Eds. J. R. Tanner, C.W. Previte-Orton and Z.N. Brooke. New York: The Macmillan Company.

Steverson, Leonard A. 2008. Bruce Smith (1892-1955). In *Policing in America: A Reference Handbook*, 139-140. Santa Barbara, CA: ABC-CLIO, Inc.

Stillman, Richard J. 2005. Introduction. In *Public Administration: Cases and Concepts*, ed. Richard J. Stillman, 8th ed. 1-6. Boston, MA: Houghton Mifflin Company.

Stokes, Susan. 1998. Pathologies of Deliberation. In *Deliberative Democracy*, ed. Jon Elster, 123-139. Cambridge: Cambridge University Press.

Stone, Christopher E. and Heather H. Ward. 2000. Democratic policing: A framework for action. *Policing & Security* 10, (April): 11-45.

Sturba, James P. 1998. Habermas and Foucault. In *Social and Political Philosophy: Classical Western Texts in Feminist and Multicultural Perspective*, 2nd ed., 463-465. Belmont, CA: Wadsworth Publishing.

——. 1998. Rawls and Hospers. In *Social and Political Philosophy: Classical Western Texts in Feminist and Multicultural Perspective*, 2nd ed., 401-464. Belmont, CA: Wadsworth Publishing.

Sunshine, Jason and Tom R. Tyler. 2003. The role of procedural justice and legitimacy in shaping public support for policing. *Law & Society Review* 37, no. 3: 513-548.

Susser, Bernard. 1992. The behavioral ideology: A review and retrospective. In *Approaches to the Study of Politics*, ed. Bernard Susser, 76-100. New York: Macmillan Publishing.

——. 1992. Introduction. In *Approaches to the Study of Politics*, ed. Bernard Susser, 1-2. New York: Macmillan Publishing Company.

Swanson, Charles R., Leonard Territo and Robert W. Taylor. 1993. *Police Administration: Structures, Processes, and Behavior*, 3rd ed. New York: Macmillan Publishing.

——. 2012. *Police Administration: Structures, Processes, and Behavior*, 8th ed. Upper Saddle River, NJ: Prentice-Hall.

Tankebe, Justice and Alison Lieblling. 2013. Legitimacy and criminal justice: An introduction. In *Legitimacy and Criminal Justice: An International Exploration*, eds. Justice Tankebe and Alison Leibling, 1-6. Oxford: Oxford University Press.

Terris, Bruce J. 1967. The role of the police. *Annals of the American Academy of Policitical and Social Science* 374, (November): 58-69.

Theodoulou, Stella Z. and Rory O'Brien. 1999. Where we stand today: The state of modern political science. In *Methods for Political Inquiry: The Discipline, Philosophy, and Analysis of Politics*, eds. Stella Z. Theodoulou and Rory O'Brien, 1-12. Upper Saddle River, NJ: Prentice-Hall.

Thurman, Quint, C. and Michael D. Reisig. 1996. Community-oriented research in an era of community-oriented policing. *American Behavioral Scientist* 39, no. 5 (March-April): 570-586.

Trinkle, Georjean and Todd A. Miller. 2013. Collaborative partnerships to solve community issues. *The Police Chief* 80, no. 10 (October 2013): 26-27.

Trojanowicz, Robert and Bonnie Bucqueroux. 1990. *Community Policing: A Contemporary Perspective*. Cincinnati, OH: Anderson Publishing Company.

Tully, James. 2002. The unfreedom of the moderns in comparison to their ideals of constitutional democracy. *Modern Law Review* 65, no 2. (March): 204-228.

Tyler, Tom R. [1990] 2006. *Why People Obey the Law*. Princeton: Princeton University Press.

———. 2014. What are legitimacy and procedural justice in policing? And why are the becoming key elements of police leadership? In *Legitimacy and Procedural Justice: A New Element of Police Leadership*, ed. Craig Fischer, 6-35. (March 2014) Washington, D.C.: Police Executive Research Forum. http://www.policeforum.org/assets/docs/Free_Online_Documents/ Leadership/legitimacy%20and%20procedural%20justice%20- %20a%20new%20element%20of%20police%20leadership.pdf (accessed April 5, 2014).

Tyler, Tom R. and Jeffery Fagan. 2008. Legitimacy and cooperation: Why do people help the police fight crime in their communities? *Ohio State Journal of Criminal Law* 6, no. 3: 231-275.

Tyler, Tom R. and Yuen J. Huo. 2002. *Trust in the Law: Encouraging Public Cooperation with the Police and Courts*. New York: Russell Sage Foundation.

Tyler, Tom R. and Jonathan Jackson. 2013. Future challenges in the study of legitimacy and criminal justice. In *Legitimacy and Criminal Justice: An International Exploration*, eds. Justice Tankebe and Alison Leibling, 83-104. Oxford: Oxford University Press.

U.S. Agency for International Development. 2002. *Foreign Aid in the National Interest: Promoting Freedom, Security, and Opportunity.* Washington D.C.: U.S. Agency for International Development. http://www.usaid.gov/fani/Full_Report--Foreign_Aid_in_the_ National_Interest.pdf (accessed November 26, 2007).

U.S. Department of Health and Human Services. 2008. § 1304.50 Program governance. In *Head Start Performance Standards.* ttp://eclkc.ohs.acf.hhs.gov/hslc/standards/Head%20Start%20 Requirements/1304/1304.50%20Program%20governance..htm (accessed October 11, 2012).

U.S. Department of Justice. 2003. *Principles of Good Policing: Avoiding Violence Between Police and Citizens.* Revised September of 2003. http://www.justice.gov/crs/pubs/principles ofgoodpolicing final092003.pdf (accessed November 20, 2010).

———. Bureau of Justice Assistance. 2005. Intelligence-led policing: The new intelligence architecture, by Marilyn Peterson. In *New Realities: Law Enforcement in the Post-9/11 Era.* September 2005. BJA. https://www.ncjrs.gov/pdffiles1/bja/ 210681.pdf. (accessed August 14, 2012).

———. National Institute of Justice. 2000a. *National Evaluation of the COPS Program – Title I of the 1994 Crime Act*, by Jeffery A. Roth, Joseph F. Ryan, *et al.* August of 2000. NIJ. https://www.ncjrs.gov/pdffiles1/nij/183643.pdf (accessed August 2, 2012).

———. National Institute of Justice. 2000b. The COPS program after 4 years – national evaluation, by Jeffery A. Roth and Joseph F. Ryan. In *National Institute of Justice: Research in Brief.* August of 2000. NIJ. http://www.nij.gov/pubs-sum/183644.htm (accessed July 20, 2012).

———. Office of Community Oriented Policing Services. 2009a. *Advancing Community Policing Through Community Governance: A Framework Document*, by Drew Diamond and Deidre Mead Weiss. June 2009. COPS. http://cops.usdoj.gov/ Publications/ e0509 19202-AdvCommunityPolicing_final.pdf (accessed August 2, 2012).

———. Office of Community Oriented Policing Services. 2009b. *Community Policing Defined.* April 2009. COPS. http://www.cops.usdoj.gov/Publications/ e030917193-CP-Defined .pdf (accessed August 2, 2012).

———. Office of Community Oriented Policing Services. 2009c. *Law Enforcement Intelligence: A Guide for State, Local, and Tribal Law Enforcement Agencies*, by David L. Carter. 2nd ed. January 2009. COPS. http://www.fas.org/irp/agency/doj/lei.pdf (accessed August 14, 2012).

———. Office of Community Oriented Policing Services. 2014. *National Center for Building Community Trust and Justice: Improving the Justice System by Enhancing Procedural Justice, Reducing Bias, and Supporting Racial Reconciliation – FY 2014 Competitive Grant Announcement.* http://www.ojjdp.gov/grants/solicitations/FY2014/NCBCTJ.pdf (accessed April 19, 2014).

U.S. Library of Congress. Congressional Research Service. 2002. *Crime Control: The Federal Response*, by JoAnne O'Bryant and Lisa Seghetti. CRS Report IB10095. http://digital .library.unt.edu/ark:/67531/metacrs2349/m1/1/high_res_d/IB10095_2002Sep12.pdf (accessed August 9, 2012).

———. Congressional Research Service. 2010. *Community Oriented Policing Services (COPS): Current Legislative Issues*, by Nathan James. CRS Report R40709. http://www.fas.org/sgp/crs/misc/R40709.pdf. (accessed July 20, 2012). Washington D.C.: Office of Congressional Information and Publishing, September 15, 2010.

Vinogradoff, Paul. 1913. Foundations of society (origins of feudalism). In *The Cambridge Medieval History: The Rise of the Saracens and the Foundations of the Western Empire*, vol. 2. 630-654. eds. H.M. Gwatkin and J.P. Whitney. New York: The Macmillan Company.

———. 1922. Feudalism. In *The Cambridge Medieval History: Germany and the Western Empire*, vol 3. 458-484. Eds. H.M. Qwatkin, J.P. Whitney, J.R. Tanner and C.W. Previte-Orton. New York: The Macmillan Company.

Vitek, Jo. 2013. Community capacity building and partnerships in action. *The Police Chief* 80, no. 10 (October 2013): 50-58.

Vito, Gennaro F., William F. Walsh and Julie Kunselman. 2005. Community policing: The middle manager's perspective. *Police Quarterly* 8, no. 4 (December): 490-511.

Vogel, Robert, Evelina Moulder and Mike Huggins. 2014. The extent of public participation: ICMA survey explores public engagement and the tenor of civic discourse. *Public Management* 96, no. 2 (March 2014): 6-10.

Walker, Samuel. 1999. *The Police in America: An Introduction*, 3rd ed. Boston: McGraw-Hill College.

Walsh, William F. and Gennaro F. Vito. 2004. The meaning of COMPSTAT: Analysis and response. *Journal of Contemporary Criminal Justice* 20, no. 1 (February): 51-69.

Wedeen, Lisa. 2002. Conceptualizing culture: Possibilities for political science. *American Political Science Review* 96, no.4 (December): 713-28.

Weisberg, Herbert F., Jon A. Krosnick and Bruce D. Bowen. 1996. *An Introduction to Survey Research, Polling, and Data Analysis*, 3rd ed. Thousand Oaks, CA: Sage Publications.

Weisburd, David, Stephen D. Mastrofski, Ann Marie McNally, Rosann Greenspan and James J. Willis. 2003. Reforming to preserve: COMPSTAT and strategic problem solving in American policing. *Criminology & Public Policy* 2, no. 3 (July): 421-456.

Weisburd, David, Cody W. Telep, Joshua C. Hinkle and John E. Eck. 2010. Is problem-oriented policing effective in reducing crime and disorder? *Criminology & Public Policy* 9, no. 1: 139-172.

Whitehead, Alfred North. [1929] 1979. *Process and Reality*. New York: Free Press.

Whitehead, Laurence. 2002. *Democratization: Theory and Experience*. New York: Oxford University Press.

Williams, E.J. 2003. Structuring in community policing: Institutionalizing innovative change. *Police Practice and Research* 4, no. 2: 119-129.

Willis, James J., Stephen D. Mastrofski and David Weisburd. 2007. Making sense of COMPSTAT: A theory-based analysis of organizational change in three police departments. *Law & Society Review* 41, no. 1 (March): 147-188.

Willis, James J., Stephen D. Mastrofski and Tammy Rinehart Kochel. 2010. The co-implementation of compstat and community policing. *Journal of Criminal Justice* 38, no. 5 (September-October): 969-980.

Wilson, James Q. [1968] 1978. *Varieties of Police Behavior: The Management of Law and Order in Eight Communities.* Cambridge, MA: Harvard University Press.

———. [1989] 2000. *Bureaucracy: What Government Agencies Do and Why They Do It.* New York: Basic Books.

Wilson, James Q. and George L. Kelling. 1982. The police and neighborhood safety. *Atlantic Monthly* 211 (March 1982): 29-38.

Wilson, Jeremy M. 2006. Law and order in an emerging democracy: Lessons from the reconstruction of Kosovo's police and justice system. *Annals of the American Academy of Political and Social Science* 605, no. 1: 152-177.

Wilson, O.W. 1950. *Police Administration.* New York: McGraw-Hill Book Company.

Wilson, O.W. and Roy Clinton McLaren. 1972. *Police Administration.* 3rd ed. New York: McGraw-Hill Book Company.

Wilson, Woodrow. 1887. The study of administration. *Political Science Quarterly* 2, no. 2: 197-222.

Winkates, James. 2000. The transformation of the South African national defense force: A good beginning. *Armed Forces & Society* 26, no. 3 (Spring): 451-472.

Worrall, John L. 2010. Do Federal law enforcement grants reduce serious crime? *Criminal Justice Police Review* 21, no. 4: 459-475.

Worrall, John L. and Jihong Zhao. 2003. The role of the COPS office in community policing. *Policing: An International Journal of Police Strategy & Management* 26, no. 1: 64-87.

Zhao, Jihong and Quint C. Thurman. 1997. Community policing: Where are we now? *Crime & Delinquency* 43, no. 3 (July): 345-357.

Zhao, Jihong, Matthew C. Scheider and Quint Thurman. 2002. Funding community policing to reduce crime: Have COPS grants made a difference? *Criminology & Public Policy* 2, no. 1 (November): 7-32.

Zhao, Jihong, Ni He and Nicholas Lovrich. 2006. The effect of local political culture on policing behaviours in the 1990's: A retest of Wilson's theory in more contemporary times. *Journal of Criminal Justice* 34, no. 6 (November-December): 569-578.

Index

9/11 Terrorist Attacks, 8, 20, 105, 138, 140, 141, 143, 178
Accountability, 1, 15, 33, 58, 65, 66, 67, 71-74, 100, 140, 149, 161, 165, 178
Almond, G., 36, 37, 63
Area studies, 34, 37
Assumptions, 3, 5, 7, 13, 20, 23, 24, 26, 31-34, 49, 157, 173
Autonomy, 98, 99, 100, 114
Bayley, D., 7, 31-38, 65, 72, 76, 77, 78, 100, 107, 108, 115, 130, 149, 160-65, 178
Bessette, J., 41, 42, 64
Bias, 4, 6, 7, 20, 21, 27, 29, 137, 158
Bohman, J., 43, 46, 53, 66, 71
Bratton, W., 18, 100, 122, 138, 139, 140, 161
Bryne grants, 125
Bureau of Justice Assistance (BJA), 173
Bureaucracy, 57, 97, 101, 105, 135
Call-in, 173
Chambers, S., 42-44, 49, 52, 55-63, 71, 159
Citizen juries, 42, 60, 69
Citizen participation, 7, 9, 74
Civil society, 3, 57, 152
Coercion, 37, 58, 168

Commission, 4, 5, 12-14, 21-28, 95, 96, 101-104, 109, 111, 116, 115, 120, 122, 124, 127, 130, 133, 144, 150, 151, 175
Community Crime Prevention District (CCPD), 134
Community engagement, 4, 5, 8-11, 31, 41, 42, 105, 108, 115-118, 130, 131, 138, 142, 147-149, 162, 165, 166, 175-178
Community input, 3, 7
Community partnerships, 117, 131, 142, 144
Community policing, 12-20, 26-31, 42, 43, 63, 75, 76, 77, 101, 105-117, 118-131, 148, 157-165,
Community policing practice, 4, 5, 21, 27, 30, 76, 107, 115, 138, 160
Community relations, 14, 16, 26, 103, 104, 109, 155, 158
Community-policing, 17, 19, 139, 143
COMPSTAT, 20, 122, 135-140, 142, 147, 159, 161
Consensus, 33, 46, 49, 61, 71-73, 77, 78, 104, 127, 132, 163
Cooperation, 15, 27, 46, 47, 48, 49, 116, 170

COPS MORE, 126
COPS Office, 19, 117, 123-130, 138, 167
Cordner, G., 19, 30, 124, 136
Corruption, 1, 35, 38, 86, 88, 94, 95, 144
Crank, J., 75-78, 100, 114, 153, 154, 159
Crime Control and Prevention Districts (CCPD), 134
Crime fighting, 8, 94, 149
Crime prevention, 128
Criminology, 32, 63, 97
Critical junctures, 176
Dahl, R., 33, 34, 36, 37
Decentralization, 18, 77, 87, 108, 113, 114, 115, 120, 121, 122, 124, 138, 161
Deliberation, 2, 20, 41, 43, 44, 50, 51, 52, 53, 56, 59, 60, 62, 64, 65, 66, 67, 68, 69, 70, 71, 72, 73, 74, 77, 104, 149, 159, 161, 163
Deliberative democracy, 3, 4, 5, 6, 9, 12, 42, 49, 50, 52, 57, 60, 61, 63, 64, 65, 67, 68, 69, 70, 71, 72, 73, 74, 119, 149, 152, 158, 159, 164, 177
Deliberative democratic forums, 65, 73, 74
Deliberative democratic practices, 5, 10, 69, 71, 73, 74, 160, 161, 165, 166, 178
Deliberative democratic theory, 2, 4, 5, 6, 8, 11, 33, 41, 43, 46, 52, 59, 60, 63, 76, 115, 119, 131, 147, 149, 158, 159, 160, 161, 165, 177, 179
Deliberative opinion polls, 42, 68

Democracy, 2, 5, 6, 10, 11, 18, 21-23, 31-38, 42, 52, 54, 57, 60, 64, 65, 68-73, 76, 89, 101-103, 105, 116, 131, 148-150, 154-159, 162-165, 177
Democratic governance, 7, 39
Democratic policing, 5, 7, 8, 10, 32, 33, 65, 72, 150, 161, 162, 164, 165, 179
Democratic principles, 7, 8, 37, 39, 72, 150, 164, 178
Democratic theory, 4-6, 9, 11, 21, 32-36, 41-44, 52, 60, 63, 131, 148, 154, 158, 160, 170, 177
Democratization, 32, 33, 34, 35, 36, 38, 76, 77, 150, 155, 162, 163, 165, 178
Deterrence, 168, 170-173
Dialogue, 14, 17, 20, 29, 32, 33, 51, 52, 57, 61, 62, 72, 106, 132, 160, 161, 163, 164, 170, 174
Diamond, L., 34-38, 162
Direct democracy, 42, 73
Disadvantaged, 14, 24
Discourse, 2, 20, 33, 41, 43, 52, 53, 54, 55, 56, 58, 60, 61, 62, 64, 65, 68, 69, 71, 73, 150, 159, 161, 163, 165, 166, 174, 179
Discourse ethics, 52-62, 161, 179
Drug Market Intervention Initiative (DMI), 170-173
Dryzek, J., 2, 41, 42, 43, 60, 64, 70, 73
Easton, D., 168
Effectiveness, 6, 15, 17, 26, 27, 30, 33, 66, 69, 74, 94, 97, 98, 102, 127, 128, 131, 132, 136-138, 147, 148, 153

Index

Efficiency, 3, 4, 6, 7, 8, 10, 15, 18, 45, 47, 72, 76, 88, 90, 91, 94, 96, 97, 98, 99, 100, 101-106, 110, 112, 114, 117, 118, 127, 135-137, 153-156, 177, 178
Efficiency-oriented, 4, 45, 105, 118, 135, 156
Engagement, 4, 9, 30, 36, 41-43, 52, 53, 72, 113, 118, 131, 138, 148-150, 160, 162, 166, 179
England, 77, 78, 82, 83, 85, 86, 89, 90
Eras, 16, 151
Evidenced-based policing, 140
Factions, 22, 88, 92
Federalist Papers, 23, 64
Feudalism, 78, 83
Fishkin, J., 42, 60, 68, 69, 73, 161
Frankpledge, 80-82
Goals, 4, 6, 19, 32, 57, 105, 136, 139, 148, 150, 156, 173, 179
Goldstein, H., 2, 13-18, 103, 105-117
Governance, 1, 8, 9, 21, 71, 79, 83, 85, 86, 132, 133, 151, 160-162
Grants, 8, 78, 124, 126, 128, 130
Gutmann, A., 2, 25, 42, 44, 49, 59-72, 159, 164
Habermas, J., 53-73, 157, 159, 161, 179
Held, D., 2, 4, 21-27, 31, 41-44, 53, 59, 60, 65- 68, 73, 157, 158, 165
High Point Strategy, 167, 170-174
Historical institutionalism, 129, 151, 175
Hot-spot policing, 140
Ideal speech situation, 58, 59, 61

Impartiality, 59, 62, 67, 68, 71, 72, 91
Influentials, 172
Informants, 144, 190
Institution, 6, 7, 18, 33, 60, 74, 78, 89, 109, 113, 129, 151, 162, 165, 177
Institutional density, 176
Institutions, 1, 2, 14, 21, 22, 33-35, 39, 45, 47, 54, 57, 60, 61, 64, 69, 70, 74, 80, 89, 129, 154, 163, 176
Intelligence, 143-144
Intelligence-led policing, 20, 135, 137-144, 147, 159
Interest group, 4, 22, 24, 27-29
International Association of Chiefs of Police (IACP), 166
Involvement, 3, 7, 9, 13, 16, 19, 20, 24, 31, 35, 42, 109, 115, 116, 131, 132, 141, 159, 160, 161, 175
Isomorphism, 129
Jackson State University, 24
Justice, 1, 2, 10, 11, 13, 24, 37, 38, 43, 44, 45, 46, 47, 48, 49, 56, 63, 70, 79, 80, 81, 82, 87, 110, 124, 125, 152, 153, 158, 162, 167, 168, 169, 170, 178
Justice as fairness, 46, 49
Kelling, G., 1, 3, 6, 8, 16, 19, 77, 89-91, 94-105, 111, 113, 123, 127, 133, 135, 136, 151-156, 175
Kennedy, D., 167, 170-174
King, M.L., 45
Law Enforcement Assistance Administration (LEAA), 17, 124

Legitimacy, 2, 3, 6, 8, 9, 10, 14, 37, 38, 41, 42, 46, 50, 51, 52, 54, 55, 61-74, 101, 102, 119, 130, 131, 137, 144-149, 151-158, 165, 167-170, 176, 178
Legitimate, 24, 36, 42, 44, 50-54, 57, 59, 67, 71, 101, 127, 149, 152, 156
Legitimation, 54, 131, 154
Local control, 75, 77, 83, 87
Local government, 78, 85, 86, 87, 88, 90, 99, 124-126, 132, 134, 135, 166, 176
London model, 84, 89, 91, 92, 98
Manin, B., 4, 49, 50, 51, 52, 64, 192
Manning, P., 29, 31, 77, 78, 89, 92, 101, 119, 135, 150, 152, 164
Manor, 78, 79, 80, 83
Maple, J., 138-140
Military, 33, 34, 35, 37, 38, 45, 78, 79, 84, 91, 92, 114, 121
Mini-publics, 70, 73
Minorities, 13, 14, 23, 24, 25, 52, 70, 102, 104, 171
Models of policing, 4, 8, 18
Moore, M., 2, 3, 6, 8, 16, 19, 127, 132, 135, 137, 148, 149, 151-155, 177
National Advisory Commission on Criminal Justice Standards and Goals, 14, 15, 17, 25, 106, 109, 111, 114, 116
National Commission on the Causes and Prevention of Violence, 13, 24, 25
National Institute of Justice (NIJ), 107, 119, 130, 131

National Research Council, 12, 27, 107, 108, 111, 113, 115, 116, 117, 118, 119, 128, 151, 154, 155, 158
Near miss, 176, 177
Neighborhood, 14, 19, 26, 27, 29, 73, 103, 108, 116, 120, 139, 143, 160, 171, 172, 177, 178
Nightwatchman, 87
Norms, 4, 11, 25, 31, 33, 39, 48, 58, 59, 62, 64, 69, 71, 72, 78, 83, 87, 101, 114, 120, 163, 168, 173
New Public Management (NPM), 136, 137, 141
Order maintenance, 19, 99, 120, 137
Organizational restructuring, 115, 121
Organizational theory, 121
Organizational transformation, 113, 117
Overt drug market, 170, 171, 172
Partnership, 14, 18, 106, 116, 131
Path dependence, 175
Philosophy, 3, 9, 10, 16, 18, 25, 32, 45, 51, 56, 63, 96, 105, 108, 116, 117, 131, 135, 139, 178
Pierson, P., 76, 129, 175, 176
Pledge system, 81, 86
Pluralism, 4, 11, 20-31, 42, 49, 64, 88, 144, 156, 157, 158
Pluralist, 20, 22, 23, 27, 29, 31, 41, 62, 156, 157, 158
Police administration, 97, 124, 127, 136, 160
Police Executive Research Forum (PERF), 167
Police legitimacy, 148, 149, 151, 152, 153, 155, 159
Political science, 2, 11, 32, 36, 131

Index

Practical discourse, 57, 61
President's Commission on Campus Unrest, 24, 197
President's Commission on Law Enforcement and Administration of Justice, 13, 14, 23-25, 81-83, 86-90, 95, 105, 110, 111, 122
Principles of good policing, 164
Problem solving, 54, 59, 117, 123, 143
Problem-oriented policing, 17, 18, 106, 110, 112, 127, 128, 139, 141, 143
Procedural justice, 158, 167-169
Professional model, 15, 16, 99, 100, 105, 114, 118, 120, 121, 126, 148
Professionalism, 33, 98, 104, 151, 153-155, 177
Progressive Era, 7, 76, 94, 118, 135
Progressives, 94, 95, 99, 135
Public administration theory, 8, 135, 136
Public participation, 115, 130, 166
Public relations, 16, 103-105
Publicity, 65, 66, 72
Race, 26, 27, 103, 156
Rawls, J., 4, 32, 44-52, 62-71
Reciprocity, 65, 71
Recommendations, 5, 8, 12, 13, 15, 23, 24, 25, 37, 69, 95, 96, 101, 103, 106, 111, 115, 116, 143, 165
Reform era, 16
Reiss, A., 28, 29, 150, 174
Relationship, 3-6, 9, 11, 13-18, 41, 46, 56, 72, 74, 76, 99, 101, 103, 104, 116, 123, 150, 162, 177

Report of the President's Commission on Campus Unrest, 24
Resistance, 4, 113, 120, 121, 122, 123, 135
Responsiveness, 1, 33, 35, 65, 71, 72, 105, 109, 149, 161, 165, 178
Riots, 13, 23, 88, 92, 175
Role confusion, 118, 119, 120
Rule of law, 34, 35, 101, 148, 152, 153
Salons, 55, 73
Schumpeter, J., 21, 22, 34
Shared governance, 161
Sheriff, 80, 82, 84, 86
Sklansky, D, 1, 31, 34, 75, 157, 158, 164
Skolnick, J., 28, 107-109, 115, 130, 150, 174
Social science, 4, 12, 26, 30, 63
Sociology, 32, 36, 157
Spoils system, 94
Strategic communications, 58
Surveys, 21, 26, 27, 30, 73, 166
Team policing, 14, 16, 17, 106, 107, 111, 114, 122
Technology, 19, 96, 99, 104, 114, 117, 126, 137, 142, 161
Themes, 5, 11, 12, 15, 20, 21, 43, 55, 64, 72, 109, 136, 160, 161
Thompson, D., 2, 25, 42, 44, 49, 59-69, 72, 73, 159, 164
Tolerance, 19, 65, 172, 178
Training, 13, 18, 28, 30, 34, 98, 104, 106, 114, 117, 123, 130, 149, 150, 159, 175, 177
Transparency, 1, 33, 65, 66, 71, 161, 165, 169, 178

Trojanowicz, R., 2, 3, 12, 16, 17, 18, 95, 96, 100, 102, 103, 106, 107, 111, 112, 115, 116, 123, 130, 132, 138, 141, 178
Trust, 154, 168, 169
Tyler, T., 167, 168, 169, 170
U.S. Department of Justice, 38, 117, 124, 126, 128, 130, 131, 142-144, 149, 164-167
Unanimity, 50, 51, 67, 72, 99
Utilitarianism, 4, 20, 22, 23, 26, 31, 168
Violent crime, 19, 23, 133, 170
Violent Crime Control and Law Enforcement Act of 1994, 19, 126
War on crime, 133
Ward, 80, 82, 87, 88, 90, 91, 95, 135
Watch, 73, 80-89, 99, 100, 152
Watchmen, 86, 87
Whitehead, L., 36, 37, 38, 77, 150, 155, 156, 162, 163, 164, 165, 177
Wilson, J., 19, 29, 33, 35, 38, 76, 94-98, 101, 109, 113, 123, 124, 133, 150, 174
Wilson, O.W., 97, 98, 101
Zero-tolerance, 19, 140, 171

CPSIA information can be obtained at www.ICGtesting.com
Printed in the USA
BVOW05*1656120415

394989BV00001B/1/P